# BECOMING A PUBLIC BENEFIT CORPORATION

# Stanford SOCIAL INNOVATION Review | Books

Edited in collaboration with the *Stanford Social Innovation Review*, this book series examines important topics across philanthropy, nonprofits, business, government, and social enterprises. The series reflects top scholarship and expertise and provides reputable and high-quality works for practitioners and scholars. We showcase work by emerging and established authors from academia, research, and practice to advance the field of social innovation.

We invite submissions on issues including, but not limited to, advocacy, collaboration, design thinking, scaling, organizational development, leadership, philanthropy, technology, measurement and evaluation, innovation, impact investing, sustainability, and governance.

*Edited by Eric Nee and Johanna Mair*

# BECOMING A PUBLIC BENEFIT CORPORATION

*Express Your Values, Energize Stakeholders,*
*Make the World a Better Place*

Michael B. Dorff

**STANFORD BUSINESS BOOKS**

AN IMPRINT OF STANFORD UNIVERSITY PRESS • STANFORD, CALIFORNIA

Stanford University Press
Stanford, California

Special discounts for bulk quantities of Stanford Business Books are available to corporations, professional associations, and other organizations. For details and discount information, contact the special sales department of Stanford University Press by emailing sales@www.sup.org.

Printed in the United States of America on acid-free, archival-quality paper

Library of Congress Control Number:
2023944607

ISBN 9781503632806 (cloth)
ISBN 9781503637849 (ebook)

Cover design: Martyn Schmoll

# CONTENTS

## ACKNOWLEDGMENTS

Writing is often a lonely process. Authors spend countless hours sitting alone in an office, staring at a computer screen. The computer screen stares back, rarely offering a comforting word or smile. Thankfully, I was blessed during the writing of this book with a number of friends and family members who cheerfully kept me company along the multiyear journey that has culminated in this book's publication.

As with my first book, my father, Elliot Dorff, a renowned and highly prolific scholar of Jewish law and medical ethics, was my primary reader and cheerleader. He pored over the early drafts, looking for (and too often finding) flaws in logic, obscure arguments, grammatical errors, and clumsy writing. My readers and I owe him a great debt for his tireless efforts to make the book as pleasant and sensible a read as possible.

I am equally indebted to a number of friends and colleagues who provided invaluable suggestions on how to improve the book's substance. Therese Maynard read an early draft of the book proposal, and her suggestions helped shape the book at its very earliest stages. Similarly, the participants in the Southern California Corporate Law Scholars Colloquium—especially Victor Fleischer, Elizabeth Pollman, and Frank Partnoy—helped me think through my goals for this book while it was still just the germ of an idea.

Miguel Padro also provided generously of his time, wisdom, and expertise when I was first thinking about what a book like this should contain. Miguel has supported me at any many points in my career, and I am deeply grateful for his friendship. At a much later stage, participants in the National Business Law Scholars Conference also provided helpful comments. I am particularly grateful to Joan Heminway, who not only provided very useful feedback on the manuscript but, as my friend and mentor for many years, has helped me develop as a scholar—and a person—in manifold ways. Patrick Corrigan is also deserving of special mention for his detailed and incredibly thoughtful comments on Chapter 9 on public entities. That chapter is much improved thanks to his comprehensive knowledge of the securities laws. Although she tragically passed away before I had gotten very far on this project, Lynn Stout served as a supportive mentor and teacher to me through much of my career. I hope she would be proud of this work; she certainly played a major role in forming the scholar who wrote it. Mike Downer provided helpful guidance on striking an appropriate balance between critiquing the current system and acknowledging its many benefits. Susan Mac Cormack, R. Todd Johnson, Jay Mitchell, and Andrew Kassoy provided crucial background on the historical origins of the benefit corporation (BC) and public benefit corporation (PBC), a history that they themselves shaped. These new forms would not exist without their tireless efforts to bring them into existence.

Of all my colleagues, though, I am most indebted to my close friends and sometimes coauthors Russell Korobkin and Steven Solomon. Russell patiently listened while I babbled on about BCs and PBCs on our weekly walks together through the Santa Monica mountains and provided gentle guidance as I wrestled with issue after issue. I am sure he will be relieved that we can now discuss other topics! Steven debated me vigorously while we were writing our article together about venture capital funding of PBCs.[1] His sharp critiques honed my thoughts on these new entities and helped me understand both their strengths and weaknesses. For this intellectual gift, as well as for his unceasing support and friendship, I am eternally grateful.

Southwestern Law School has provided me with an intellectual and spiritual home for twenty years. It has provided financial support throughout the lengthy writing process as well as the time I needed to complete the work, including a sabbatical at a crucial time in the writing process. I am also grateful to the school for awarding me the inaugural Kenneth and Harle Montgomery Foundation Distinguished Scholar Award on the basis of this project, and to Bryant Garth and the Foundation for establishing the award at Southwestern. Most important, though, Southwestern provided me with fabulous students who served as my research assistants. These students not only found information and sources for me, they also edited drafts of the manuscript and gave me incredibly helpful comments on both style and substance. Kristen Abajian, Abe Bran, Brigitta Cymerint, Jenny Eaton, Andrew Hyman, Eden Moalem, and Katie Trinh: I cannot express how much I appreciate all of your hard work, good thoughts, and steady encouragement. I am honored to have taught you and proud now to call you my colleagues.

This book would not exist without the vision and encouragement of Steve Catalano at Stanford University Press (SUP). Steve believed in this project even more than I did and championed it throughout the long writing and publication process. I could not think of a better home for this book than SUP or a better editor for it than Steve. I am equally indebted to Kate Wahl, Stanford's gracious editor in chief, who took over the project when Steve left the Press for other opportunities; to Richard Narramore, Steve's successor, who brought the book over the finish line; Richard's able deputy, Cindy Lim, who kept everything on track and coached through the marketing process; and to Gigi Mark, Stanford's excellent senior production editor who ensured the final product was the best possible version of this book. I am deeply grateful to Steve, Kate, Richard, Cindy, Gigi, and all their SUP colleagues for shepherding this book through to publication.

Finally, I thank Tanya, Zoe, and Miles for allowing me the enormous amounts of time it took to write this book and for kindly indulging me when I insisted on talking about it far too often. My children, Zoe and Miles, are truly my inspiration. We owe them—and all the children in their generation and those generations that will follow them—our very best efforts to build an economy that works for all of us and treats the planet and its resources responsibly. I believe and hope that the BC/PBC movement will be an important step in building that more ethical and responsible economy and will help us leave the world better than we found it.

*BECOMING A PUBLIC BENEFIT CORPORATION*

# *INTRODUCTION*

Benefit corporations began with a basketball shoe and a mixtape. Jay Coen Gilbert and two Wharton classmates founded a basketball shoe and apparel company while in graduate school. Named "And1," after a play where a player is fouled while successfully making a shot, thereby gaining two points and a free throw, the company took off after launching a marketing campaign organized around highlight reels of street basketball players performing trick moves, or "mixtapes."[1] Bart Houlahan joined the company early on and became its chief financial officer, chief operating officer, and president.[2]

Gilbert and Houlahan inaugurated a number of progressive corporate policies at And1. For example, the company offered parental leave benefits, implemented an employee ownership program, and donated 5 percent of its annual profits to local charities. It also took steps to protect workers at its upstream suppliers, negotiating a code of conduct covering workplace safety and minimum wages. When they ultimately sold the company in 2005, though, the buyer dropped many of these policies and ran the company more traditionally.[3]

Gilbert and Houlihan were dismayed at the changes to their company after the sale. Although they had not consciously identified their management style as socially responsible, they recognized that their employees' work lives had been markedly better under the their own management. They spent some time thinking deeply about how they could change that result the next time they started a company and spoke to other business leaders about the problem as well. After considering and abandoning a number of ideas, they ultimately hit on the concept of a certification program for prosocial companies: they would create a test that would measure the social benefits a company produced for society and certify companies that passed the test as being better for the world.[4]

Along with Andrew Kassoy, a Wall Street investor, they founded B Lab, a nonprofit corporation, and designed an extensive questionnaire for companies—the B Impact Assessment—that asked companies to evaluate themselves along four dimensions: governance, workers, the community, and the environment. The assessment scored companies on a 200-point scale; companies that scored 80 or higher qualified for B Lab's certification and could market themselves as "B Corps" if they paid B Lab the requisite fee.[5]

B Lab's founders feared that certification alone would fail to achieve their goal of creating companies with durable social missions. A B Corp could easily drop its certification and revert to traditional profit-focused management after a sale or because the owners changed their priorities. They realized that some states have corporate statutes that permit, but do not require, corporations to prioritize the welfare of employees and other corporate constituencies over the pursuit of profits, and they experimented with using those statutes to create a more durable legal commitment to social purpose. Some states did not have constituency statutes, however. Their attempt to persuade one such state, the economic powerhouse of California, to adopt a constituency statute failed, but that failure ultimately bore productive fruit. California's governor vetoed the legislature's constituency bill, but in his veto message, he included a recommendation that the state create a new form of business organization that was between a for-profit corporation and a nonprofit corporation. A group of California lawyers established a drafting group—led by Susan Mac Cormac from Morrison and Foerster and R. Todd Johnson from Jones Day (together with other corporate lawyers, including Jay Mitchell from Stanford Law School; Will Fitzpatrick, former general counsel of Omidyar Network; Rob Wexler of Adler and Colvin; and Keith Bishop, former California commissioner of corporations)—that worked for two and a half years on a new form, devoting thousands of pro bono hours to the project. Ultimately, they created the form that is now known in California as the social purpose corporation.[6]

As the California group's work neared completion, the B Lab trio decided to create their own new form of business organization, the benefit corporation, to serve the same goal of providing a more lasting legal framework for founders of companies with prosocial values. With the help of some volunteer outside attorneys (William H. Clark Jr. of Drinker Biddle & Reath LLP with others, including many from the California group, providing helpful comments), B Lab drafted model benefit corporation legislation (referred to here as the Model Act) and began lobbying state legislatures to add benefit corporations (BCs) to their menu of business organization options. The first legislature to accept their invitation was Maryland's, which passed the first BC legislation in the nation in 2010. A number of states followed fairly swiftly over the following two years, including California, Illinois, New Jersey, New York, Pennsylvania, and Virginia. California also passed legislation authorizing the Mac Cormac/Johnson team's social purpose corporation (then known as the flexible purpose corporation).[7] Noticeably missing from this list was Delaware, the state with the most impact for corporate law. (I explain why this tiny state is of such gargantuan importance to corporations in Chapter 2.) The omission was not for lack of B Lab's efforts. B Lab well understood Delaware's importance and tried from the beginning to persuade the state legislature to authorize BCs. Delaware, though, resisted at first.

Perhaps due to the singular importance of Delaware's corporate law to the nation as a whole, Delaware has an unusual process for passing amendments to its corporation statute. Any changes the legislature makes to the state's corporate law must have the approval of experts in the field. Amendments to the law start with the Council of the Delaware State Bar Association's Section of Corporation Law, not the Delaware General Assembly, though the assembly does have the final word on whether it will enact the council's recommendations. The council consists of a number of highly prominent Delaware corporate lawyers.[8] At the time B Lab brought the Model Act to the council, its chair was Frederick (Rick) Alexander, then a partner at Morris, Nichols, Arsht & Tunnell LLP, a highly respected Delaware law firm.

Alexander and the council were deeply skeptical of B Lab's proposal. They felt that Delaware's corporate law was already functioning very well, and they did not see the need to risk tampering with a successful system. Even members of the council that were concerned with corporations' deleterious effects on the environment and society did not believe the solution lay with creating an entirely new type of corporation. Instead, they thought the responsibility for restraining bad corporate actors rested with the government. If corporations were polluting the environment, for example, the government should pass more stringent environmental requirements or better enforce the existing restrictions. They did not see changes to corporate governance rules as a meaningful part of the solution.[9]

B Lab persisted, marshaling the assistance of entrepreneurs and investors who liked the idea of a form of business organization that was designed to harness the powerful forces of capitalism to solve social problems rather than aggravate them. Eventually B Lab persuaded the council to create an alternative business form for companies that wanted to do more than earn a profit. But the council was not satisfied with the Model Act and decided to draft its own statute, even renaming the entity as a "public benefit corporation" ("PBC.").[10]

Interestingly, Rick Alexander, the council's chair, who doubted the need for benefit corporations when B Lab began its lobbying efforts, ultimately became a fierce advocate for the cause. He not only led the drafting of the Delaware PBC statute but left his law firm and joined B Lab as its head of legal policy. He has since founded a new organization, The Shareholder Commons, which aims to persuade investors to foster responsible capitalism in the companies whose shares they own.[11]

Whether we call it a BC or a PBC, this new form raises all sorts of fascinating questions and challenges that we discuss in depth in subsequent chapters. We go through the details of the BC's and PBC's legal features and how they vary from state to state in Chapter 3. For now, it is enough to know that these entities' boards of directors have a legal duty to consider the interests of other groups, such as employees, customers, communities, and perhaps even the environment, when making business decisions. Shareholders remain important—these are, after all, for-profit companies—but shareholders are one of several groups whose interests directors must consider when charting the corporation's course.

Although the form is still quite new, thousands of companies have already chosen to adopt it. These range from tiny companies with no employees to enormous companies whose brands are household names. Patagonia, Athleta, Danone North America, Ben & Jerry's Homemade, Allbirds, and Warby Parker are all BCs or PBCs. Some of these, such as Patagonia, are privately held companies whose owners have embraced conscious capitalism. Others, like Athleta and Danone North America, are wholly owned subsidiaries of international public companies, or, like Allbirds and Warby Parker, publicly traded companies themselves. BCs and PBCs have adopted a wide range of social causes, from the environment to their employees' well-being to advancing a host of different charitable goals. Some pursue all of these social ends. What they have in common is a determination to reshape capitalism so that the pursuit of profit does not produce troubling results for the rest of us.

As exciting and inspiring as this idea is, it also raises a host of practical questions. For example, why would entrepreneurs who want to make money choose a legal form that might sometimes require them to sacrifice financial returns for other ends? Why would any sane investor put capital into such an entity? What counts as a social purpose that a BC or PBC can pursue? How can a BC or PBC balance the trade-offs between profit and purpose? This book explores these questions and others, such as how well these new forms guard against companies exaggerating the social benefits they produce (referred to as "purpose washing") and how going public is likely to affect these social purpose organizations.

The theme that runs through our discussion of BCs and PBCs is that these forms are good *reinforcement* tools but not good *enforcement* tools. The BC and PBC statutes grant permission to organizations that want to pursue social enterprise to do so. They also provide some tools to improve that pursuit and reinforce the existing motivation to work on some societal problem or otherwise run the business in a way that is more cognizant of its impact. In both ways—by sending a clear message to the managers of BCs and PBCs that the law does not prevent them from sacrificing profit for social purpose and by providing a supportive framework—BCs and PBCs represent a significant legal advance for the social enterprise movement. As we will see, though, the statutes are not particularly effective at forcing companies that lack sincere purpose goals to prioritize purpose over profit when the two conflict. Like a good workout partner, the BC or PBC legal forms can encourage those with the desire to make a difference to do so, but they cannot make management get up early in the morning and hit the social purpose gym. Much of this book focuses on the legal framework of BCs and PBCs, but it is important to remember that law is only part of the story. Corporate culture and law must work hand in hand for BCs and PBCs to separate themselves meaningfully from traditional capitalism. For companies that truly embrace a social purpose, BCs and PBCs can be powerful tools. For those that do not, the new forms have little power to humanize their quest for profits.

My goal is to provide practical guidance on these issues without descending into too much technical jargon. This book is designed to be easily accessible to entrepreneurs, investors, and students without any legal background, while remaining precise enough for lawyers seeking information about these new forms. I also aim to present a balanced take on all of these issues. My purpose is to provide a clear understanding of both the opportunities and the challenges the new forms present so that readers can make up their own minds about whether BCs and PBCs are for them.

That said, I freely confess that the ambition of the social entrepreneurs and investors who have adopted this movement as their own inspires me. Every time I meet entrepreneurs who have built companies around these ideals, I come away with a sense of amazement at their imagination, idealism, and daring. These new forms represent a serious challenge to the way we have traditionally thought companies should be run. BCs and PBCs are not themselves a complete solution to any of the problems that come with capitalism's many benefits. But they do provide a useful tool for people to test their ideas on how to produce quality goods and services while taking care of the employees who provide them, the customers who buy them, the investors who enable them, and the planet on which we all live. I hope this book will embolden you to join the experiment.

Before we can plunge into a discussion of these new business entities, we first need to ensure that we understand the traditional corporate model. The first chapter of the book therefore begins by asking, Why do corporations exist?

# ONE

## *WHAT IS A CORPORATION'S PURPOSE?*

Volkswagen perpetrated a global fraud in 2015, inflicting billions of dollars in losses on its customers. It did this on purpose: its most senior officers actively participated in deceiving its customers and government officials. But here's the most remarkable part: the Volkswagen employees who carried out the fraud did not profit personally. Instead, they acted primarily for the benefit of total strangers whom they would never meet: Volkswagen's shareholders. In doing so, they were in a sense obeying what traditional legal and management authorities say is their duty as agents of the corporation: maximizing profits for the company's shareholders.

The story is likely familiar since it received massive coverage from the popular press. Volkswagen had rigged its emission controls software so that when it detected that a car was having its tailpipe emissions tested, it would ramp down the engine's performance, thereby reducing emissions. At other times, when the engine performed normally, the car's emissions exceeded legal requirements in many countries, including the United States. When the fraud came to light, governments imposed enormous fines on the company, and Volkswagen's chief executive officer was forced to resign.[1]

Volkswagen's story is just one of a number of shocking examples of corporate misbehavior that involved little direct personal benefit to the perpetrators. Facebook permitted Cambridge Analytica to access information about tens of millions of users, enabling Cambridge Analytica to create narrowly targeted ads to encourage voters to support Donald Trump in the 2016 presidential election.[2] Guidant sold a defectively designed defibrillator even after discovering the defect.[3] A. H. Robins marketed the Dalkon shield after learning that it was causing severe infections and even deaths in users.[4] Firestone knowingly sold defective tires, causing scores of deaths.[5] Ford Motor continued to sell its Pinto model while aware of a dangerous defect that could set the car on fire in a rear-end collision.[6]

The list of corporate scandals could easily fill a chapter by itself. More broadly, critics have blamed many of society's ills on corporations. Corporations have been accused of playing a role in producing global warming and all of its associated costs from sea-level rise to droughts to floods to more frequent and intense storms. Businesses have produced millions of tons of single-use plastic, much of which ends up in a landfill or the ocean, to the point where some have predicted that we will soon have more plastic in the ocean than fish.[7] Companies have moved factories and the jobs attached to them from communities that supported them for generations, leaving behind towns and cities bereft of good jobs and neighborhoods full of abandoned homes and boarded-up windows. Corporations have also been blamed for the vast increase in income inequality in the United States.[8] And some companies have produced unreasonably dangerous products and continued to sell them to their customers even after discovering the risk as we saw just above.

While critics can point to these negative impacts corporations have had, it is important to note at the outset that corporations have also produced tremendous good for us all. They are an enormously successful method of organizing capital and labor to produce goods and services. Without corporations, it is difficult to imagine how our economy could have achieved the tremendous growth it has experienced in the past century and a half. My point here is not that corporations are evil. To the contrary, corporations form the linchpin of our economy. But we should recognize that the prosperity corporations have produced has often come at a steep cost. We should therefore ask ourselves if we can make changes to corporate governance that would help us secure the abundance that corporations continue to provide while reducing the associated harms. To achieve that goal, we must first understand what motivates the individual human beings who run corporations.

In all of the scandals noted here, the corporate employees who carried out the misdeeds may have benefited indirectly by making themselves appear more successful at their jobs and perhaps by receiving bonuses or increasing the value of their stock options. But their personal rewards were a tiny fraction of the amount gained by the corporation and its shareholders. In extreme cases, these employees committed serious crimes that hurt or killed people, primarily for the financial benefit of the corporation's shareholders.

Why? Why would executives who spent decades building their careers risk everything on a fraud for the benefit of strangers? Less dramatic but more common, why would directors ever agree to pollute the oceans, abandon their friends and neighbors, or aggravate income inequality while gaining little or nothing personally? While we may never know the entire answer, much of the explanation lies at the feet of a decades-old doctrine of US corporate law: shareholder primacy.

## What Is Shareholder Primacy?

Shareholder primacy states that a company's board of directors—the group ultimately responsible for running corporations—must focus on maximizing the return for shareholders. The directors must do so even if the returns come at the expense of other groups that have tied their futures to the company, such as employees, customers, suppliers, and the communities in which the companies do business. Shareholder primacy says that if boards can increase long-term profits by 1 percent by firing one thousand employees, they should do it. If they can improve profit margins slightly with a new manufacturing process that will pollute the environment more, they should do it (as long as the new pollution does not run afoul of the environmental laws). If they can reduce expenses by moving their manufacturing base away from a city that has nurtured it for generations, then the law requires them to move.

Shareholder primacy is the dictate that most people who run corporations—the officers and the members of the board of directors—believe they must obey. From this perspective, shareholders are the entire reason corporations exist. All of the other groups who contribute to the enterprise's success must look out for themselves. The corporation's job is to extract as much value from these other groups as possible while paying them as little as possible, maximizing shareholders' wealth.

In this chapter, we examine this idea that took companies that were rapidly improving their workers' lives and transformed them into machines for making the rich even richer. It is the same idea that led many corporations to close factories in communities that had supported them for decades, destroying entire towns that depended on the jobs those factories provided. And it is the same idea that encouraged corporations to intervene in politics in an effort to loosen the regulations that were intended to police bad corporate behavior, including those designed to protect our planet from environmental degradation and the ravages of global warming.

## What Can Psychology Teach Us about Corporate Behavior?

To understand the impact the shareholder primacy doctrine may have on corporate conduct, we first need to establish how people behave when they are part of a group. We know that human beings are often kind, honorable, and benevolent, but that they can also be cruel, devious, and maleficent. People are seldom only good or only evil; most of us act differently at different times, and our decisions often stem from a mixture of motives. Few people have characters so strong that they always choose the same way. Even when facing similar decisions, we may act differently based on a host of factors, from how someone treated us earlier that day to whether the object of our attention bears a passing resemblance to an ex-lover.

Most important for purposes of this book, our choices often depend on the behavior of those around us. Peer pressure is a familiar concept when dealing with teenagers, but the phenomenon exerts an equally powerful effect on adults. We often behave differently based on our read of the room.

A famous set of experiments to demonstrate the power of peer pressure in the laboratory were performed by social psychologist Solomon Asch in the 1950s at Swarthmore College. Asch wanted to explore people's willingness to go along with the group, even when they knew that the group was objectively wrong. He handed experimental subjects a card with three printed lines and asked subjects to identify which of the three matched the length of a line on a second card. This was a very simple task; almost everyone answered the question correctly when alone.

Asch tested how people's answers would change when influenced by peers. He put subjects in a room with several confederates, then asked the confederates to answer the question before turning to the subject. When the confederates answered the question correctly, so did the subject. But when the confederates all chose the wrong line (following Asch's instructions), the experimental subjects often followed along, choosing the line they knew did not match. In fact, about 70 percent of the subjects chose the wrong answer at least once under the influence of their companions' unanimous (but wrong) choice.[9]

These results are surprising, but the consequences of choosing the wrong line seem minimal. Surely when there are real stakes involved, when people's lives will be seriously affected by what someone does, people will stand up for what is right, won't they?

Stanley Milgram conducted a series of experiments at Yale beginning in 1961 that shed some light on this question, though under circumstances that tested subjects' willingness to resist an authority figure rather than a group of peers. Milgram told his subjects that they were conducting an experiment on the value of electric shock punishment in aiding learning. The subjects were assigned the role of teachers and sat in a room where they could not see the supposed student (who was actually in on the experiment) but could hear him. The "teacher" would ask the "student" questions and shock the student whenever the student's answer was incorrect, using higher and higher levels of electricity with every wrong answer. No actual shocks were ever administered, but the teachers heard prerecorded reactions to the shocks they thought they were administering. The reactions included vigorous protests and eventually demands to be free before falling silent. Teachers who became reluctant to continue administering the shocks were given a series of prompts to encourage them to continue, such as, "It is absolutely essential that you continue." If they continued to refuse after four such prompts, the experiment ended. The experiment also ended if the teacher gave the maximum shock three times. Sixty-five percent of the teachers administered the highest level of shock.

Philip Zimbardo conducted an experiment at Stanford in 1971 with parallel results. He randomly assigned volunteer college students to take on the role of either prisoners or guards in a simulated prison. The guards quickly fell into their roles. Many began to abuse the prisoners in a variety of ways. Guards forced the prisoners to repeat their assigned identity numbers and punished them with extended exercise whenever they made mistakes. They also punished prisoners by forcing them to urinate and defecate into a bucket in their cell and then refused to permit the prisoners to empty the bucket. Guards confiscated the prisoners' mattresses at times, forcing them to sleep on concrete, and stripped some prisoners, leaving them naked. The experiment was originally planned to run for two weeks but was canceled after six days when a graduate student objected to the experiment's morality.

Both Milgram's and Zimbardo's experiments have been criticized on ethical and methodological grounds, but they demonstrate the human capacity to do horrible things when someone perceived to be in authority orders them to do so (the experiment administrator in the Milgram study and the "prison warden" in the Zimbardo simulation). This effect is particularly strong when reinforced by peers. If everyone around us is behaving the same way, we tend to believe that that behavior is appropriate.

Corporate culture takes full advantage of this tendency to inculcate behavior in employees that furthers corporate goals. Companies teach new employees, "This is how things are done here," or conversely, "That's not how we do things here." Strong corporate cultures can imbue employees with purpose, a sense of community and belonging, and a desire to advance the company's mission. This is helpful to the company because the employees become more dedicated and efficient. Employees also may benefit from a healthy corporate culture because they feel that their work serves a noble aim, even if that aim is just helping their team, a group of people they value and respect. Whether the culture is healthy or not, the orders that come from the company's leaders will tend to be followed, as the Milgram experiment showed. And when employees are surrounded by others who echo leadership's message, the effect is magnified, as we saw in the Asch and Zimbardo experiments.

Organizing people into cohesive groups not only magnifies the extent of obedience to authority, it also multiplies the power of those who wield that authority. An individual can write a symphony, but it takes a highly coordinated group to perform one. Or for a less enlightened example, one person can operate a street corner drug sale operation, but it takes an international criminal gang to produce the drugs, smuggle them across borders, and distribute them around the world. Gathering people into groups multiplies resources while at the same time legitimizing even highly nefarious behavior as acceptable under the organization's code of conduct. The end result is that those who lead these groups can become enormously powerful.

## Are Corporations Serving Our Needs?

The power these groups have can be used to achieve tremendous good for humanity. The modern corporation is arguably the most successful innovation in human organizational behavior since the Roman Empire. Humanity is materially richer now than at any previous moment in recorded history, and much of the credit should go to the corporate form. Corporations have organized staggering amounts of capital, labor, and natural resources to produce the greatest pile of wealth humanity has ever seen. They have built roads, bridges, railroads, and airports. They have developed life-saving medications and the hospitals that administer them. They have defeated Malthusian predictions of global starvation by wringing previously inconceivable amounts of food from farms. They have made all of humanity's knowledge available on a device that can fit in a pocket and manufactured that device cheaply enough for billions to afford one. In short, corporations have wrought miracles, all in the name of shareholder value.

But those miracles came at a price, demonstrating that leaders' power can also be used for great ill. Corporations used up irreplaceable natural resources to build our infrastructure. They left millions without medical insurance and bankrupted hundreds of thousands who could not afford to pay their medical bills.[10] They soaked our farmland with chemical fertilizers and fed us genetically modified plants, both of which will have unpredictable impacts on our health and the broader environment.[11] They provided communication tools that made us feel paradoxically more alone and bereft of community.[12] They acquired their competitors and concentrated power into fewer and fewer hands, giving themselves the power to set prices and suppress innovation that threatened their market position.

For good or ill, there is no denying that corporations possess massive amounts of power. The largest corporations are wealthier than many countries. If we think of a corporation's annual revenues as roughly analogous to a country's gross domestic product, then Apple's 2018 revenues of $265.6 billion would rank it forty-first among the world's nations, just below Finland and above Egypt, Portugal, Greece, and New Zealand.[13] If we instead compare Apple's revenues to governmental budgets, then Apple would rank fifteenth, just above Russia and Sweden.[14]

We can appreciate all the benefits corporations have conferred on us and still be wary of how such large, wealthy institutions make decisions. Even if we assume that on net, corporations have improved our lives, we can and should still ask how they can do a better job with fewer ill effects.

For example, while corporations undeniably improved the standard of living for the US middle class between 1945 and the early 1970s, the middle class's progress has slowed to a crawl since then compared to the upper class's progress.[15] While the highest earners' income has risen very quickly since 1979, the vast majority of US income earners (those in the bottom 90 percent) have seen their real wages rise at about one-tenth the rate of those in the top 1 percent (15 percent compared to 138 percent).[16] Even this stark statistic masks how dire the situation has become. Generally the less people earn, the slower their wages have grown. The wages of those smack in the middle (at the 50th percentile) rose only 6 percent from 1979 to 2013, and those near the bottom (at the 10th percentile of income earners) actually saw a real decline of 5 percent during those decades.[17]

Why did companies improve incomes for the working and middle class for the first few postwar decades, yet fail to do so in more recent decades? Many causes undoubtedly contributed to this shift, from the decline in unions' power to the rise of globalization and the growing automation of many jobs. But we can also ask "why?" for each of these contributing causes. Why did unions decline? Why did globalization occur? Why did companies automate so many jobs?

A large part of the answer to these questions is corporate directors' and officers' belief that their primary responsibility—perhaps their sole responsibility—is to run the company so as to maximize shareholders' return. The social psychology literature tells us that individuals often conform to groups. When a group adopts a purpose, its members are likely to see the pursuit of that purpose as a legitimate goal, at least when doing so does not conflict with other moral values and—as the Milgram and Zimbardo experiments so vividly demonstrated—sometimes even when it does. This tendency is especially strong when those in authority endorse that purpose. Groups use legitimizing language that distances the ethically questionable aspect of actions that meet their goals and tend to ignore or avoid arguments the majority opposes.[18]

Directors whose boards have adopted shareholder primacy as their dominant guiding value may therefore conform to the group's moral judgment. They may adopt a mind-set that suggests that it is the government's responsibility to police the ethical lines of a corporation's behavior, while the directors' task is to make as much money for shareholders as possible. They may also rationalize prioritizing shareholders with arguments that shareholders *deserve* to be the focus of boards' attention. For example, defenders of shareholder primacy sometimes argue that corporations will be more efficient if the "residual claimants" have unified interests. An enterprise's residual claimants are those who receive whatever is left over after all those with fixed claims on the company's revenue stream have been paid in full. Shareholders are typically seen as the residual claimants in a corporation because they have no right to any defined payment, as opposed to other corporate constituencies such as employees and creditors who have a contractual right to set payments. The argument is that corporate boards will do a better job managing the company for one set of residual claimants than if they try to balance the needs of groups with opposing interests, and shareholders should fill this role because the absence of a contractual right to a fixed payment makes them uniquely vulnerable.[19]

Corporate governance law assists in this moral outsourcing by ordering directors and officers to maximize shareholder value under the shareholder primacy doctrine. Corporate agents who instead divert company resources to improving employees' lives, cleaning up the environment, or supporting the communities in which the company functions face the possibility of personal liability for doing so in a shareholder suit. An emotionless, risk-neutral agent might ignore this possibility, since the threat of this sort of liability is not terribly realistic. The law grants great deference to officers' and directors' decisions under a doctrine called the "business judgment rule," a concept we discuss in Chapter 2. As long as directors can make a coherent argument that their actions will lead to larger corporate profits eventually, they are almost certain to escape liability.

The deference courts grant to corporate boards does grant wide latitude to boards to take good care of their employees, invest in their communities, and protect the environment. The ESG (environmental, social, and governance) movement demonstrates that many corporate boards are taking advantage of this freedom to craft corporate strategies that sacrifice short-term profits for the sake of the environment, social goals, and good governance. For example, Dick's Sporting Goods chose to stop selling guns at hundreds of its stores, sacrificing significant profits. The board could argue, though, that the move might prove profit maximizing. The directors could claim that the company's decision boosted its reputation, making at least some customers more eager to shop there and increasing overall sales. Although the company sacrificed the profits from gun sales, profits overall might rise as customers who favor gun control chose to shop at Dick's Sporting Goods rather than at Big 5 or some other competitor. An irate shareholder who sued the board over this decision would have very little chance of overcoming this argument under the deference afforded under the business judgment rule. In this particular case, the rationale seems to have worked out in practice: sales increased at stores where the company no longer sold guns.[20] But this type of argument—that the board is sacrificing immediate profits to boost the company's reputation and therefore increase profits over the long run—will almost always protect boards from liability for violating the duty of care.

Despite this latitude to sacrifice short-term profits, the law's shareholder primacy mandate has a real legitimizing impact, culturally, rhetorically, and emotionally. Actual liability for violating the rule is not very likely, but directors whom the law instructs to maximize profits are likely to engage in a sincere effort to do so. Often the quest for profits over the long run will result in boards' choosing policies that protect the environment and promote the welfare of employees and communities, but these goals may also diverge. When they do, directors are likely to choose profits over purpose, as the law requires.

Legal scholars have echoed the message that it is the government's job to decide on the outer limits of proper corporate behavior.[21] Directors and officers must play within the rules, but as long as they do, their duty is to make every effort to "win" by earning as much money for shareholders as possible. We might then understand why officers and directors would fear violating the shareholder primacy norm, even if objectively, the liability risk they face is minimal.

One profound problem with allowing corporations to export their moral compass to the government is that the law permits corporations to influence governmental decisions about the rules of the game. Even before the Supreme Court's *Citizens United* decision in 2010 solidified corporations' ability to participate directly in elections, corporations had long influenced the legislative process by lobbying for their preferred rules.[22] Individual directors and officers also helped shape policy with their (already legal) campaign contributions. Now that corporations can try to persuade the public to vote for their preferred candidates directly by paying for political advertisements and making campaign donations, boards must decide where to direct their company's powers of suasion.

Here, the discussion comes full circle. Directors, we now know, owe a duty to maximize the value of the company on behalf of its shareholders. Their efforts should therefore aim at crafting a friendly regulatory environment that provides as many advantages as possible to the business. In many cases, directors may reasonably see their duty as requiring them to try to soften rules that protect the environment, consumers, employees, and competitors. How reassured should we be, then, when companies defer to governmental regulation to define the acceptable bounds for their behavior?

Shareholder primacy presents a difficult conundrum to those of us who care about our country's and planet's well-being. The doctrine instructs directors to focus exclusively on increasing corporate profits and to look to the law outside of corporate governance—such as minimum wage statutes and environmental regulations—for guidance on the limits of permissible action. But then the law governing lobbying and political speech permits both corporations and their executives and directors to try to shape the rules that in turn describe the outer bounds of legal corporate behavior. Assuming that shareholder primacy governs those rule-shaping efforts as well, corporations are required to take all legal steps to eliminate any rules that stand in the way of their maximizing profits. This seems a deeply troubling result.

At this point, we might justifiably be wondering how corporate law has gotten so twisted up. Corporate law is a technical and sometimes difficult subject, but at its core, law in a democratic society is supposed to reflect that society's values. This is true even of technical areas like corporate law. We value economic development, and corporations have certainly provided that. But we value development because we believe that a growing economy will improve everyone's lives, not just those of the wealthy. That notion seemed to work well for the first few decades after World War II, but it has largely failed us since the 1980s. Corporate law—and shareholder primacy in particular—seems to bear a good part of the blame for that failure, so it is worth asking why a democratic country has adopted such a troubling fundamental rule to guide its most important economic actors.

### Who Determines Corporate Law?

To understand the rationale behind shareholder primacy, we must start with a few basics about corporate governance law in the United States. For many topics, both federal and state law have the power to set legal standards. They both have authority, for example, over environmental regulation, workers' wage and hours rules, and consumer protections. When it comes to the law that governs the relationship among shareholders, officers, and directors, however—what is generally termed "corporate governance law"—state law provides most of the rules. Federal law, especially federal securities law for public companies, sometimes intervenes, but traditionally state law controls most corporate governance issues.

With fifty states, plus the District of Columbia and territories such as Puerto Rico, Guam, and the US Virgin Islands, how do corporations know which state's laws cover their corporate governance disputes? The answer is surprisingly simple: the board chooses. Each corporation must register in a single state or territory by filing its documents with that state's secretary of state and paying a special tax, called a franchise tax, for the privilege of existing under that state's laws. Corporations are free to choose any state they like; they are not required to have a significant business presence in their state of incorporation. A state whose headquarters is in California, does most of its business in Florida, and whose investors mostly live in New York is free to register in North Dakota if it so pleases. In addition, corporations may change their state of incorporation at will by filing the appropriate documents and paying the required fees. For as long as a corporation is registered in a state, the laws of that state will govern the relationship among its officers, directors, and shareholders under the "internal affairs doctrine."[23]

The internal affairs doctrine creates an incentive for state legislatures to craft their corporate governance laws to please corporate boards in order to lure more corporations to register in their state. Boards, not the shareholders, choose the state of incorporation, and incorporation comes with corporate franchise taxes. States competing for those franchise tax revenues have an interest in enacting corporate governance laws that will appeal to the corporate directors who choose the state of incorporation. In 2021, for example, Delaware's state government projected that the incorporation tax (which includes not only the corporate franchise tax but also parallel taxes for other business entity forms and the fees foreign corporations pay to do business in Delaware) would account for 28 percent of the state's budget.[24]

In a highly influential law review article, William Carey argued that this dynamic creates a "race to the bottom" for state legislatures, as they compete to attract directors by protecting them from shareholder suits.[25] If this view is correct, we should expect to see state corporation statutes that make it very difficult for shareholders to prevail in any conflict with the board.

Other scholars, most notably Ralph K. Winter, have argued that the dynamic creates a "race to the top," at least for publicly traded companies.[26] Strategic directors will recognize, argued Winter, that shareholders will respond to the selection of the state of incorporation by discounting the shares of companies that incorporate in a state that makes it unduly difficult for shareholders to hold directors accountable for their misdeeds. In other words, a shareholder considering an investment in a company will check the company's state of incorporation. If that state's laws make it undesirably difficult to sue directors when they violate their duties to shareholders or define those duties too loosely to provide meaningful curbs on bad corporate behavior, the shareholder will refuse to invest without a price discount that compensates for the added risk caused by the director-favoring rules. Shares of companies incorporated in states that protect directors too much will then trade at a significant discount to those registered in states whose laws better enable shareholders to deter directors' misdeeds. Directors, anticipating this reaction by shareholders, will choose to incorporate in states that provide higher share prices rather than those that provide better director liability protection. Presumably directors' compensation packages will incentivize them to make this choice. State legislatures, understanding all of this, will enact corporate governance statutes that provide shareholders with a meaningful ability to punish directors who govern the corporation badly.

Whether the race is to the bottom or the top, it has a clear winner: Delaware. Despite its small population and even smaller geographical size, Delaware is by far the most important and influential state for corporate law.[27] The majority of public companies and a supermajority of Fortune 500 companies are registered in Delaware.[28] Delaware's influence reaches even further than the corporations it governs directly; other states' courts, knowing that Delaware courts have vastly more experience and expertise in regulating corporate governance, often adopt Delaware's rulings as their own. As we think about the development and effects of shareholder primacy, then, we have to pay special attention to Delaware.

### How Did Shareholder Primacy Become the Law?

Oddly for such a fundamental rule of corporate law, shareholder primacy is not dictated by any state statute, even in Delaware. Instead, the doctrine traces back to a famous case dealing with the nascent auto industry in Michigan in 1919.[29] The Dodge brothers, the founders of the eponymous car company, held a 10 percent stake in the then privately held Ford Motor Company. Ford Motor was enormously successful. Demand for its Model T outstripped its factories' ability to produce new cars. The company was hugely profitable and by 1915 had paid its shareholders over $40 million in dividends. This amount was only a fraction of its profits, however; by 1916, the company had another $112 million in surplus over capital, including over $50 million in cash.

Henry Ford, the company's founder, president, and majority shareholder, announced in 1916 that the company would no longer pay out large "special" dividends but would instead limit its payouts to shareholders to

$2 million per year. The remaining profits would all be reinvested into the business to build more factories and hire more workers. The Dodge brothers sued Ford Motor and Henry Ford, demanding that the company pay out more of these profits to them as dividends.

The Dodge brothers' suit also complained that Henry Ford was running the company as almost a charitable endeavor, aiming to benefit workers and customers rather than the shareholders. They pointed to a newspaper story that had quoted Henry Ford as saying, "My ambition, is to employ still more men; to spread the benefits of this industrial system to the greatest possible number, to help them build up their lives and their homes."[30] As support of this accusation, the Dodge brothers also pointed out that the company had originally priced the Model T at $900 but reduced its price sharply each year so that it was down to $360 in 1916. The Dodge brothers claimed that this reduction in price, when the company could not meet existing demand at higher prices, was a dereliction of Henry Ford's duty to the company's shareholders to maximize the company's profits. The company could easily have sold every car it produced at a higher price, yet Henry Ford insisted on lowering the price every year.

The Dodge brothers also protested Henry Ford's plans to expand the company by building a second factory, using what they saw as their money, the company's retained earnings. The Dodge brothers asked the court to order Henry Ford to refrain from carrying out his expansion plans, to distribute at least 75 percent of the accumulated surplus to the shareholders, and to require the company to pay out all of its profits to the shareholders going forward, except as required for emergency business purposes.

Henry Ford admitted that his purpose was to benefit his workers and spread the perks of capitalism, but he also argued that the planned expansion was in the company's best interests. His lawyer argued humanitarian motives were legally permissible, or at least mixed motives were, and that corporations were even permitted to engage in charitable activities so long as they were incidental to the business and not its core purpose.

The Michigan Supreme Court drew a distinction between incidental charitable activities and a "general purpose and plan to benefit mankind at the expense of others."[31] The former it declared legal, but the latter was beyond the powers of the board. The court went on to state, in blunt terms:

A business corporation is organized and carried on primarily for the profit of the stockholders. The powers of the directors are to be employed for that end. The discretion of directors is to be exercised in the choice of means to attain that end, and does not extend to a change in the end itself, to the reduction of profits, or to the nondistribution of profits among stockholders in order to devote them to other purposes.[32]

This language is arguably the clearest and most definitive statement of the shareholder primacy doctrine anywhere, and it is the reason this case appears in virtually every corporate law textbook. It serves as the source text for anyone claiming that shareholder primacy is the law of the land.

Ironically, the rule the court laid down in *Dodge* played no analytical role in deciding the case's outcome. In legal parlance, the statement of shareholder primacy—definitive sounding as it was—was "merely dicta." Dicta are judicial asides that are not necessary for the determination of the case. They are not considered binding legal authority, though courts may consider them to the extent they find them persuasive.

The *Dodge* court ruled that Henry Ford was free to continue with his business expansion plans. This ruling was an application of another foundational corporate law doctrine, the business judgment rule. In essence, this rule states that courts will not second-guess boards' business decisions so long as they are reasonably informed, untainted by self-interest, and made in good faith. Courts generally do not feel qualified to run corporations. They also do not want to subject directors to personal liability based on information that developed long after the directors made their decision. For both of those reasons and to ensure that corporations remain able to recruit qualified directors, courts generally defer to boards' business decisions.

In *Dodge*, the court ruled that Henry Ford could decide for himself how to run the company. Acting in his capacity as a director and with the consent of his fellow board members, Ford's decisions were entitled to deference under the business judgment rule. The court, after delivering its lecture on shareholder primacy, essentially took Henry Ford at his word that his actions would ultimately benefit the shareholders. In fact, the court trusted Henry Ford's good intentions toward the shareholders in the face of his representation that he was motivated by a desire to help his employees and society generally. To justify this move, the court pointed out that the company's phenomenal success up until that point was pretty good evidence that Henry Ford knew what he was doing. The court wrote:

> We are not, however, persuaded that we should interfere with the proposed expansion of the business of the Ford Motor Company. In view of the fact that the selling price of products may be increased at any time, the ultimate results of the larger business cannot be certainly estimated. The judges are not business experts. It is recognized that plans must often be made for a long future, for expected competition, for a continuing as well as an immediately profitable venture. The experience of the Ford Motor Company is evidence of capable management of its affairs.[33]

On the dividends issue, the court was less deferential, ordering the company to pay out substantial dividends. But that issue did not turn on Henry Ford's supposedly charitable motivations either. Instead, the court pointed out that the company had plenty of money to pursue all of Ford's expansion plans, keep a substantial sum of money in reserve for emergencies, and still pay out tens of millions in dividends. The nonpayment of dividends, or the payment of inadequate dividends, raises the specter of a conflict of interest between those in control of the company—in this case, Henry Ford—and the minority shareholders. Controlling shareholders have many powers at their disposal they can use to abscond with the company's profits, freezing out the minority and depriving them of the reasonable value of their stock. Because of this potential for a conflict of interest, courts are far less deferential when evaluating a possible minority freeze-out than when they are passing judgment on an ordinary business decision.

Again, though, neither the court's decision on the company's expansion plans nor its ruling on dividends turned in any way on Henry Ford's alleged humanitarian intentions. Nevertheless, we now explore the court's powerfully confident language in laying down the shareholder primacy doctrine and how it has influenced both corporate behavior and the law.

## Do Corporate Leaders Believe in Shareholder Primacy?

Although orthodox corporate law has embraced shareholder primacy for a century, executives and directors did not internalize it wholeheartedly as a management norm until many decades after *Dodge*. During the 1950s and

1960s, executives believed they should prioritize customers and employees rather than shareholders when making corporate decisions.[34] Respected management theorists such as Peter Drucker reinforced these views by arguing that treating employees well, for example, would ultimately benefit the company (and therefore comply with shareholder primacy, though that was not Drucker's concern).[35] These managerial attitudes may help explain why workers during those decades saw healthy increases in real pay, in sharp contrast to the more anemic growth in workers' pay in recent decades. The law may have mandated shareholder primacy, but managers largely ignored this obligation, protected by the business judgment rule and by shareholders who either shared management's views about the importance of other corporate constituencies or were too passive to bother challenging them.

This managerial view changed during the late 1970s and early 1980s as the country tilted rightward. Ronald Reagan captured the presidency while arguing for the deregulation of business. And Milton Friedman, the Nobel Prize–winning economist from the University of Chicago, pushed hard to persuade managers that they should focus exclusively on maximizing profits for shareholders.

Friedman wrote an article in the *New York Times Magazine* in 1970 entitled "The Social Responsibility of Business Is to Increase Its Profits."[36] The title of the piece aptly summarized its thesis. Friedman argued forcefully that corporate executives' duty was to the company's owners, the shareholders. Directing corporate resources to social causes such as improving employees' wages or investing in a greener manufacturing process than required by law essentially amounted to picking the shareholders' pockets. Friedman argued, "Businessmen who [advocate socially aware management] are unwitting puppets of the intellectual forces that have been undermining the basis of a free society these past decades.[37]

Friedman's sharp attack on corporate social responsibility resonated with a broader cultural movement of the 1970s: the rise of economic analysis in other fields of study, especially political science and law. Perhaps the culture was receptive to this hard-nosed, tough-sounding mode of thinking for other reasons: a desire for rules and order after the free-wheeling 1960s, a search for solutions to the relative decline of the United States in the face of renewed global competition, or just a natural pendulum swing in attitudes.

Regardless of why Friedman's ideas took hold, there can be little doubt that they found fertile ground in the minds of directors and officers. Perhaps the best evidence of his influence are the changes in executive compensation that took place beginning in the late 1970s. Prior to this time, companies paid their CEOs primarily in cash salaries. Companies sometimes used bonuses that were tied to short-term corporate results, but these seldom amounted to a significant percentage of an executive's compensation package.

Beginning in the 1970s and accelerating greatly through the 1980s and 1990s, major corporations began incorporating various forms of pay that tied executives' compensation to the company's stock price. By 2006, S&P 500 firms typically tied about half of a CEO's pay to the company's stock price, generally through awards of stock and stock options.[38] The rationale that boards generally cited for this shift in pay structure was that they wanted to incentivize CEOs to manage corporations for the benefit of the shareholders. Although they may not have cited Friedman, this change in pay structure amounted to a full-throated endorsement of his view. CEOs whose pay depended largely on increasing the company's stock price would presumably try to run the company in a way that boosted that price.

Do CEOs have meaningful control over share prices? Can CEOs even control the company metrics that influence share prices? There is little empirical support for either proposition. There are also serious reasons to doubt whether incentive pay works in this type of context at all, even if CEOs could influence share prices by working harder or smarter. But these are topics for another book. (Shameless plug: I've already written it.[39]) More to the point, whether or not tying pay to stock price helps to increase the stock price, the attempt demonstrates boards' adoption of shareholder primacy as their core purpose.

Federal tax law implicitly endorsed this view when the Clinton administration attempted to bring CEO pay down to more earthly levels. Congress passed section 162(m) of the tax code to bar companies from deducting CEO pay in excess of $1 million from the company's income. The theory was that companies would be deterred from paying their executives over $1 million because every dollar of CEO pay over that amount would have to come from the corporation's after-tax income, making that pay considerably more expensive to the company. Congress added an exception to the bill, however, for performance-based compensation, which included stock options and performance shares (stock issued to executives only if the company meets certain performance goals). The net effect of the provision was to encourage companies to tie pay over $1 million to the company's performance, especially its share price, so that the company could continue to pay executives out of pretax money, which can be considerably cheaper than paying out of after-tax money. This policy makes sense only if Congress believed that tying CEO pay to a company's stock price was a good idea, and the only apparent reason why this would be a good idea is if Congress believed in shareholder primacy. (In an interesting postscript, the Trump administration eliminated the performance-pay exception to section 162(m) as part of the Tax Cuts and Jobs Act of 2017.)

### Is Shareholder Primacy Still the Law?

The few courts to have the opportunity to consider shareholder primacy as a legal matter mostly followed Friedman and the *Dodge v. Ford Motor* dicta. The Delaware Supreme Court initially seemed to tip its hat in the other direction, in *Unocal Corp. v. Mesa Petroleum Co.*, but then reversed course sharply the following year to assert its adherence to shareholder primacy.[40] In a classic hostile takeover case, *Revlon, Inc. v. MacAndrews & Forbes Holdings, Inc.*, the court ruled that boards could only consider other corporate constituencies besides the shareholders instrumentally, as a means ultimately to enrich the shareholders. As the court wrote, "While concern for various corporate constituencies is proper when addressing a takeover threat, that principle is limited by the requirement that there be some rationally related benefit accruing to the stockholders."[41] In *Revlon*, the Delaware Supreme Court quickly arrested its movement toward some alternative theory of corporate governance and reasserted its adoption of orthodox shareholder primacy.

The Delaware Supreme Court has not squarely addressed this question since *Revlon*, but the prestigious Delaware Court of Chancery has, in a case dealing with two famous brands: Craigslist and eBay.[42] Craig Newmark founded Craigslist in 1995 as an email list for events taking place in San Francisco. Since that time, Craigslist—under the leadership of James Buckmaster, the company's CEO—had grown into the dominant website for classified advertisements in the United States. Despite its success and large market share, Craigslist remained a small company, with only a few dozen employees at the time of the lawsuit in 2010.

Craigslist remained small in part because of its unusual culture and business strategy. Newmark and Buckmaster showed little interest in converting their commanding market share into profits. Instead, they let most people advertise on Craigslist for free. What little revenue Craigslist earned came from job postings in some cities and apartments listings in New York City, both of which cost the advertisers money to list on the site. Otherwise, Newmark and Buckmaster believed that Craigslist should be operated as a public service.

Craigslist had only three shareholders at the time of the lawsuit: Newmark, Buckmaster, and eBay. At that time, eBay owned about 28 percent of the company's outstanding shares, leaving Newmark and Buckmaster together firmly in possession of a majority stake. Nevertheless, Newark and Buckmaster (the court refers to them as Craig and Jim) took several steps to protect the company's mission from eBay's efforts to adopt a profit-maximizing strategy. eBay sued to invalidate these steps and won. The court's explanation of its holding is worth quoting at some length to provide a concrete sense of the Delaware courts' wholehearted endorsement of shareholder primacy:

> Jim [Buckmaster] and Craig [Newmark] did prove that they personally believe craigslist should not be about the business of stockholder wealth maximization, now or in the future. As an abstract matter, there is nothing inappropriate about an organization seeking to aid local, national, and global communities by providing a website for online classifieds that is largely devoid of monetized elements. Indeed, I personally appreciate and admire Jim's and Craig's desire to be of service to communities. The corporate form in which craigslist operates, however, is not an appropriate vehicle for purely philanthropic ends, at least not when there are other stockholders interested in realizing a return on their investment. Jim and Craig opted to form craigslist, Inc. as a *for-profit Delaware corporation* and voluntarily accepted millions of dollars from eBay as part of a transaction whereby eBay became a stockholder. Having chosen a for-profit corporate form, the craigslist directors are bound by the fiduciary duties and standards that accompany that form. Those standards include acting to promote the value of the corporation for the benefit of its stockholders. The "Inc." after the company name has to mean at least that. Thus, I cannot accept as valid for the purposes of implementing the

Rights Plan a corporate policy that specifically, clearly, and admittedly seeks *not* to maximize the economic value of a for-profit Delaware corporation for the benefit of its stockholders—no matter whether those stockholders are individuals of modest means or a corporate titan of online commerce. If Jim and Craig were the only stockholders affected by their decisions, then there would be no one to object. eBay, however, holds a significant stake in craigslist, and Jim and Craig's actions affect others besides themselves.[43]

*Revlon* and *eBay* seem quite clear: shareholder primacy is the law in Delaware for traditional corporations.[44] Nevertheless, some respected scholars have questioned whether this is really true under Delaware law, as we discuss in the next section.

### Does Shareholder Primacy Have Any Real Legal Bite?

The most prominent critique of the conventional view that Delaware law requires boards to attempt to maximize shareholder profits came from Lynn Stout, a Cornell law professor. Stout argued that the deference courts offer boards of directors under the business judgment rule means that boards are free to consider other constituencies besides shareholders when determining corporate actions. All they need to have is some stated rationale—even a poorly reasoned one—for why considering these other constituencies will ultimately help the corporation's bottom line. She wrote, "As long as [directors] do not take [corporate] assets for themselves, they can give them to charity; spend them on raises and health care for employees; refuse to pay dividends so as to build up a cash cushion that benefits creditors; and pursue low-profit projects that benefit the community, society or the environment."[45]

Stout was certainly correct that the business judgment rule affords directors tremendous latitude in forming corporate strategy. But she conflated deference to boards in forming *tactics* with permission to pursue different *goals*. Delaware law seems quite clear that shareholder primacy is the mandatory goal for corporate boards; they have no latitude to choose a different one, short perhaps of a statement granting them permission to do so in the company's founding document, the certificate of incorporation. (As Stout acknowledged, most certificates of incorporation say simply that the corporation is authorized to pursue any lawful purpose, a phrase that has not been interpreted as opting out of shareholder primacy.[46])

Directors of Delaware corporations are free to pursue whatever tactics they can claim in good faith they are adopting to maximize shareholder value. But they are not permitted to take actions that they acknowledge will harm the shareholders' financial interests in order to help other corporate constituencies. As Leo Strine, the former chief justice of the Delaware Supreme Court has written, "Despite attempts to muddy the doctrinal waters, a clear-eyed look at the law of corporations in Delaware reveals that, within the limits of their discretion, directors must make stockholder welfare their sole end, and that other interests may be taken into consideration only as a means of promoting stockholder welfare."[47]

Still, boards have the power to use the latitude both Stout and Strine acknowledged exists under the business judgment rule to pursue the welfare of other corporate constituencies, as long as their actions are ultimately intended to increase profits for shareholders. As a practical matter, then, there may not be much difference between Stout's and Strine's visions of Delaware law. The paucity of lawsuits where shareholders attempt to enforce a board's duty to pursue shareholder welfare indicates that this distinction may be without a real difference. Cases like *eBay*, where the shareholder primacy doctrine was actually enforced, are exceedingly rare; in fact, *eBay* may be the only example in this century.

Some might argue that part of the reason for the lack of suits may be that many states have somewhat softened the shareholder primacy rule. The majority of states—though not Delaware—have passed constituency statutes that authorize directors to consider other corporate constituencies such as employees, customers, suppliers, and communities when making corporate decisions. Even in these states, though, directors are not required to consider the welfare of these other constituencies, and these other constituencies do not have the right to sue directors who ignore them. Courts have decided few cases that turn on these statutes, and the bulk of these involve hostile takeover attempts, with the defending board invoking the statute as an excuse for turning down a hostile offer. This is not terribly surprising, as most states adopted these statutes to help defend their corporations from hostile takeovers. These statutes have not had much impact on the corporate purpose debate within boardrooms and do not seem to have shaped directors' behavior.[48]

Whether or not their states had a constituency statute, boards used their latitude under the business judgment rule to aid other groups quite often in the first decades after World War II, especially to improve employees' welfare. They even used—and continue to use—this latitude to give money away to charities, arguing that donations to popular causes can improve a company's public image and ultimately its sales.[49]

The law on shareholder primacy may play an important role in shaping managerial culture and thereby corporate behavior. But whatever work the shareholder primacy doctrine is doing is not through the realistic threat of imposing personal liability on directors and officers. That dynamic suggests that the linchpin to change corporate behavior is to transform managerial culture rather than to edit the liability rules. But it also suggests that reforming the law may prove an effective path to shape culture and behavior, regardless of any actual pecuniary impact of the new rules.

## Is Shareholder Primacy Weakening?

We have seen that without any amendment to the law, companies markedly changed their behavior after the 1970s. There are signs now that the cultural pendulum may be shifting back in the pro-constituency direction again. Several highly influential corporate authorities have recently embraced the idea that corporations should strive to do more than maximize profits for shareholders. A change in the law, such as the creation of a new type of business organization, has the potential to accelerate this shift by legitimizing the new attitudes.

Larry Fink, the founder and CEO of BlackRock, the largest asset manager in the world, wrote a letter to CEOs in 2017 that endorsed the stakeholder view, rejecting shareholder primacy. He wrote:

> Society is demanding that companies, both public and private, serve a social purpose. To prosper over time, every company must not only deliver financial performance, but also show how it makes a positive contribution to society. Companies must benefit all of their stakeholders, including shareholders, employees, customers, and the communities in which they operate.[50]

Similarly, Marc Benioff, the chair and co-CEO of Salesforce, a cloud software company with a market capitalization over $100 billion, issued a call to companies to manage their businesses for the benefit of all stakeholders (such as employees and communities) and not just for shareholders. In an editorial for the *New York Times*, he wrote:

> Every C.E.O. and every company must recognize that their responsibilities do not stop at the edge of the corporate campus. When we finally start focusing on stakeholder value as well as shareholder value, our companies will be more successful, our communities will be more equal, our societies will be more just and our planet will be healthier. [51]

The cry by establishment figures for a new (or perhaps a return to an old) way of thinking about corporate purpose has not been limited to a few progressive corporate leaders. The Business Roundtable, an association of CEOs of major US companies, released a new Statement on the Purpose of a Corporation in 2019 in which it abandoned shareholder primacy and called for a stakeholder view. The statement, which pledged the CEO signatories' commitment to their customers, employees, suppliers, and communities, in addition to their shareholders, concluded, "Each of our stakeholders is essential. We commit to deliver value to all of them, for the future success of our companies, our communities and our country."[52]

Fink, Benioff, and the Business Roundtable all called for voluntary shifts to stakeholder theories of management. Senator Elizabeth Warren of Massachusetts. however, was not content with relying on a gradual shift in corporate culture. In 2018, she proposed a mandatory legal shift when she introduced the Accountable Capitalism Act (ACA), a bill with a number of important provisions, but the most interesting for our purposes was a rejection of shareholder primacy. The ACA would require US corporations with over $1 billion in annual revenue to obtain a new, federal corporate charter that would require them to consider the welfare of all corporate stakeholders in making corporate decisions.[53] In a press release announcing the bill, Senator Warren argued that "we need to end the harmful corporate obsession with maximizing shareholder returns at all costs."[54]

The ACA may never become law, but for entrepreneurs interested in a business entity form that prioritizes all of a company's constituencies, not just shareholders, and that also encourages companies to adopt social causes as part of their core mission, there is now a new form that does just that: the benefit corporation (BC). Advocates argue that the BC, along with its close cousin the public benefit corporation (PBC), have the potential to tame capitalism's worst impulses while harnessing its enormous power to solve numerous social problems, from homelessness to global warming and from world hunger to health care. Critics have countered that this new legal form will aggravate agency costs by providing cover to directors and officers to entrench themselves and pursue their own interests at shareholders' expense. The BC may fool constituents into thinking it is achieving real social progress while in reality, these critics maintain, it only provides a convenient mask for traditional corporate avarice.[55]

———

Which of these predictions turns out to be true depends most of all on you, the readers of this book. We have already seen that managerial culture likely matters more than the law in determining corporate actions. Will you adopt this new form for the companies you form or invest in or represent? How will you tackle the many challenges it poses? And how will you use it? Will you see it as a tool to make a reasonable profit and change the world for the better? Or will you try to take advantage of the BC's positive image for your own private benefit?

Before we can get into any of that, we need a much more nuanced understanding of both traditional corporate law and the new provisions governing BCs. In this chapter, we discussed the history of corporate purpose in the United States, learning that the current view is that the purpose of corporations is to maximize profits for shareholders (shareholder primacy). BCs and PBCs change that purpose by statute to a broader, stakeholder view, with implications that we explore throughout the book. Chapter 2 outlines the basic framework of US corporate governance law. (Experienced lawyers may be tempted to skip this chapter, but I suspect even they may find my take on this topic helpful in understanding the chapters that follow.) Chapter 3 then explains how BCs and PBCs are different from traditional corporations. Together, these two chapters will give us the tools we need to explore the questions we will tackle in the rest of the book.

# TWO

# CORPORATE LAW BASICS

To understand how BCs and PBCs are different from traditional corporations, we first need to look at how traditional corporations run. Some of this material will be familiar to many readers, but much of it will be new even to readers with significant business experience.

## Who Runs the Corporation?

Surprisingly, given the shareholder primacy rule, the law delegates the most power within the corporation not to the company's owners, the shareholders, but to its board of directors. The corporate law statutes of every state empower the board to make most corporate decisions. For example, Delaware's statute states, "The business and affairs of every corporation organized under this chapter shall be managed by or under the direction of a board of directors."[1]

One of the most important decisions the board makes is the appointment of the senior officers, especially the CEO. This decision is critical because the board, although legally empowered to run the company, typically cedes day-to-day control to the officers. The officers turn to the board for guidance and authority only for major decisions. For large public companies, the full board typically meets only once per quarter, though it has committees that may meet more often than that.

The reason that officers, rather than directors, make most corporate decisions is that directorships are typically part-time positions, especially at public companies. The directors generally have full-time jobs at other companies, often as a senior executive. As a result, they do not have the time or incentive to devote much time to the company's affairs. Of necessity, they rely on the senior executives to tee up issues that require their attention and to make recommendations for how those issues should be resolved. Despite the law empowering them to run the company, directors serve more of a monitoring role than an active managerial role in large corporations. Only when major decisions arise, such as the decision to sell the company, do directors truly fulfill a managerial role.[2]

For smaller, privately held companies, board members are generally the company's founders and representatives of some of the major investors. For these companies, directors and officers can be the same people, with the company founders filling both roles simultaneously, at least for some of the board slots. These boards are likely to take a much more active managerial role rather than the monitoring role of public company boards, since the directors—as either company founders or major investors—have much more at stake than the typical director of a large, public company.

Shareholders' main role in governance is to elect the directors, though they also get to vote on certain major decisions, such as a possible merger with another company. (Shareholders' ability to vote on acquisitions can depend on the transaction's structure, but the technicalities involved are too much in the weeds for our purposes in this book.) In public companies, shareholders have traditionally been viewed as passive, except perhaps when a possible sale of the company for a large premium is in the offing. Otherwise, historically, shareholders of public companies seldom owned a sufficiently large chunk of stock to wield much influence over the board. The rise of institutional shareholders—especially the tremendous concentration of stock in the hands of mega-shareholders like BlackRock, Vanguard, and State Street—has strengthened shareholders' hands, though it remains unclear to what extent these shareholders care to use their influence over typical management issues.[3]

Some public companies do have a controlling shareholder, that is, a single shareholder or coherent group of shareholders who together hold enough votes to elect a majority of the board. This happens most frequently when the company's founders have retained a controlling interest before going public, selling only a minority of the shares to investors. It can also happen with the use of dual-class shares: founders sometimes create two classes of stock, with one class having the right to one vote (or even no votes) per share and the other having the right to many votes (sometimes even thousands of votes) per share. The point of dual-class stock is to keep control in the founders' hands, even after the founders have sold off a majority of the company's equity to investors. This move is sometimes justified as a way to ensure the company is managed well by keeping control in the hands of the founders, who care about the company's long-term interests, and out of the hands of short-term arbitrageurs or hedge funds out for a quick buck. But dual-class shares can also insulate the founders from the other shareholders' legitimate concerns, sometimes leading to self-dealing or poor management.[4]

The story is dramatically different in closely held companies, those owned by just a handful of shareholders (like the typical start-up). These companies' shareholders possess tremendous power. Shareholders in all companies can fire the directors and elect new ones, but that power is more theoretical than actual in public companies. Even massive shareholders like BlackRock are unlikely to own the requisite majority of shares to fire a director, and for a number of reasons, institutional shareholders are generally reluctant to coordinate with their competitor investors when deciding how to vote their shares.

In closely held companies, in contrast, the shareholders can have the practical ability to exercise this power, giving them much more influence over the board and, through the board, the company. Investors in closely held companies also may negotiate for special governance rights, like the right to appoint a representative to the board or the right to block (or require) dividends, that give them even more power.

The relative power of these three groups—directors, executives, and shareholders—depends greatly on the company's capital structure (especially the degree to which ownership is concentrated and whether there are dual-class shares), and whether any shareholders have negotiated special governance rights for themselves as a condition of investing. In the frequent case where none of the shareholders are actively involved in running the business, it is crucial that the board of directors and executives who do manage the company are accountable to the relatively passive shareholders. Without some mechanism to ensure that the directors and executives will run the company honestly, potential shareholders will be reluctant to invest in the corporation. The more accountable that directors and officers are to shareholders for their actions in running the corporation, the more likely shareholders will be to invest. Somewhat paradoxically, then, the company's founders—who will generally serve as officers and directors and be vulnerable to liability in shareholder suits—should *want* the law to hold them accountable for their bad behavior, at least when that bad behavior hurts shareholders.

To see why this is true, imagine you are an investor. A company's founders meet with you to pitch you on buying equity in their company. You like the company's business model and believe it has tremendous potential for growth. But you are less sure that you trust the founders. They seem like they might take your money, invest it in the business, and then find a way to divert the company's profits to themselves once they no longer need you. One solution to this problem is to negotiate with them at length over contractual protections. You might insist on rights to regular reports on how the company is doing, for example, or even ask for a seat on the board of directors to help you monitor the company's progress directly. The founders might resist these points, though, and if your investment is small compared to the company's overall need for capital, you may lack the necessary leverage to get the terms you want. Plus, negotiating all these terms is time-consuming and, if lawyers are involved (as they should be!), expensive. How can the founders persuade you to trust them so that you can make the investment both you and they want you to make?

In order to help solve this problem, the courts have developed a number of special duties, called "fiduciary duties," that directors and officers owe to the corporation and its shareholders under state law. The most important of these for day-to-day management are the duties of care and loyalty, but there are also some specialized duties that arise in the mergers and acquisitions context that shape a board's response to a buyout offer. (During this discussion, I will refer to Delaware law and the Delaware court cases that shaped it since Delaware law remains the closest analogue we have to a national corporate governance law.)

## What Is the Duty of Care?

The duty of care requires directors and executives to act as a reasonably cautious person would in managing the business.[5] When the company is considering whether to launch a new product, for example, the board and the senior officers must investigate the likelihood the product will succeed in the market and produce profits to the extent a reasonably cautious board and reasonably cautious officers would. This is far from a bright-line test; reasonable people—and reasonable judges—might well differ on what a reasonably cautious person would do.

Remember also that courts judge corporate conduct after the fact, when the outcome of the decision has materialized. Directors and officers are in the much less fortunate position of having to predict how their decisions will come out. Judges might be forgiven for suffering from some hindsight bias in these cases, finding that the defendants' decision was clearly mistaken when things turned out badly even if it might have seemed reasonable to most people at the time it was made.

Not only do corporate fiduciaries risk courts' hindsight bias from the duty of care, but they also face a second risk: judges' inexperience managing a business. Even on Delaware's specialized corporate court, the Court of Chancery, judges' prior experience seldom prepares them to run a complicated business. These judges typically come from sophisticated private firms where they practiced corporate law. In fact, Chancellor Kathaleen St. J. McCormick and all four vice chancellors currently serving on the court came from private law practice.[6] They are experts in corporate governance and other areas of business law, but they have little or no experience managing a corporation themselves.

Outside of Delaware's Court of Chancery, judges frequently come from the ranks of the local district attorney's office, so their dominant experience is prosecuting criminal cases.[7] They typically lack any meaningful business experience. At most, they might have experience representing companies, generally in litigation, but this is inadequate preparation for making the types of business decisions that boards and executives must address. Judges are therefore a poor choice of referee for deciding whether directors and officers should be personally liable for having made an unreasonable decision.

Judges are well aware of their deficits in this area and have crafted the law governing duty-of-care suits to compensate for their institutional shortcomings. Although the duty of care asks corporate fiduciaries to exercise ordinary care when running the company—to act as an ordinarily prudent person would—the law imposes liability only on fiduciaries who violate the business judgment rule. As we discussed in Chapter 1, the business judgment rule is, in essence, a rule of deference to corporate management. It recognizes that by reviewing business decisions, courts run the risk of displacing directors and officers as the de facto managers of the corporation. Courts will intervene as a second-best solution when there is strong reason to suspect that a corporate board cannot be trusted to make an objective decision, such as when the directors have a conflict of interest or act in bad faith. In those cases, the judges' lack of business experience and hindsight bias are outweighed by the directors' self-interest or bad faith. But when courts believe the board is trustworthy, they generally defer to the board's judgment.

Imagine, for example, a company faced with flagging sales for its core product, a brand of laundry detergent. The company has several options. One response would be to launch an aggressive and expensive new advertising campaign to remind consumers of the laundry brand they have always known and loved, a nostalgia play. Some of Coke's ad campaigns could be seen this way, such as its famous commercial in which a young boy cheered up the famously fierce NFL defensive tackle, "Mean" Joe Greene, with a Coke.[8] An alternative would be to try to create a new, hipper image for the brand, persuading consumers to think differently about a brand they are already familiar with. We might think about Dos Equis's "most interesting man in the world" campaign as an example of this approach. That campaign revolutionized the public image of a beer brand that was well over a century old by associating it with a made-up character with hyperbolic personality traits. Ads described this man with memorable lines such as, "His charm is so contagious, vaccines have been created for it."[9] A third possibility would be for the company to create an entirely new brand to attract a different market segment, as when Toyota created the Lexus badge to go after the luxury car market.

Suppose our company's board decides on the first option. The company spends millions of dollars on a brand-new campaign touting the familiar virtues of its old brand in an exaggerated way, showing how clothes washed in its brand evoke warm, fuzzy feelings in everyone who smells them. The flagship commercial shows a well-known celebrity bringing peace between police and protesters from the Black Lives Matter movement just by letting the participants smell his clothes.

Unfortunately, the new ad campaign is a total failure. Critics immediately slam the ad's racial insensitivity, and the company pulls the ad after only a few showings. The millions of dollars the company spent on creating the ad and buying time on television are entirely wasted. The company's stock price plummets, with the market reacting not only to the wasted money but also to the company's now damaged reputation. Angry shareholders sue.[10]

Should the directors who made the strategic decision to try a nostalgia campaign face personal liability for this decision? What about the corporate officers who agreed to launch the commercial that created the controversy? At least that decision, if not the higher-level conceptual decision by the board to try a nostalgia campaign, seems pretty foolish, especially in hindsight. And the decision caused extensive damage to the company—damage that someone should pay for. Imposing liability on those responsible would likely deter future corporate officers from such carelessness.

Nevertheless, this lawsuit is almost certainly dead on arrival under the business judgment rule. Courts understand that they do not have the training or expertise to run corporations, nor do they generally have any desire to do so. For a court to rule for shareholders in their suit against the corporation's officers, the judge would have to rule on the wisdom of the executives' decision. Such a ruling would require the judge to lay down a rule, something that could be followed by other courts in the future and would guide executives' future decisions in all companies that stated what executives were required to do. Imagine what such a rule would look like.

Could a judge hold that all nostalgia campaigns are forbidden to companies? That would certainly seem like an overreaching decision since these campaigns are often successful. What about a rule barring racially insensitive advertising? That narrower rule seems less likely to force companies to give up on profitable opportunities, but its interference with free speech might run afoul of the First Amendment. Also, racial sensitivity is a benchmark that often depends on the audience and the time period. Messages some perceive as perfectly acceptable might be seen by others as at least insensitive, and perhaps offensive. And our sense of what is appropriate to say about race has changed dramatically over time. This sort of variability makes a legal standard difficult to apply for both executives trying to predict how a court will rule when making a decision about corporate strategy and for courts having to make such rulings.

To avoid having to dive into these incredibly complex and difficult decisions, and in recognition of courts' institutional deficiencies in policing substantive business decisions, courts have largely decided to duck the entire area. Instead of acting as Monday morning quarterbacks for the business world, courts have stayed firmly in an arena where they feel comfortable: process. The business judgment rule is primarily about the process by which companies make their decisions; as long as the fiduciary (someone who owes fiduciary duties, such as a director or an executive) made a decision that was informed, disinterested, and in good faith, the decision will almost never result in liability. The only exceptions are for waste, meaning that the company gave up something of value in a transaction where it received essentially nothing in exchange, and for irrationality, meaning that the decision was so poor that no sane adult would make it. Courts apply these exceptions very rarely, so rarely in fact that one well-known Delaware judge compared their likelihood to the odds the Loch Ness monster exists.[11]

At first glance, the requirement that fiduciaries be informed before making a decision seems as if it could open up directors and officers to a real chance of personal liability. One can easily imagine cases about the substance of a decision being recast as targeting fiduciaries for failing to inform themselves adequately before making the decision. Shareholders angry about the ad campaign described above, for example, might argue that the executives failed to inform themselves adequately about the likely public reaction to the ad. A simple focus group would likely have revealed the problem. Failing to use some standard techniques to test an ad before launching it might amount to a sort of business malpractice.

This case would almost certainly fail too, as have most attempts to sue corporate fiduciaries for failing to inform themselves adequately. This is not to say that this strategy can never succeed; in some cases, courts have found directors liable for failing to inform themselves.[12] But the Delaware courts have decided to demand very little of directors and officers, asking only that they not be grossly negligent in informing themselves before making a business decision.[13] As a result, shareholder suits against directors and officers for breach of the duty of care seldom succeed. (There is a statute in Delaware that corporations can use to make these suits even tougher for shareholders to win by absolving directors from liability for all breaches of the duty of care.[14] Duty-of-care suits are uphill battles, though, even in corporations that have not chosen to avail themselves of this additional protection.)

## What Is the Duty of Loyalty?

The duty of care covers companies' ordinary business decisions, and as we have now seen, in the vast majority of cases, courts will defer to the directors' and officers' business judgment. Some transactions, however, draw special scrutiny from courts. Among them are self-dealing transactions by fiduciaries, fiduciaries' efforts to compete with the corporation, purposeful attempts to harm the corporation or violate the law, the erection and maintenance of provisions to prevent hostile takeovers of the company, and (at least sometimes) the sale of the company. For all of these transactions, courts are more suspicious that corporate fiduciaries may be taking advantage of their position to gain some personal benefit at the corporation's expense. The business judgment rule therefore will not apply. Instead, the courts have invented specialized legal tests for each of these situations.

Generally when a corporation buys or sells something, it is dealing with an outsider. Since the bargain is at arm's length, with both sides having every incentive to negotiate for the best deal they can, the courts will not examine these transactions closely. There are times, though, when the corporation transacts with one of its own officers or directors. For example, suppose Director is a member of the board of directors of an auto manufacturer (Auto) and also owns a steel plant (Plant). If Auto buys steel from Plant, then Director is on both sides of the transaction. As a director of the corporation, the law requires Director to try to get the lowest price possible for Plant's steel. But as Plant's owner, Director will naturally want to negotiate the highest price possible for Plant's steel.

At one time, the law effectively barred these transactions altogether by allowing any shareholder to cancel the deal if it became disadvantageous to the corporation.[15] Contemporary courts have liberalized this rule because they recognize that these self-dealing transactions can sometimes be advantageous to the company. The company's fiduciaries presumably want the company to succeed, so they may offer better terms than an outsider would. They also know more about the company than an outsider would, and so they may feel more comfortable extending credit when an outsider might not or might be willing to extend credit on better terms than an outsider would.

Courts now view these deals through the lens of the fiduciary duty of loyalty. The law requires corporate fiduciaries to show loyalty to their corporation by putting the corporation's interests ahead of their personal interests. To ensure that they do so, courts apply the "entire fairness test" to self-dealing transactions. This test is far more rigorous and less deferential than the business judgment rule that applies to potential breaches of the duty of care. It asks fiduciaries to prove that the transaction was entirely fair to the corporation and its shareholders, looking at both the process by which the deal was negotiated and approved and the substantive fairness of the resulting transaction.[16]

This is a tough, but not impossible, test for fiduciaries to meet. The test requires courts to review transactions, taking on the business supervisory role they reject in the duty-of-care context. But they are willing to overcome their reluctance to adopt that role in the duty-of-loyalty context because the assumption that applies when the duty of care is involved—that the corporate fiduciaries are doing their best for the company—seems inappropriate when the fiduciary stands to gain personally by striking a bad deal for the corporation. Fiduciaries may be able to avoid facing this difficult standard if they obtain approval of the conflicted transaction from the independent directors or shareholders, under the theory that courts can trust these groups to safeguard the company's interests.[17]

The duty of loyalty also applies when an officer or director takes an opportunity for the fiduciary's own benefit that should belong to the corporation or competes with the corporation.[18] Similar to the conflict-of-interest transactions, with these corporate opportunity cases, courts cannot simply trust that fiduciaries are acting in the corporation's best interest when their own personal interest may be directly opposed to the corporation's interests.

Courts also enhance their scrutiny of directors' actions when directors appear to be acting in bad faith, which the Delaware courts have defined as acting with some purpose other than furthering the corporation's best interests. This can include acting with the intent to violate the law or intentionally failing to act in the face of a known duty to act.[19] (The duty of good faith is not technically a separate duty but a subset of the duty of loyalty.[20]) For example, if a company's shareholders passed a bylaw limiting the compensation the corporation's officers could receive, but the corporation's directors authorized a more generous plan than permitted in defiance of that bylaw, the directors would be liable for violating their duty of good faith.[21]

### What Special Duties Apply in the Takeover Context?

Although boards normally have the power to control a corporation's actions, that power may be limited when it comes to a decision to sell the company. A buyer can make an offer directly to the shareholders, going over the directors' heads, through a mechanism called a "tender offer." To prevent these "hostile acquisitions," directors sometimes implement "takeover defenses." A takeover defense prevents the shareholders from receiving offers the board opposes, often by imposing large costs on the unfriendly buyer or by delaying the implementation of the takeover for a long enough period to make the purchase financially untenable.

When a board installs a takeover defense, the directors are not technically engaged in self-dealing. They are not buying anything from the corporation or selling anything to the corporation. But courts realize that directors do have something to gain by protecting the company from a hostile acquisition. By definition, a hostile acquisition is one that the board would prefer to reject. The directors may have perfectly legitimate reasons for their dislike of the hostile offer; they may feel the buyer is unlikely to secure sufficient financing to complete the deal, or that they can find a different buyer who will make a higher bid, or that their own plans for the company will ultimately result in a higher share price than the one on offer.

It is also possible, though, that the directors would simply prefer to remain in office. If the directors' rejection of an offer—and adoption of takeover defenses to enforce their rejection—is rooted in a business judgment about the company's value, then courts should treat those actions like any other business decision and defer under the business judgment rule. If the directors are at least partly motivated by a desire to remain in office, though, then courts should treat their decision more like a breach of the duty of loyalty and provide meaningful review.

Perhaps because it is difficult at the outset of a case to determine the directors' motivation, the Delaware courts have elected to give all adoptions of takeover defenses a type of intermediate scrutiny. Courts neither defer under the business judgment rule nor subject these decisions to a rigorous entire fairness review. Instead, they apply something called the *Unocal* test, named after the Delaware Supreme Court decision that first adopted it. The *Unocal* test first asks if the board has properly identified a threat to the company's strategy. If the court agrees such a threat exists, the court then examines whether the board's response was proportional to the threat.[22] (The test is actually a bit more involved than I am describing here, but this description will suffice for our very limited purposes.[23]) Note that the test does not directly attempt to discern the board's motives. Still, if the board reacted to a genuine threat in a proportional way, one might infer that their motives were proper (or at least the courts appear to have accepted this as a more easily provable proxy for a motivation test).

The courts also sometimes give a form of intermediate scrutiny to another type of board action with potentially questionable motives: the sale of the company. The rationale for the courts' greater scrutiny in this context is a bit opaque. At times, the courts seem concerned that the board may choose one buyer over another in order to benefit themselves. Such cases represent a form of self-dealing that would seem to trigger a duty-of-loyalty claim and the entire fairness test rather than intermediate scrutiny. Nevertheless, the landmark case that created this type of scrutiny, *Revlon, Inc. v. MacAndrews and Forbes Holdings, Inc.*, involved such allegations and applied intermediate scrutiny, not the entire fairness test.[24] Other times, the courts seem less clear about the nature of their concern. Their concern might be the great importance of the transaction—it is hard to imagine a more important decision to shareholders than whether to sell the company—or perhaps some less defined sense that at an endgame moment like a corporate sale, the directors' incentives may become muddied.

In *Revlon*, two companies offered to purchase Revlon, Pantry Pride and Forstmann, Little. The board favored Forstmann, though Pantry Pride's offer appeared to be higher. Pantry Pride sued, alleging in part that Revlon's board chose Forstmann because it offered the Revlon directors a personal benefit to secure their approval of its bid. (Specifically, Forstmann agreed to protect the board from liability from holders of bonds Revlon had issued in an earlier stock repurchase by ensuring the notes retained their value.) Although the court could have analyzed this as a duty-of-loyalty issue, and in fact the Chancery Court did so at trial, the Delaware Supreme Court took a different path. In ruling for Pantry Pride and against Revlon's board, the Delaware Supreme Court held that once the Revlon board had determined to break up the company and sell off the pieces, the board's duty transformed from preserving the company's best interests (and those of its shareholders) to acting as auctioneers. When a transaction triggers *Revlon* duties, the board must act reasonably to obtain the highest price possible for the shareholders.

Since *Revlon*, the Delaware courts have struggled to define exactly what types of transactions trigger a board's *Revlon* duties.[25] Courts have also vacillated on precisely what they require from boards once the duties are triggered.[26] For our limited purposes, it should suffice to say that *Revlon* duties are triggered any time a corporation experiences a change of control, and that when it applies, *Revlon* requires boards to act reasonably to maximize the share price for shareholders—and only shareholders—in the immediate term. They cannot reject an offer under the rationale that they have a better plan to raise the company's value over the long term. Instead, they must sell the company to the highest bidder.[27]

## How Can Shareholders Enforce Directors' Fiduciary Duties?

Directors owe all of these fiduciary duties—the duty of care, the duty of loyalty, the duty of good faith, the *Unocal* duty, and the *Revlon* duty—to their corporation. Any violation of these duties is therefore an offense to the corporation. A violation of a fiduciary duty that harms the corporation naturally also hurts the shareholders, since their stock will be worth less if the corporation declines in value. But the shareholders' harm in such cases is derivative of the corporation's more direct harm. If the company is worth less because it has suffered an injury, that injury will also lower the company's stock price, thereby indirectly hurting shareholders. Although shareholders are harmed whenever a villain harms the corporation, they do not have the right to sue the villain directly. When a corporate fiduciary harms the corporation itself, as opposed to harming an individual shareholder directly, the claim against that fiduciary belongs to the corporation, not to the individual shareholders. The corporation suffered the harm, so the corporation owns the right to sue for a remedy.

Nevertheless, the courts have recognized that the corporation might not always act as aggressively as it should to protect itself when fiduciaries violate their duties. To see why this is so, imagine a fairly typical case where a shareholder complains that the board violated its duty of care by making an abysmally poor business decision. Suppose the corporation in question manufactured bicycles, and the board decided to invest heavily in a new model with square wheels, with predictably disastrous results. The board made a colossally foolish decision; if any ordinary business decision violates the duty of care, this one should. They could not have informed themselves very well if they believed square wheels would function on a bicycle. Their decision may actually be one of those very rare cases that qualify as irrational. This should be an open-and-shut case.

There is, however, one important wrinkle: the directors are the defendants in this case, and the court is very likely to hold them personally liable for the corporation's losses. But the directors are also the people empowered to make the corporation's decisions, including the decision of whether to have the corporation bring a case against . . . those same directors. Even the most ethically upstanding directors would be hard-pressed to vote to sue themselves. The directors may also prove reluctant to sue the senior officers they appointed and supervised, at least in some cases.

We therefore face a dilemma. The very people who are most likely to have breached their fiduciary duties are the same people charged with enforcing those duties on the corporation's behalf. Aphorisms about foxes guarding henhouses spring readily to mind. In order to enforce fiduciary duties and prevent them from becoming effectively meaningless, we need a mechanism that will empower someone to bring suit against the directors and officers who also has an incentive to do so.

At first blush, shareholders seem the ideal group for this role. They are the closest analogue to an owner that we have in the corporation, and the analogy seems particularly apt in this context. If the fiduciaries harm the corporation, the shareholders' equity stakes will decline in value. The shareholders therefore seem to have an incentive to bring a lawsuit to recover that lost value on the corporation's behalf.

Unfortunately, there is a major flaw in the theory that the shareholders will ride to the rescue, at least when we are dealing with a publicly held corporation. In a public company, the largest shareholder typically owns a few percentage points of the outstanding equity, and most shareholders own far less than that. Pretend for a moment that the company's largest shareholder in this case owns 1 percent of the company's stock. And imagine that the board's square wheels experiment cost the company half its value, causing its market capitalization (the value of the company measured as the price per share times the number of outstanding shares) to decline from $100 million to $50 million. Lawsuits are expensive, especially sophisticated claims with large potential damages like this one. Suppose that we can litigate this claim to its conclusion for the relatively thrifty price of $5 million. Will our largest shareholder be willing to foot the bill?

The odds of winning this case look pretty good from the shareholder's perspective, but there is always some chance of losing. Unfortunate facts turn up in discovery, the judge may unexpectedly rule against the shareholders on some key legal issues, or the judge may see the case differently than the plaintiffs do. Let us say that the shareholders have an 80 percent chance of winning the case. The expected value from the corporation's perspective is the chance of winning times the amount of damages minus the cost of suing. In this case, that would be 80 percent × $50 million − $5 million or $35 million. Easy decision: the corporation should absolutely bring this case. But the corporation will not do so because the directors who decide what the corporation does are also the defendants. Instead, we must ask whether any shareholder will bring the case.

The expected value from our largest shareholder's perspective looks a bit different, because the shareholder does not receive the full amount of the damages awarded; the corporation does. The shareholder benefits from any damage award only to the extent of the shareholder's equity stake, which in this case is 1 percent. So if the shareholder sues, the expected return to the shareholder (as opposed to the corporation) is the percentage of ownership times the chance of winning times the amount of damage minus the cost of suing, or 1 percent × 80 percent × $50 million — $5 million. The shareholder should expect to *lose* $4.6 million. That is, the shareholder can expect to spend much more on legal fees and the other costs of suing than he or she is likely to earn back from the suit. We could be more optimistic and assume our largest shareholder owns 10 percent of the company instead of 1 percent, but even this larger shareholder should expect to lose $1 million.

In some cases, the numbers might turn out better for the shareholders, where the combination of a large shareholder, large damages, and a relatively low cost of suit would result in a positive expected return to the individual shareholder from suing. Those cases might still suffer from the free-rider effect, with the largest shareholders reluctant to bear the entire burden of bringing suit when *all* the shareholders benefit from the recovery in proportion to their ownership stakes. Choosing to sue might put the shareholder at a disadvantage relative to the other investors.

To solve this problem, the law created a special kind of lawsuit, the "derivative suit." This is a lawsuit by a shareholder on behalf of the corporation. If the suit is successful, the court awards damages to the corporation, with the shareholders indirectly sharing the recovery equally on a per share basis through the increase in the corporation's value. The corporation also pays for the legal fees incurred in bringing the successful suit, either as a proportion of the amount recovered—a contingency fee—or, if the suit resulted in a substantial nonpecuniary benefit to the corporation, by paying the lawyers' hourly fees. If the suit fails, the corporation owes the lawyers nothing.[28]

Derivative suits still require a shareholder to bring the case, and someone must advance the legal fees and other costs, taking the risk that the defendants will win and the plaintiff shareholder will be stuck paying the legal fees without any contribution by the corporation. Without someone willing to take on this risk, there will be no derivative suits, and directors and officers will have little incentive to obey their fiduciary duties.

The hero of our story, the character who takes on this risk and enables the corporate governance system to function, is the lawyer. There are law firms that specialize in these cases. They find a shareholder to act as the putative plaintiff, but the real party at interest is the law firm. The firm risks its lawyers' time and the firm's capital to pursue the case, betting that it will win enough of these cases and collect sufficient fees to make the risk worthwhile.

The hero of this story is the lawyer, but the lawyer is also the monster. If derivative suits are too easy to bring and win, lawyers will bring lots of cases where the claims are not particularly strong, where the corporate fiduciaries behaved appropriately. They will bring these frivolous cases because the corporate fiduciaries have a strong incentive to settle them, even if the claims are not especially good. If the fiduciaries settle the cases, the corporation or its insurers will pay the damages. But if the case proceeds to trial and results in a verdict against the fiduciaries, it is quite possible that neither the corporation nor its insurers will cover the fiduciaries' resulting liability.[29] As a result, it may be easy for lawyers to extract some settlement value out of quite weak cases. If the law enabled lawyers to bring these cases too easily, corporations could suffer death from a thousand cuts.

The law therefore must strike a balance. On the one hand, it cannot make these cases too hard to bring, or no lawyer will take on the risk associated with bringing them and directors' and officers' fiduciary duties will become mere formalisms, without any teeth. On the other hand, if the law makes these cases too easy to bring, lawyers will open the floodgates of litigation and corporations will drown. The law has therefore tried to impose some barriers to bringing these cases without making them insurmountable. Reasonable people could differ as to whether the law has gone too far in one direction or the other or has found a good balance.

The first barrier to entry for derivative suits requires the suing shareholder to own stock in the company throughout the relevant time period. This requirement consists of two rules. The shareholder serving as plaintiff in the suit must have owned stock in the corporation at the time the alleged wrongdoing occurred (the "contemporaneous ownership test") and must remain a shareholder throughout the length of the suit (the "continuous ownership rule").[30] The second barrier is the demand requirement. Before filing suit, the shareholder must either make a demand on the board to have the corporation sue the alleged wrongdoers or state in a court pleading that any such demand would be pointless.[31]

Since the plaintiff in these cases will be suing the directors for breach of their duties to balance, it seems unlikely that those same directors will agree to have the corporation sue themselves, as we have discussed. But the fact that the directors are the defendants in the suit is not sufficient under Delaware law to allow the plaintiff to skip demand as futile.[32]

The shareholder plaintiff must allege something more. Delaware requires the shareholder plaintiff in a derivative action to demonstrate a reasonable inference that the directors cannot be trusted to make an unbiased decision about the lawsuit. If the board lacks a majority of trustworthy directors, demand will be excused as futile. There are three ways a director might be disqualified as untrustworthy: (1) if the director gained some important personal benefit from the conduct that is the basis of the lawsuit; (2) if the director faces a substantial chance of personal liability in the lawsuit; or (3) if the director has a relationship with someone in either of the first two categories that would prevent the director from making an unbiased decision about the suit.[33]

Finally, a plaintiff who succeeds in meeting both the stock ownership requirements and the demand futility requirement still faces the possibility that the court will dismiss the case at the board's request some point after the litigation has begun, sometimes years after the plaintiffs filed their initial complaint. Although states vary on this issue, under Delaware law, the board may appoint an independent committee of directors to evaluate the lawsuit and determine if it is in the company's best interest.[34]

Recall that a derivative claim technically belongs to the corporation. The law allows a shareholder plaintiff to bring the claim only because the organization entrusted with making the corporation's decisions—the board of directors—is interested or dependent and therefore untrustworthy. Once the board has delegated its power to a committee that *is* trustworthy, Delaware courts permit that committee to ask the court to dismiss the derivative action. The court will not defer to this committee entirely because Delaware judges recognize that this committee, while apparently independent, was appointed by a board that the court already determined was either interested in the lawsuit or dependent on those who were. The committee is somewhat tainted by its origins.

Delaware courts therefore apply a two-step test, first inquiring into the committee's independence and good faith and the reasonableness of the investigation it made into the merits of the lawsuit. If the court finds that the committee has failed to meet its burden of demonstrating its directors' independence or good faith and that it made a reasonable investigation, the court will allow the case to continue. If the committee meets its burden on these issues, the court applies the second step, using its own business judgment to decide whether the lawsuit is in the corporation's best interest.[35]

———

At this point, we have a basic understanding of the roles that directors, officers, and shareholders all play as well as the core duties that directors and officers owe the corporation and its shareholders. Directors and officers must act reasonably in managing the corporation, but liability for violating this duty of care is measured by the very deferential business judgment rule. They owe a duty to put the corporation's interests first, and liability for violations of this duty of loyalty is measured by the quite strict entire fairness test. Finally, there are two duties that apply in the context of mergers and acquisitions. The *Unocal* duty applies when the board adopts an antitakeover device and requires the board to respond to a threat in a proportional way. The *Revlon* duty applies when the company is being sold in certain types of transactions and requires the board to act as auctioneers, selling the company to the highest bidder. All of these duties are evaluated against the backdrop of the corporation's overall purpose: maximizing profits for the shareholders. In the next chapter, we discuss how these rules change for benefit corporations under B Lab's Model Act and for public benefit corporations under Delaware law.

## THREE

# HOW ARE BCs AND PBCs DIFFERENT?

When B Lab invented the benefit corporation, it drafted a model statute that states could pass as legislation without having to come up with their own versions. B Lab calls its proposed legislation the "model benefit corporation legislation." For brevity, I refer to this draft statute as the Model Act or sometimes just the Act. Most states that have authorized BCs have passed some version of the Act. A number of states have made changes to it before passing it, and B Lab itself has changed the Act over time. All of this makes discussing the law a bit of a moving target, but I refer here to the most recent version of the Model Act as of this writing (dated January 13, 2016).[1] The changes states have made are generally not critical, and my goal is not to turn my readers into lawyers but to give you a good grounding in the core concepts.

Rather than tweak the Model Act, Delaware decided to draft its own statute from scratch. Because Delaware law is so important to corporate governance and because Delaware's statute is different from the Model Act in some significant ways, I examine Delaware public benefit corporations separately.

## How Do BCs Run?

### *What Is a BC's Purpose?*

The most important change the Model Act makes to traditional corporate governance rules is that it changes the traditional purpose of the corporation: to make money for the corporation's shareholders. We have already explored how that profit-maximization goal has likely contributed to a host of problems, from income inequality to global warming. The whole point of the BC is to reverse the shareholder primacy rule in an effort to harness capitalism to solve social problems, some of which capitalism helped create. So it should not surprise anyone that the Model Act adopts a different rationale for why BCs exist. The Model Act states, "A benefit corporation shall have a purpose of creating a general public benefit."[2]

The first part of the sentence is clear enough, but what in the world is a "general public benefit"? Fortunately, the Act tells us, defining *general public benefit* as "a material positive impact on society and the environment, taken as a whole, from the business and operations of a benefit corporation assessed taking into account the impacts of the benefit corporation as reported against a third-party standard."[3] There is a lot to unpack there, so we will take the key pieces one phrase at a time.

We'll start at the beginning with *material positive impact*. We should take the easiest word first. The word *material* is a term of art in the law, but its meaning is fairly intuitive. Essentially, the Act is saying here that the "positive impact" has to be meaningful, not trivial. This is the furthest thing from a precise standard, but the general intent should be reasonably clear. And because this is a term of art in the law, courts have interpreted it many times in reported cases, which makes it feasible for lawyers who have read those cases (or can look them up) to make fairly good predictions about whether something is "material." *Impact* should not give us much trouble; the Act wants BCs to have some effect.

*Positive* is the only word in this phrase that should give us serious pause. On first glance, you might have passed right over it; "positive" means the opposite of "negative," something that tends to be good rather than bad. This is where we get into a deep philosophical quagmire. What effects count as "positive"? Some uses of the term should be unambiguous. If the BC feeds the hungry, that should count. Cures terrible diseases? Check. Provides clean, renewable energy? No question. But there is a lot that we disagree on in the United States, sometimes passionately. What if the BC provides abortions to women who want them and who lack health insurance or other means to pay for the procedure? Some people would likely call that a positive impact, providing free women's health care to those in need. Others might think it equivalent to murdering infants. Now we see the problem.

The Model Act solves this problem by ducking it cleanly: it never defines *positive*. We can gain some sense of the intended meaning from the definition of "specific public benefit," something we will get to a bit later in this chapter. That definition contains a list of actions that count as a "specific public benefit"—things like "improving human health" and "promoting the arts."[4] Those goals all look quite uncontroversial, but the final item on the list is a catch-all: "conferring any other particular benefit on society or the environment."[5] What counts as a "benefit" for society? "Benefit" sounds awfully similar to "positive" and opens the same can of worms. We will see shortly that there is some language in there about measuring the positive impact against a standard developed by a third party. But the rules for choosing a third-party standard do not say anything about what that standard is allowed to consider "positive" or a "benefit." In the end, then, the Act is carefully neutral as to what counts as positive.

Does this mean that the whole enterprise is pointless? After all, if *anything* can count as a positive impact, then what is the difference between a BC and a traditional corporation? Oil extraction companies provide an indisputably valuable commodity that most people still need. Could Chevron convert to a BC? We discuss these questions when we cover permissible social purposes in Chapter 4.

### Can a BC Also Adopt a Specific Public Benefit?

We just learned that a BC must have the purpose of providing a general public benefit. As we discussed, the definition of *general public benefit* is somewhat inchoate and leaves a lot of room for the board to shape the company's mission. We also discussed this flexibility as a possible criticism of the BC form: if a BC can stand for absolutely any value, some might argue that the form stands for nothing.

Perhaps for this reason, some companies may want to declare more clearly what their vision is. They may want to do this to communicate their mission to outside audiences, such as customers, employees, or communities. They may also want to adopt a specific mission to guide future directors and corporate officers as they decide how to run the business. The company founders may not be involved in active management forever, after all, and they may want to take steps to encourage the company to stay on the path they blazed.

The Model Act provides an optional mechanism for BCs to declare clearly that they plan to pursue not just general social goals but a specific one. BCs must identify any "specific public benefit" they embrace in the corporate charter, a document that is roughly analogous to the corporation's constitution and, like a constitution, is relatively difficult to amend. (Amendments to the corporate charter generally require the approval of a majority of the directors as well as a majority of the voting shares.) Just as BCs have a great deal of flexibility in choosing how to pursue a general public benefit, they also have the discretion to choose from a wide range of possible specific public benefits. Authorized specific public benefits include:

1. providing low-income or underserved individuals or communities with beneficial products or services;

2. promoting economic opportunity for individuals or communities beyond the creation of jobs in the normal course of business;

3. protecting or restoring the environment;

4. improving human health;

5. promoting the arts, sciences, or advancement of knowledge;

6. increasing the flow of capital to entities with a purpose to benefit society or the environment; and

7. conferring any other particular benefit on society or the environment.[6]

Again, BCs have no obligation to adopt a specific public benefit. The Model Act empowers them to do so if they want to distinguish themselves or express a more tailored vision of the good they do for society for internal or external audiences. Any specific benefit a BC adopts legally becomes part of its own best interests, along with the general public benefit. The BC's board is then permitted to pursue that specific public benefit and balance that specific benefit against its other goals, such as earning profits.[7]

*Should BC Directors Pursue Profit or Purpose?*

Hand in glove with the change in purpose of BCs is the directors' and officers' duty to consider that expanded purpose when running the business. Remember that fiduciaries of a traditional corporation must make business decisions with the intent of maximizing profits. That task can be incredibly complex, even though the goal is singular. For officers and directors of a BC, though, the task may be quite a bit more challenging. The Model Act requires them to consider the effect of any decision on the BC's shareholders; its employees, subsidiaries, and suppliers; its customers, to the extent they are beneficiaries of either the BC's general public benefit or specific public benefit; the welfare of every community in which the BC, its subsidiaries, or its suppliers have offices; the local and international environment; the BC's own interests, both immediate and over the longer term; and the BC's general public benefit purpose and any specific public benefit purpose the BC has adopted.[8] That is quite a juggling act!

As if that were not enough, the Model Act also gives directors and officers permission to consider "other pertinent factors or the interests of any other group that they deem appropriate."[9] While "pertinent" might be seen as some limit on the broad discretion the Act grants here, courts are unlikely to read it that way. The ending phrase "that they deem appropriate" likely applies to both the "other pertinent factors" and the "interests of any other group" and seems to grant essentially unfettered discretion to the board and the officers to consider anything they want.

BC directors and officers may choose which factors to prioritize. They may also decide to emphasize different factors at different times or in different contexts. The Model Act gives them a great deal of latitude, stating that they "need not give priority to a particular interest or factor" unless the BC's corporate charter says that they will emphasize certain aspects of the general public benefit or some specific public benefit that the BC has adopted.[10]

With so many factors to consider, this balancing task may seem overwhelming at first. But when we look more closely, we can see that it is not really very different from what managers of a traditional corporation do. Traditional corporations need to care about their customers' well-being because dissatisfied customers will stop buying what the company is selling. Their concern for their customers may stem from a desire for profits rather than a direct motivation to help, but the net effect is the same. Similarly, managers of traditional corporations must pay some attention to their employees' satisfaction. Unhappy employees tend to be less productive, which lowers the company's profits. They also sometimes leave, imposing large search and training costs on the firm trying to replace them.[11] Traditional corporations also have to think about their suppliers, because if their suppliers are losing money, they will go out of business and the company will need to find new sources.

Running a BC is not the same as running a traditional corporation. It requires more purposeful thought about the well-being of customers, employees, and suppliers for their own sake and not just as profit-producing instruments. In addition, a BC must consider other factors as well, such as the environment and the communities in which it and its subsidiaries and suppliers operate. Again, those interests must be considered for their own sake and not as a means to maximize profits (such as by improving customer loyalty). My point is not that running a BC is the same, but that the difference in complexity from the task of running a traditional corporation is one of degree, not of kind. Running a traditional corporation is a complex task; running a BC is a more complex task. The increase in difficulty may be significant, but it should not prove overwhelming. And if we believe that BCs and PBCs can help us meaningfully soften the adverse impacts of capitalism, some increase in managerial complexity may prove a reasonable trade-off. Nothing worthwhile is easy.

Although BCs empower directors to prioritize values such as employee welfare or environmental sustainability over profit, the enormous discretion granted their boards also permits them to choose profit over purpose. The statute requires a sincere consideration of purpose; it does not dictate any particular outcome. Again, though, the point of the BC is to obtain better results on average. The statutory mechanisms that require self-reflection, consideration of interests other than profit, and disclosure should encourage more socially valuable decisions by directors who sincerely desire to run companies in a more holistic way. But these mechanisms only *encourage* different decisions; they do not *require* them. A BC board can use the flexibility the statute provides to choose profits over purpose, so long as it sincerely considers the public benefit before doing so. A BC that elected the most profitable course every time, though, and acted indistinguishably from a traditional corporation would raise a red flag that its board was not truly considering other options.

### Who Can Sue to Enforce BC Directors' Duties?

The primary enforcement mechanism is a new type of lawsuit that shareholders can use against the BC's directors: a benefit enforcement proceeding. Shareholders who own at least 2 percent of a class of the BC's stock (or at least 5 percent of the equity of the BC's parent company, if there is one) may bring a benefit enforcement proceeding for any failure of the BC to create a general public benefit or any specific public benefit the BC has included in its corporate charter as part of its purpose. They may also bring a benefit enforcement proceeding for any violation of a duty established by the Model Act.[12]

The benefit enforcement proceeding works only for duties created by the Model Act; shareholders who want to bring other types of claims—such as breaches of the duties of care or loyalty, claims under *Unocal* or *Revlon*, or other civil actions such as claims for breach of contract or a tort like negligence—must follow a different procedure. (Claims for breaches of fiduciary duty outside the Model Act often have to be brought as derivative claims, as we discussed in Chapter 2.) The benefit enforcement proceeding is also the only way anyone can sue to enforce the rights and duties created by the Model Act; the Model Act forbids any other type of suit.[13]

The Model Act states that benefit enforcement proceedings are brought "derivatively."[14] This statement might indicate that these cases are derivative suits and require plaintiffs to overcome all the hurdles that generally come with derivative suits addressed in Chapter 2: the contemporaneous and continuous ownership rules, the demand futility requirement, and the possibility of dismissal after evaluation by an independent board committee. It is, however, possible that the Act may have used that word only descriptively, indicating that the plaintiffs in these cases are suing for harm done to the corporation rather than directly to individual shareholders. There are no reported cases that have tested this question yet. Courts could hold that benefit enforcement proceedings should not be subject to the usual obstacles imposed on derivative suits if they believe the incentives to bring these suits are lower than in a typical derivative claim. Remember that these obstacles are designed to strike a balance between providing too much incentive to lawyers to bring these actions—which could result in a lot of frivolous litigation—and providing too little incentive—which could result in directors and officers ignoring their fiduciary duties to balance and produce social benefits.

To the extent that these suits are rooted in claims that the board is focusing too much on profits and neglecting the company's social goals, lawyers may not have a great deal of incentive to sue. The corporation is unlikely to suffer any pecuniary harm from underemphasizing social goals in order to maximize profits, and the attorneys' fees are commonly calculated as a percentage of the financial recovery garnered by the suit. It is possible for attorneys to persuade a court to award them hourly fees if the suit succeeds in conferring a material benefit on the company, but this is a riskier proposition than suing for a large damage pool. Courts could reasonably decide to forgo some or all of the requirements for traditional derivative suits in order to encourage lawyers to sue directors of BCs that produce too little social benefit. The statutory language leans against this, but it is sufficiently ambiguous to allow a court to find that the statute did not intend to import all of the features of a derivative suit into the benefit enforcement proceeding.

The point of the benefit enforcement proceeding is to ensure that BCs are achieving their missions, a worthy goal. We need some method of preventing BCs from becoming indistinguishable from traditional corporations. If the BC experiment is going to succeed, that will have to mean that they behave better in some meaningful way than traditional corporations do. Suing directors and officers, as well as the BCs themselves, when the BCs fail to live up to what they say they will do feels very appealing. The looming threat of liability seems to work reasonably well in some other contexts to deter bad behavior and adds the benefit of compensating the victims. There are, though, significant limits to the benefit enforcement proceeding that may prevent it from serving this critical function very effectively, even without the barriers imposed in derivative suits. We hold off on discussing those though, until Chapter 5.[15]

### Must BCs Disclose Their Social Performance?

The second way the Model Act tries to ensure that BCs behave meaningfully better than traditional corporations—in addition to the threat of director liability—is by requiring them to report on what they are doing for the world. The theory is that when a company has to tell the public about what it is doing, it will be more likely to do the right thing. When a company reports bad conduct, it is likely to damage its reputation and suffer all sorts of setbacks, from declining sales to greater difficulty attracting and retaining its workforce. In order to avoid those ill effects, BCs under a disclosure obligation—knowing that the public is watching—might choose to behave in a way they can be proud to reveal. As Justice Brandeis famously stated, "Publicity is justly commended as a remedy for social and industrial diseases. Sunlight is said to be the best of disinfectants; electric light the most efficient policeman."[16]

The Model Act's primary drafter was William H. Clark Jr., a well-respected corporate lawyer who made a career of advising public companies on their corporate governance. The federal securities laws require public companies to disclose a lot of information about their financial results and business plans, with the goal of giving investors the information they need to make good decisions about which stocks to buy and sell. Corporate lawyers like Clark are therefore steeped in a culture of disclosure, so it is no surprise that Clark would have turned to disclosure as a tool to help shape BCs' behavior.

The Model Act requires BCs to prepare a "benefit report" every year that must include a number of items. The two most important are a narrative description of the general (and any specific) public benefit the BC provided and an assessment of "the overall social and environmental performance" of the BC measured against a third-party standard.[17] The other items mostly pertain to the role of the benefit director, if the BC has one. I examine these in the next section.

The narrative description requirement is fairly straightforward. The Model Act requires a BC to discuss the ways it pursued a general public benefit and the extent to which it succeeded in producing one. As already noted, the general public benefit can include a wide range of activities such as cleaning up the environment, progressive policies for employees, donating some profits to charity, and a host of other items. If a BC has adopted a specific public benefit, then the Act requires it to do the same for the specific public benefit—report on both efforts and achievements. If the BC has encountered obstacles in translating its efforts into achievements, it must detail those as well. Finally, each BC must set forth the process it used to choose its third-party standard by which it measures its social performance.

The assessment of the BC's social and environmental performance requires a little more explanation. In order to make the assessment meaningful, the Model Act requires BCs to apply a standard created by a third party, not by the BC itself. Otherwise the assessment could easily become meaningless, with BCs setting the bar low and then congratulating themselves for leaping over it. To avoid this, the Act sets up fairly rigorous criteria for third-party assessments. A BC can choose any assessment that meets the criteria and apply it to itself.

The standard must be *comprehensive*, in that it includes measures of the company's impact on its workforce (and the workforce of its subsidiaries and suppliers), customers who are beneficiaries of its general or specific public benefit purpose, community and societal factors, and the local and global environment. The standard must be *credible*, meaning that the entity that drafted it must have the necessary expertise to evaluate a company's overall social and environmental performance. Credibility also speaks to the process with which the developer created the standard. The Act demands that the third party give voice to multiple stakeholders and provide a public comment period so that anyone the developer did not invite to participate in the drafting can provide criticisms and suggestions for changes. Finally, the third-party standard must be *transparent* about both the way the standard was developed and how it works. In terms of the standard's substance, the public must have access to information about the criteria the standard uses to measure a company's social and environmental performance and the weight the standard gives to each of those criteria.

The standard's author cannot be an entity that the BC controls. The standard developer must disclose the identities of everyone who controls or influences the developing entity (such as its directors, officer, and owners). He or she must also disclose the process it uses to decide on changes to the standard's substance and how it chooses new members of its governing body. And the developer must reveal where it gets its money, so that the public can discern whether the developer's funding sources are related to the BC itself or the BC's industry.[18]

If the standard's authoring organization or anyone affiliated with the authoring organization (such as the author's directors, officers, or significant shareholders) has any connection with the BC or the people affiliated with it, the benefit report must disclose that connection.[19] The Act chose to require disclosure of this relationship. An alternative would have been to ban BCs with any such connections from using that third-party standard. That is likely the intent here—to discourage BCs from using standards written by organizations that have ties to the BC or its officers, directors, or significant shareholders by forcing them to make potentially embarrassing disclosures if they do use those standards—but disclosure is an indirect (and perhaps less effective) way of achieving that goal.

Once a BC has chosen a third-party standard that complies with these rules, it must continue to use that standard in subsequent years' benefit reports. If the BC does decide to change standards, the benefit report must explain why it switched.[20] The Act presumably wants to prevent BCs from strategically changing the measuring standards in order to inflate their results. Again, the Act chose the disclosure route rather than an outright ban on switching, perhaps out of concern that a ban would be overly rigid and unworkable.

Since B Lab wrote the Model Act, it should come as no surprise that its own measurement tool for socially conscious businesses, the B Impact Assessment (BIA), meets the Model Act's requirements. The BIA has many strengths, and it is by far the most popular choice for BCs' third-party standard, but it is not necessarily the best standard for all BCs. (The choice of a third-party standard is beyond the scope of this book, but I have written about the BIA's strengths and weaknesses elsewhere.[21])

A benefit report that no one can access would be largely pointless, so the Model Act requires BCs to make their benefit reports available to the public. Every BC must provide a copy of each year's benefit report to its shareholders within four months of the end of its fiscal year. In addition, it must post its benefit reports on its website, assuming it has one. If a BC does not have a website, it must send a copy of the benefit report to anyone who asks for it. BCs must also file a copy of each benefit report with the secretary of state's office of the state in which they registered.[22] Note, though, that compliance with these requirements has not been all that one might hope, a topic for Chapter 5.

*Can a BC Appoint a Director or Officer with Special Duties*
*to Enforce Its Social Purpose?*

BCs are for-profit businesses, and one can easily imagine a BC's directors and officers becoming so focused on maximizing profits that they neglect the BC's other social priorities. It might prove helpful to designate one or two directors or officers, or both, who "own" the company's social mission. If the social goals are these fiduciaries' primary focus, they are less likely to get lost in the day-to-day challenges of keeping the company afloat. Having someone whose job it is to remind the other people running the company that the BC is about more than earning a profit could prove quite helpful to sustaining the BC's social aspects.

The Model Act's authors recognized this possibility and provided BCs with two options: the benefit director and the benefit officer. The benefit director is indistinguishable from the other directors on a BC board: the shareholders elect him or her the same way and can remove that person the same way, as long as the director is independent of the BC (meaning that the benefit director is not a full-time employee of the company). Other than this independence requirement, there are only two differences between the benefit director and the other directors.

The first difference is that the benefit director has the additional obligation of preparing an annual statement that reports on whether during that year, the BC acted in compliance with its general public benefit purpose and any specific public benefit purpose it adopted. The compliance report must include the benefit director's views on whether the board and the BC's officers obeyed their duty to consider the impact of the company's actions on the various corporate constituencies and the environment. The BC then includes this compliance report in its annual benefit report.[23]

The second difference is that the Model Act protects the benefit director from personal liability in regard to some of his or her decisions. In many states, corporations have the option of protecting all of their directors from personal liability for violating the duty of care by including a provision in the corporate charter opting into that protection.[24] The Model Act goes a step further and extends this protection to *benefit* directors automatically whether or not the BC has protected the other directors.

The Act is not very clear on precisely how far this protection extends. The relevant provision states that "a benefit director shall not be personally liable for an act or omission in the capacity of a benefit director unless the act or omission constitutes self-dealing, willful misconduct, or a knowing violation of law."[25] These three conditions limit the protection to violations of the duty of care; benefit directors are still vulnerable to personal liability for violations of their duty of loyalty and for acts in bad faith.

The harder condition to understand is the one that limits the protection to acts or omissions "in the capacity of a benefit director." Since the Model Act says that benefit directors have the same powers and duties as other directors, that phrase could be read expansively to mean that benefit directors are protected from liability for violations of the duty of care for *any* act they perform in their capacity as a director. That reading would have the effect of automatically giving benefit directors the full scope of the protection that directors can receive when corporations opt into the protective provision in their corporate charters, even if the BC has not chosen to do that. That seems a strained reading to me. Why should benefit directors get this protection when the corporation has chosen not to give it to the other directors? The more likely interpretation is that benefit directors are protected when they act as *benefit* directors specifically, not for any act they take as a director. Since the only action that benefit directors take that is unique to them is to provide the annual compliance statement, the better reading of this protection is that it is limited to that act. In other words, benefit directors cannot be held personally liable for violations of their duty of care for providing the annual compliance statement. They also share the same protection as other BC directors from personal financial liability for failing to consider interests other than profits and from failing to pursue or create a general or specific public benefit.[26]

In addition to offering the option of creating a benefit director, the Model Act also includes the possibility of appointing a benefit officer, who has the duty of preparing the BC's annual benefit report. Otherwise, the benefit officer is no different from any other corporate executive. The Act does not grant benefit officers any special protection from liability in connection with their role, the way it does for benefit directors. Benefit directors can also take on the task of benefit officer, if that seems advisable, but their dual role will not offer them any additional liability protection.[27] The Act extends that protection only to actions taken in the capacity of a benefit director.[28]

*How Can a Traditional Corporation Convert to a BC?*

Many of the existing BCs began life in that form. For them, the adoption of the BC legal form was simple. All that was required was that the founders obey the general rules for founding corporations in that state and that they put a provision in the corporate charter that stated that the company was a benefit corporation.[29]

Many existing corporations, of course, might choose to convert to BC status now that the option is available. Patagonia and Kickstarter are two prominent examples of companies whose prosocial missions—respectively, protecting the environment and promoting the arts—long predated the availability of the BC form. Both companies converted after the legislatures in their states of incorporation (California and Delaware, respectively) passed authorizing legislation.

For companies like Patagonia that were originally formed as traditional corporations, the process requires a few extra steps. First, the company must amend its corporate charter to state that the company is a benefit corporation, which requires the approval of the board of directors. Any vote by the board requires that a quorum of the directors (usually a majority) attend the meeting and then that a majority of the directors present approve the resolution at issue.

Then the amendment must be approved by the shareholders. A shareholder meeting also requires a quorum (again, usually a majority of the shares) to count as a valid meeting. For ordinary matters, once a quorum is present, all that is needed for a resolution's approval is a majority of the shares represented at the meeting (technically, the approval of a majority of the votes represented, which is not always the same as the number of shares). To convert to a BC, though, the Model Act requires a higher threshold: two-thirds of the votes of each class of outstanding stock must approve the conversion for it to become effective.[30] Alternatively, a traditional corporation can become a BC by merging with an existing BC, with the existing BC as the surviving corporation. The merger also must be approved by both the board and a two-thirds vote of each class of outstanding stock.[31]

## How Do PBCs Run?

When Delaware opted into the BC movement in 2013, it decided not to adopt the Model Act and instead drafted its own statute from scratch. Delaware refused even to keep the name of the new entity; in Delaware, these entities are called public benefit corporations (PBCs) rather than benefit corporations. This change in nomenclature has caused some—in my view, entirely unnecessary—confusion. (This confusion compounds the already existing confounding of the legal forms—whether a benefit corporation or a public benefit corporation—with holders of B Lab's certification—"B Corps.") Many important commercial states such as California and New York already had what they term a "public benefit corporation" form, the wording those states use for a nonprofit corporation. While Delaware's drafting effort seems a bit overdone—it could have just edited the portions of the Model Act it wanted to change—it is in keeping with its role as the leader in US corporate law that it chose to write its own statute rather than follow B Lab's lead.

Despite that decision to change the form of the statute entirely, the Delaware PBC statute's substantive elements are often similar to the Model Act's BC form. Certainly, the themes overlap. Like BCs, PBCs have a broader purpose than earning profits, and their boards of directors are required to balance those broader goals against the desire for earnings. The specifics of how Delaware defines and protects these broader purposes, though, are materially different in a Delaware PBC.

### What Are PBCs' Purpose?

The Delaware statute defines PBCs as for-profit entities that are "intended to produce a public benefit or public benefits and to operate in a responsible and sustainable manner."[32] That raises the question of what counts as a "public benefit." Delaware defines *public benefit* as "a positive effect (or reduction of negative effects) on 1 or more categories of persons, entities, communities or interests (other than stockholders in their capacities as stockholders) including, but not limited to, effects of an artistic, charitable, cultural, economic, educational, environmental, literary, medical, religious, scientific or technological nature."[33] The Model Act defined *public benefit* for BCs as "a material positive impact on society and the environment, taken as a whole, from the business and operations of a benefit corporation assessed taking into account the impacts of the benefit corporation as reported against a third-party standard."[34]

These definitions use different language, but the intent seems to be broadly similar. The Model Act asks for a positive impact on society. a requirement that closely tracks Delaware's mandate that PBCs have a positive effect (or reduce a negative effect) on "persons, entities, communities or interests," which sounds like a description of "society." But from there, the two definitions diverge. Delaware's statute goes on to list specific categories of public benefit and requires only that a PBC pursue at least one of those categories. In contrast, the Model Act requires BCs to produce a positive impact on society and the environment "taken as a whole," a requirement that is more demanding than Delaware's. A Delaware PBC chooses a specific benefit that it will pursue, but a Model Act BC must create a broad positive impact on society generally. (The Model Act does have an analogous list of specific public benefits, but the Act places its list in the definition of "specific public benefit," something that is optional for BCs.[35])

The reason Delaware includes a list of specific social benefits in its definition of "public benefit" is that it does not require PBCs to foster a general public benefit, in contrast to the Model Act's requirement of BCs. Instead, PBCs are required to adopt one or more specific public benefits.[36] Not only does Delaware law not require PBCs to pursue a general public benefit, it does not even offer that as an option. Instead, Delaware PBCs define for themselves what particular good causes they will pursue by listing those goals in their corporate charters.

Delaware's approach avoids the difficult definitional questions the Model Act faced in trying to outline how a corporation can pursue a "general public benefit," but it does so at the cost of abandoning all attempts at any degree of standardization. With one exception, this is probably more a difference of style rather than substance. Remember that the Model Act's very broad definition of a general public benefit provides a great deal of freedom to BCs to choose how they will create a positive impact on society. Still, the goal of the Model Act is more ambitious, even if the practical impact of that ambition may be minimal. The exception where the differences may have some bite is the Model Act's mandate that the general public benefit include a positive impact on the environment. This is the one part of the

Model Act's general public benefit requirement that seems clear. For Delaware PBCs, the environment is just one option among many on their menu of social impact choices. A Delaware PBC could choose to work to heal the environment, but it is not required to do so. Under the Model Act, helping the environment is mandatory.

An additional, probably less consequential, difference in the two statutes' definitions of corporate purpose is that the Model Act requires assessment against a third-party standard and reporting as part of the very definition of *public benefit*. Delaware does not. In fact, as we will see a bit later, Delaware makes the use of a third-party standard entirely optional for PBCs and contains a more lenient reporting requirement.

### What Is a PBC's Specific Public Benefit?

Delaware law requires each PBC to choose at least one specific public benefit it will pursue. This does not mean that Delaware PBCs are necessarily providing narrower public benefits than Model Act BCs are. PBCs are free to choose to adopt as many specific public benefits as they like. For example, a PBC might choose to create a positive workplace for its employees, enact green policies that reduce energy and plastic use, and donate a percentage of its profits to helping the homeless. There does not have to be any material difference between how a PBC functions and how that same company would operate if it instead organized as a BC, especially when we think about the very broad definition of a general public benefit the Model Act adopts for BCs. On the other hand, a PBC could elect to focus on only one or two areas, which might make it look quite different from a BC that takes its duty to create a general public benefit seriously.

The list of specific public benefits available to PBCs in Delaware is very broad, much like the comparable list in the Model Act. Both statutes essentially leave it up to the company's discretion to define for itself what it means to be a "good" company. Delaware's list includes benefits that are "artistic, charitable, cultural, economic, educational, environmental, literary, medical, religious, scientific or technological [in] nature."[37] Note that Delaware specifically listed religious benefits, even though the Model Act did not (though the Model Act's catch-all provision should probably be read as broad enough to include religious benefits).

Much of this list overlaps with the Model Act's list of specific public benefits, though the two statutes sometimes use different terminology. Both statutes include art, charity, the environment, medicine, and science. They also both list economic benefits, though they describe them somewhat differently. Delaware adds cultural, educational, literary, religious, and technological benefits, but most of these could fit into a broad reading of the Model Act's categories ("advancement of knowledge," for example, could include education as well as scientific progress) or, if not, would be covered by the Model Act's catch-all provision. And like the Model Act, Delaware's statute permits companies to add other categories beyond those listed in the statute. The Model Act has a catch-all provision that covers "any other particular benefit on society or the environment," while Delaware simply says its list is "not limited to" the enumerated categories.[38]

### Should PBC Directors Pursue Profit or Purpose?

The Delaware statute requires PBC boards to balance profit against other prosocial interests in much the same way that the Model Act requires BC boards to do so. The Model Act lists some of these other interests specifically, though not exclusively, but the Delaware statute is more general. Delaware requires PBC boards to manage the PBC "in a manner that balances the stockholders' pecuniary interests, the best interests of those materially affected by the corporation's conduct, and the public benefit or public benefits identified in its certificate of incorporation."[39] Both statutes require boards to pursue the stockholders' financial interests. Delaware's broad inclusion of "those materially affected" by the company's operations would include many of the specific categories of internal interest groups the Model Act lists, such as the company's employees (and the employees of its subsidiaries), communities where it or its subsidiaries have offices, and perhaps the environment.

Delaware's language could also be read to include some of the more distantly affected groups, such as the employees and communities of the company's suppliers, but these are more uncertain. A lot hinges on courts' future interpretation of the word *materially* in Delaware's statute. *Material* in the law means "important."[40] Not every impact will count as material, and courts will have considerable discretion in deciding how broad they want this requirement to be. The courts might choose to adopt a bright-line test that either includes suppliers' conduct or excludes it categorically, but it seems more likely that they will determine whether suppliers' treatment of their employees, their communities, and their local environments is the material result of the PBC's conduct on a case-by-case basis. A bright-line test would be easier to apply, but materiality is typically seen as a fact-specific inquiry, which would be more consistent with case-by-case treatment. Overall, then, Delaware's balancing requirement is likely to end up being somewhat narrower than the Model Act's, at least when it comes to PBCs' suppliers.

The same will likely be true of Delaware's treatment of the environment. The Delaware statute does not specifically mention the environment as one of the interests that PBC directors must balance. In some cases, a company's treatment of the environment might well result in a sufficiently material effect on identifiable individuals to trigger the "those materially affected by the corporation's conduct" test. This seems especially likely when the PBC is polluting the local environment, since those effects will often be easier to identify concretely. But as a PBC's environmental impact becomes more diffuse—as it becomes harder to identify specific people or groups directly and materially affected—Delaware courts are less and less likely to insist that PBC boards take that impact into account when contemplating corporate action.

This result will be different for PBCs that list the environment as one of the specific public benefits the company commits to pursue. Delaware law does require PBC boards to consider the specific public benefit(s) identified in the PBC's certificate of incorporation when making corporate decisions. If the corporate charter includes the environment (local or global) as one of the company's specific public benefits, then the board must consider the environment. Materiality will still matter here, even though the statute does not use the word when describing the board's consideration of the PBC's specific public benefit(s). Delaware law requires the board to balance different interests: profits, the company's material impact on others, and the company's specific public benefit(s). Balancing different interests necessarily requires the board to think about how important a given decision will be to each of those interests.

For example, suppose a PBC that manufactured heavy-duty farm equipment listed the reduction of greenhouse gases as its only specific public benefit. Because each of its products was very expensive, the company had long relied on in-person meetings with farmers as its core sales strategy. These meetings required a great deal of travel, often by plane, which produced a significant volume of greenhouse gases. One of the PBC's directors proposed switching to videoconferencing sales meetings rather than having these meetings in person. A pilot study revealed that videoconferencing was less effective than in-person meetings and resulted in a 10 percent decline in sales. This decline in revenue swamped any positive impact on the PBC's bottom line from the cost savings that came from reduced travel and resulted in a 15 percent decline in profits. Nevertheless, videoconferencing was much easier on the sales staff, enabling them to spend more time with their families. Videoconferencing cut down on the PBC's greenhouse gas emissions by 5 percent. (Most of the company's carbon emissions stemmed from its manufacturing process.)

In deciding whether to adopt the new policy, the board must consider all three of these factors: the reduction in sales and corresponding decline in profits, the positive effect on the lives of the employees, and the beneficial impact on the environment. For each of these factors, materiality is key. The hypothetical posited a 15 percent reduction in profits, a significant improvement in the sales staff's quality of life, and a 5 percent decrease in greenhouse gas emissions. However we might come out on the decision with those assumptions, our analysis would clearly change dramatically if the loss in profits was instead 75 percent, with the other factors holding constant. Similarly, if we could eliminate all of the PBC's greenhouse gas emissions with this new policy, our decision might shift again. The materiality of each factor is critical to the balancing process, even without a statutory requirement that it be so.

Delaware's balancing requirement arguably has a similar effect to the Model Act's general public benefit mandate. The Act requires BCs to pursue a general public benefit, which it defines quite broadly as a material positive effect on society and the environment.[41] By requiring PBCs to balance profit against the companies' impact on those materially affected by its conduct, Delaware law effectively requires PBCs to consider their impact on society when determining corporate policy. The framework for this requirement is different, though the net effect may prove quite similar.

*Who Can Sue to Enforce PBC Directors' Duties?*

Just like the Model Act, Delaware law permits shareholders who own at least 2 percent of a PBC's stock to bring a suit against the PBC's directors if the directors fail to promote the company's social purpose adequately.[42] Delaware law is somewhat more restrictive than the Model Act, though, in three ways.

First, under Delaware law, only shareholders who own at least 2 percent of the PBC's total outstanding equity may bring suit. The Model Act permits shareholders who own at least 2 percent of any *class* of stock to sue. For companies that have only one class of stock, these rules will have the identical result, but for corporations that have issued more than one class, the Delaware rule will be more restrictive.

Second, there is no provision under Delaware law for shareholders of a PBC's parent company to sue the PBC's directors for failing to balance interests properly. The Model Act permits shareholders who own at least 5 percent of a BC's parent company to sue.

Finally, and perhaps most important, Delaware requires PBC shareholders to bring these suits as derivative actions. As we discussed in Chapter 2, a derivative action is much harder to launch successfully than the alternative, a direct action. To succeed in a derivative action, the shareholder plaintiff must meet the contemporaneous and continuous ownership requirements and must demonstrate that demand was futile. In addition, the case may be dismissed if the corporation appoints an independent committee to evaluate whether the case is in the corporation's best interest, that committee determines in good faith and after a reasonable investigation that the corporation would be better off if the suit were dismissed, and the court rules that in its own business judgment, the case is against the corporation's best interests.

The Model Act, in contrast, created a new type of lawsuit, the benefit enforcement proceeding, that shareholders may use to sue directors whom they believe are violating their duty to balance the BC's various goals. Courts may incorporate the derivative suit features into benefit enforcement proceedings under the Model Act, but that outcome is far from certain. In Delaware, there is no new type of lawsuit to handle these claims. They must be brought with a traditional derivative action with all its accompanying obstacles.

*Must PBCs Disclose Their Social Performance?*

Like the Model Act, Delaware law requires some degree of disclosure as an enforcement tool to help ensure the board remains accountable for its decisions. The state's disclosure requirement, though, is considerably narrower than the Model Act's in three significant ways. First, unlike the Model Act, which requires a benefit report annually, Delaware requires its equivalent disclosure only every other year. Second, Delaware requires PBCs to send its disclosure only to shareholders, whereas the Model Act mandates that BCs make benefit reports available to the public by posting them on the company's website or by making them available on request if the company has no website. Finally, although the content of the disclosure under the two statutes is broadly similar, there is one important difference: Delaware does not require PBCs to measure their provision of a public benefit against a third-party standard as the Model Act does for BCs. Delaware does require PBCs to assess their success in furthering whatever specific public benefit they have adopted, but that assessment does not need to involve an independent, third-party standard. PBCs are free to assess their progress in any way the board deems fit.[43]

*Can a PBC Appoint a Director or Officer with Special Duties to Enforce Its Social Purpose?*

Delaware does not expressly provide for the option of appointing a benefit director or officer. Nevertheless, its law is quite flexible. It is possible to create the position of a benefit director with the obligation to gather information on the company's progress in furthering its social mission and reporting back to the board. Delaware permits boards to form committees, even committees made up of a single director. Boards can then delegate almost any of their powers to that committee, as though the committee were the board. (There are some exceptions to this broad delegation authority, but they are not pertinent to this discussion.[44]) The benefit director would not automatically receive liability protection, as that person does under the Model Act, but a Delaware PBC could include a provision in its corporate charter that insulated all of the directors, including the benefit director, from personal liability for any violations of the duty of care.[45]

Delaware law also empowers the board to create officer positions and define officers' duties. A Delaware PBC could therefore create a position with the title of "benefit officer" and could assign that officer the duty of preparing the PBC's report on its social mission for the company's shareholders. In other words, although the Delaware PBC statute does not include any provisions that mention either a benefit director or a benefit officer, the general flexibility of Delaware corporate law allows a PBC to create these positions, just as the Model Act does.

### How Can a Traditional Corporation Convert to a PBC?

A company that chooses to begin as a PBC has only two requirements to implement that choice. It must state in its corporate charter that it is a public benefit corporation, and that charter must list one or more specific public benefits that it will pursue.[46] The company's name may reflect its PBC status such as by including the words "public benefit corporation" or the abbreviation "PBC," but this is not mandatory.[47] (Advertising PBC status in a company's name does have at least one advantage: nonpublic PBCs that do not indicate their status in the company's name must provide notice to shareholders of their PBC status before they issue stock. PBCs whose names do indicate their PBC status are exempt from this notice requirement.[48]) Including a charter provision stating the company is organized as a PBC also appears in the Model Act, but the Act does not require a BC to adopt a specific public benefit. Instead, BCs must all pursue a general public benefit (which again may have an analogous effect to Delaware's requirement that PBCs consider their impact on all those materially affected by their actions).

A traditional corporation that wants to convert to PBC status must amend its corporate charter to state that it is a PBC and adopt one or more specific public benefits. Alternatively, a traditional corporation can merge with an existing PBC, with the PBC as the surviving corporation. With either method, a conversion requires the approval of the board of directors. Approval also requires approval of a majority of the shares, a lower threshold than the Model Act imposes for conversion to a BC.[49] Delaware originally required a higher shareholder vote as well but amended its statute to make it easier for traditional corporations to convert to PBCs.[50]

———

In this chapter, we covered the differences between BCs, PBCs, and traditional corporations along seven different dimensions: (1) general public purpose, (2) specific public purpose, (3) directors' duty to balance purpose against profit, (4) suits to enforce directors' balancing duty, (5) disclosure of the company's fulfillment of its social mission, (6) appointment of a benefit director or officer, and (7) the requirements to convert from a traditional corporation to a BC or PBC.

In the next two chapters, we examine whether these new legal forms provide adequate protections against purpose washing. In Chapter 4, we study the legal requirement that BCs and PBCs pursue some social purpose and ask whether the definition of "social purpose" is too broad to be meaningful. Then, in Chapter 5, we tackle the enforcement mechanisms in BCs and PBCs and ask if they are too easily circumvented.

# FOUR

## WHAT PUBLIC PURPOSES CAN BENEFIT CORPORATIONS SERVE?

### Veeva Systems: A Case Study

When he was in high school, few would have picked Peter Gassner as a likely future tech billionaire. The son of a machine shop owner in Oregon, Gassner did not plan to attend college. He took the SAT only once, while hung over, intending to work as a roofer after graduating from high school. But then fate intervened in the form of his senior year math teacher, who, noticing Gassner had a talent for mathematics, persuaded him to take a computer science course. Gassner enjoyed the class and, after some research, realized that programming paid more than roofing without the physical punishment roofing imposed. He decided to attend Oregon State and study computer science.[1]

Gassner did not enjoy academics, even in college. He took a break at one point to work as a waiter in Hawaii for nine months. He returned to Oregon State for a time, then took another break, this time for an internship at IBM, where he saw professional software developers for the first time. They impressed him enough to persuade him to return to school. Again, though, he found school unpleasant and took another break, this time in Australia for nine months, followed by two months in Indonesia and a year in Thailand. Finally, he returned to Oregon State for one last six-month stretch to finish his degree.[2]

College may have required a few lengthy detours, but from there Gassner's career took off. He secured a job at IBM after graduation working on a database optimizer and stayed there for five years. Although he was doing well at IBM, he felt that database software was too narrow a field and decided to pursue work in software applications. A former mentor at IBM had moved to Peoplesoft and helped Gassner get hired there. Although he began as a software developer at Peoplesoft, he rose quickly and nine years later was in charge of a team of five hundred people. From there, he moved to Salesforce where he helped build the company's platform. Eventually he left Salesforce and took two years off to spend time traveling with his family.[3]

After his family trips, Gassner began looking for another interesting project to work on. Salesforce's founder, Marc Benioff, introduced him to Craig Ramsey. Ramsey had some experience selling technology products to pharmaceutical companies, and Gassner was looking to build a cloud-based technology company that provided industry-specific services. Together, they formed Veeva Systems to provide cloud-based customer relations management software to pharmaceutical companies. Veeva was a huge success and eventually went public. Today, it is traded on the New York Stock Exchange (NYSE), and Gassner is worth over $5 billion.

So far, this sounds much like countless other high-tech start-up success stories: an unlikely founder builds a company that achieves astronomical growth. Veeva's business model is entirely consistent with traditional, shareholder-centered management. Veeva's investors have done astoundingly well; they have every reason to be ecstatic with Gassner's leadership.

In 2021, Gassner made a truly surprising decision: he decided to convert Veeva into a public benefit corporation. Veeva's customers are large corporations. There is no obvious reason why Gassner would expect converting to a PBC would expand his customer base or his customers' loyalty. Nevertheless, he took the ground-breaking step of making Veeva the first NYSE-traded company to convert to a PBC.

Gassner has argued this decision was a natural one because the company was already run on a multistakeholder management model. Gassner explained, "We believe social and economic benefits go hand in hand and have always operated with the long-term view that doing the right thing for our customers, employees, and communities ultimately allows us to deliver the best results for investors."[4] In other words, Gassner believed that there is no trade-off between rewarding shareholders and treating other stakeholders well. What is best for customers, employees, and communities is ultimately also best for the shareholders' bottom line.

Delaware PBCs, though, are required to state in their corporate charters a specific public benefit that they are pursuing. What sort of specific public benefit would a company like Veeva—that believes it is pursuing profit by treating its customers and employees well—say that it is advancing? Veeva is not donating a fraction of its profits to some charitable purpose. Its business model mostly focuses on helping pharmaceutical companies sell their products, which does not seem particularly public minded. Veeva also provides its customers with databases that help develop new therapies, which sounds much closer to the mark, but that is only a portion of the company's business.

Veeva's charter provides little comfort to those who may be concerned that its goals do not veer very far from those of a traditional corporation. Its charter states, "The specific public benefits to be promoted by the Corporation are to provide products and services that are intended to help make the industries we serve more productive, and to create high-quality employment opportunities in the communities in which we operate."[5] In other words, Veeva commits itself to serve its customers and provide good jobs. Most traditional companies would say precisely the same without feeling that they are describing some high-minded public purpose.

The first benefit of making the pharmaceutical industry more productive is just a restatement of Veeva's business model: this is how it makes money for shareholders. Granted that making the pharmaceutical industry more efficient may indirectly result in better health for many people, but something similar could be said about every other company's business model. A company that does not make someone better off by providing a good or service will not stay in business very long because it will have no customers. Amazon could say that it serves the specific public benefit of making its customers' lives more efficient by allowing them to spend less time shopping for goods they need. This is true, but is it the sort of thing the drafters of the PBC statute had in mind when they required PBCs to state a specific public benefit they would provide?

The second benefit of providing good jobs is a by-product of operating a company that requires highly skilled employees. Not all companies provide such jobs; some rely primarily on unskilled labor and pay those employees minimum wage. Fast-food companies, for example, mostly hire people with few skills and pay them poorly. But most technology companies require highly skilled labor in order to operate. Hiring such people is a business necessity; the company could not succeed without it. Again, it is hard to see this as the sort of boon to the public outside of ordinary business the PBC statute drafters likely envisioned. Instead, jobs creation seems more like a natural by-product of a high-tech company's quest for shareholder profits.

Despite these substantial concerns about Veeva's stated public purpose, Veeva is a Delaware PBC in good standing. To understand how this can be true, we need to examine further Delaware's rules for PBCs' specific public benefit.

## What Type of Specific Public Benefits Does the Law Allow?

All Delaware PBCs must identify in their corporate charters one or more specific public benefits they will promote.[6] Delaware defines the term *public benefit* as "a positive effect (or reduction of negative effects) on 1 or more categories of persons, entities, communities or interests (other than stockholders in their capacities as stockholders) including, but not limited to, effects of an artistic, charitable, cultural, economic, educational, environmental, literary, medical, religious, scientific or technological nature."[7]

In contrast to Delaware's law for PBCs, the Model Act does not require BCs to adopt a specific public benefit, but it does permit them to do so. The Act defines a "specific public benefit" as including, "(1) providing low-income or underserved individuals or communities with beneficial products or services; (2) promoting economic opportunity for individuals or communities beyond the creation of jobs in the normal course of business; (3) protecting or restoring the environment; (4) improving human health; (5) promoting the arts, sciences, or advancement of knowledge; (6) increasing the flow of capital to entities with a purpose to benefit society or the environment; and (7) conferring any other particular benefit on society or the environment."[8]

Both definitions are broad and include a similar list of social causes. Delaware and the Model Act both approve of the arts, charity, the environment, medicine, and expanding human knowledge. Delaware's statute specifically singles out the provision of economic, educational, and religious benefits, while the Model Act does not specifically mention any of these three. Conversely, the Act highlights helping the poor—devoting two categories to this concept—and promoting investment in, or donations to, other prosocial organizations, while the Delaware statute contents itself with the simple mention of "charitable" causes. Neither statute's list claims to be exclusive, though; both contain broad catch-all provisions that could easily encompass the specific categories each omits.

### Do Veeva's Specific Public Benefits Qualify?

Does either of Veeva's specific public benefits—serving its customers and providing good jobs—qualify as specific public benefits under these two statutes? We should begin with Delaware's law, because Veeva is registered in Delaware and so Delaware law governs its internal operations. Serving its customers should have a positive effect on some category of persons or entities, as Delaware requires, since Veeva's customers are entities (companies), and to the extent Veeva services their marketing and research needs, it is helping them. But the Delaware statute also says something about the nature of this positive effect. The statute is broad—it does not require the type of effect to fit within one of the listed categories—but we would certainly feel more comfortable advising Veeva that it is in compliance with the statute if its purpose did fit within one of the specifically enumerated types of benefit.

Fortunately for Veeva, there is little doubt that helping pharmaceutical companies improve their businesses does fit within one of the listed benefit categories: economic. Delaware counts helping people or entities economically as a "specific public benefit." Similarly, providing high-quality jobs to Veeva's employees would presumably count as producing a positive economic effect on a category of people: those who work for Veeva. Veeva's two specific public benefits therefore seem to fit squarely within the language of Delaware's statute.

Delaware is the state of incorporation of choice for major US companies, and some scholars have argued that this is because it shapes its corporate governance law to cater to the directors and officers who run these companies, often at shareholders' expense.[9] We might therefore be suspicious that the same race-to-the-bottom dynamic might apply to any conflicts between those same favored officers and directors and other corporate constituents, such as the beneficiaries of a PBC's specific public benefit. The same cannot be said for the Model Act, though, which applies in the majority of states and therefore cannot be said to supply an advantage to one state over another in the competition for franchise taxes. Would Veeva's two specific public benefits fit within the Model Act's provisions as well as they do in Delaware's?

The answer, perhaps surprisingly, may be yes. The seventh category of specific public benefit under the Model Act is "conferring any other particular benefit on society or the environment."[10] This is a catch-all provision, and it is very broad. Veeva's business model does not seem aimed at reducing global warming or pollution, but it does try to confer a benefit on society: providing services to its customers and good jobs to its employees. The Model Act does not define what counts as conferring a "particular benefit on society," and as of this writing, there are no reported court decisions interpreting that phrase. In the absence of limiting language, the phrase is likely to be interpreted as encompassing just about anything that could be described with a straight face as a benefit. Marketing services and good jobs are certainly things that people value. Providing them would therefore seem to count as a benefit to society.

## Why Is the Law So Permissive?

At this point, you may be excused for thinking that if providing ordinary commercial services to customers—or good jobs to employees—counts as a specific public benefit, then there is no meaningful limit to the definition of a specific public benefit. After all, if helping companies market their products counts, then so should extracting oil from the ground to sell to customers or manufacturing weapons for the military. Society does seem to value gasoline and security from hostile neighbors, so providing oil or manufacturing weapons for the US military should count as a specific public benefit. But then what is the point of having a specific public benefit at all? How does identifying a specific public benefit distinguish PBCs from traditional corporations?

One answer is that the act of self-consciously identifying the specific public benefit a corporation is providing to society may encourage self-reflection that can lead to positive changes in behavior. Corporate boards that engage in the process of thinking about their company's role in the larger world may be more likely to care about enhancing the company's positive impact on others beyond the company's shareholders. Boards of traditional corporations that do not self-reflect this way may lack any spur to think beyond the company's profits. Adopting a PBC/BC form may encourage boards to think more deeply about how their company's actions affect the community.

Another answer is that revealing the specific public benefit in a public document such as a corporate charter will allow customers, employees, and other corporate constituencies to decide for themselves whether those benefits are sufficiently worthwhile to give the company "credit." There are no tax benefits for adopting a PBC/BC form; any pecuniary rewards stem from others' belief that the adoption of one of these forms means that the company will function in a way that is meaningfully better for society. Employees may be willing to work for lower pay or may stay with the company longer or work more passionately because they believe the company stands for something worthwhile. Customers may choose the company's products over those of its competitors, even if the products are more expensive, because the customers believe the company is a better corporate citizen. Suppliers may give the company better terms because they believe the company will be a more reliable and ethical business partner.

The benefits that all of these participants may provide hinge on the participants' belief that the company is better behaved in some meaningful way than its traditionally organized peers. To persuade these constituents, the company must disclose what it believes it is doing that is different from what traditional corporations do. In this way, the PBC and BC statutes act much like the federal securities laws. Federal law does not decide which stocks are worth buying and which are not. Instead, the securities laws require companies to disclose information to investors so that the investors can make informed decisions about where to place their money.[11] Similarly, the PBC and BC laws require companies to disclose what benefits they believe they are providing the public, and then the public can decide whether these benefits are worth supporting.

### Does the Law Require a General Public Benefit?

Even if the specific public benefit definition is too broad to reassure constituents that all PBCs and BCs are meaningfully different from traditional corporations, we must remember that the specific public benefit is not the only requirement under Delaware law (and is not a requirement at all under the Model Act). Both statutes require boards to run companies in particular ways that differ from the legal mandates for traditional corporations in addition to any specific public benefit they may adopt.

The Delaware statute defines a PBC in part as a company that "is intended . . . to operate in a responsible and sustainable manner."[12] The statute does not flesh out what it means for a company to behave responsibly or sustainably, so this language should likely be seen as serving a rhetorical purpose, urging companies to do the "right" thing, whatever they believe that to be. It is hard to imagine a lawsuit against a PBC that argues the PBC has failed to obey this requirement having any chance of success.

But the Delaware law also requires PBC boards to "manage or direct the business and affairs of the public benefit corporation in a manner that balances the pecuniary interests of the stockholders, the best interests of those materially affected by the corporation's conduct, and the specific public benefit or public benefits identified in its certificate of incorporation."[13] Traditional corporations face no such balancing requirement; boards of traditional corporations are required to focus solely on increasing profits for their shareholders.

In stark contrast to the specific public benefit requirement, which grants boards almost unlimited latitude to define the public benefit in any way they see fit, the balancing requirement is fairly specific. PBC boards must pay attention to *all* of those "materially affected" by the corporation's activities. Although this phrase has yet to be interpreted by a published court decision, its natural meaning is broad and demanding. The phrase presumably encompasses the company's employees, customers, suppliers, and the communities in which it operates. It should also be read to include the environment, to the extent the corporation has an impact on the local environment sufficiently to "materially affect" those who live nearby or materially affects the global environment. The phrase could be read more expansively also to include those who experience more indirect effects, such as the employees of the PBC's suppliers, so long as they felt a "material" (meaning substantial) effect from the company's actions.

Unlike Delaware, the Model Act does not require—though it does permit—BCs to adopt a specific public benefit. Instead, it requires BCs to pursue the "general public benefit," which it defines as "a material positive impact on society and the environment, taken as a whole, from the business and operations of a benefit corporation assessed taking into account the impacts of the benefit corporation as reported against a third-party standard."[14]

At first glance, the "general public benefit" requirement looks much like Delaware's command that PBCs "operate in a responsible and sustainable manner."[15] Like Delaware's provision, the Model Act's "general public benefit" mandate is defined so amorphously that it would be difficult to enforce it in a court of law. Just about any business could reasonably claim to have a "material positive impact on society" even if all it does is provide a good or service that people want. But the Model Act also requires a positive impact on the environment. Delaware's reference to "sustainable" could be read as referring to the environment as well, but it could also be read more narrowly to mean that the company's business model could keep it in business for a long period of time. I have argued that Delaware's balancing mandate should be read to include a PBC's impact on the environment, and the Model Act expressly requires BCs to improve the environment overall in a substantial way. This requirement to take the environment into consideration is at least one way in which the law governing BCs (and, I would argue, PBCs) differs from the law that covers traditional corporations.

In addition, like Delaware's statute, the Model Act requires a BC's board of directors to balance the company's pursuit of profits against other goals. (Although the Act requires boards to "consider" these other goals while the Delaware law requires boards to "balance" them, I do not think this difference in phrasing should be read as having a meaningful difference in intent, so I use the terms interchangeably.) The Model Act's balancing requirement lists a number of factors that BC boards *must* consider when making business decisions, then lists other factors that BC boards *may* consider. The list of mandatory considerations includes:

> (i) the shareholders of the benefit corporation; (ii) the employees and work force of the benefit corporation, its subsidiaries, and its suppliers; (iii) the interests of customers as beneficiaries of the general public benefit or a specific public benefit purpose of the benefit corporation; (iv) community and societal factors, including those of each community in which offices or facilities of the benefit corporation, its subsidiaries, or its suppliers are located; (v) the local and global environment; (vi) the short-term and long-term interests of the benefit corporation, including benefits that may accrue to the benefit corporation from its long-term plans and the possibility that these interests may best be served by the continued interest of the benefit corporation; and (vii) the ability of the benefit corporation to accomplish its general public benefit purpose and any specific public benefit purpose.[16]

The Model Act's list of factors BC boards must consider is certainly more detailed than Delaware's parallel list for PBCs, but it embraces the same concept of requiring BC boards to consider the well-being of all those affected by the company's actions, as well as any specific public benefit the BC has embraced. With the possible exception of the global environment (and again, I think there is a strong argument that Delaware's statute covers the global environment as well), all of the specific factors listed in the Model Act would also be encompassed by Delaware's requirement that boards consider those affected materially by the company's activities.

Despite the weakness of the specific public benefit provisions, then, the Delaware statute and the Model Act both require PBCs to behave differently from traditional corporations in a substantial way that aligns well with popular conceptions of what it means to be a "good" company. "Good" companies take into account the impact they have on others—what economists call somewhat euphemistically "externalities." Good companies pay their employees a living wage, even if the law permits them to pay less. Good companies do their best to minimize their pollution of the environment, even if it is both cheaper and legal to pollute more. Good companies get involved in their communities, even though there is no legal mandate to do so. Good companies also produce responsible products and services that perform as expected and do not pose an unreasonable risk of harm. Delaware's balancing requirement and the Model Act's general public benefit requirement encourage all of these sorts of behaviors that we tend to associate with companies we admire.

Notice that even the balancing requirement leaves PBCs' and BCs' boards with tremendous discretion. The statutes do not require these boards to choose employees, the environment, or customers over profit in any particular decision. The statutes only require boards to balance these other interests with the pursuit of profits. A PBC or BC board that always chose profits over purpose could not reasonably be said to be in compliance with the law, but a board could certainly choose profits sometimes—even often—and remain within the law's bounds.

Granting this discretion to the board is in keeping with the general deference of corporate law to boards' business decisions. As we discussed in Chapter 2, courts are reluctant to second-guess a board's judgment about what is best for the business and therefore generally defer to the board's decisions, as long as the board was reasonably informed before making the decision and did not suffer from a conflict of interest or demonstrate bad faith.[17] But this discretion is not absolute. Courts that see that a PBC board is ignoring its duty to take seriously the harm the company may cause to others in the pursuit of profit can and should hold the board to account. The extent to which courts are likely to have the opportunity to do so, however, is a difficult question, one we take up in Chapter 5. The balancing requirement imposes real duties on PBCs and BCs to behave differently—I would say better—than traditional corporations, separate and apart from any specific public benefit the company may adopt.

One way to think about this is that in a sense, all PBCs and BCs are required at a minimum to adopt a public benefit purpose of attempting to avoid unreasonable negative externalities. It is doubtful that any business can avoid imposing all negative externalities; even nonprofit organizations seem unlikely to achieve perfection by this measure. But organizing as a PBC or BC means that the board must make meaningful efforts to avoid harmful externalities, consistent with the need to earn a reasonable profit. Some BCs or PBCs may choose to be far more ambitious than this in their pursuit of purpose, through the specific public benefit mechanism or otherwise. All of them, though, must adopt this "negative externality minimization" purpose as a baseline. Embracing this purpose would fundamentally set these new entities apart from their traditional corporate cousins.

Many companies may find this externality avoidance conception helpful in contemplating how to make their commitments to social purpose more concrete, and I suspect it will often capture much of our intuition about what it means for a company to be a good corporate citizen. Nevertheless, I do not mean to suggest the externality conception is the only way to think about corporate virtue. For one thing, it may fail to cover a category of positive behaviors that "good" companies often engage in, such as donations to charity or paying above-market wages. These positive behaviors are not really about reducing negative externalities, but they would be included, I suspect, in most people's concepts of what a "good" company does. Still, avoiding negative externalities would be an excellent place to start for a company that wants to be socially responsible.

At least theoretically, then, PBCs and BCs should behave differently— better, from a societal viewpoint—from traditional corporations. Veeva should remain in good standing as a PBC—and not vulnerable to possible shareholder enforcement suits—only so long as its board operates the company in a way that fulfills its externality minimization duty.

As we will see in Chapter 5, though, the balancing duty of PBC and BC boards of directors is not easy to enforce. Neither the Delaware statute nor the Model Act provides a sufficiently robust enforcement mechanism to lend much comfort that companies will feel compelled to balance conscientiously shareholders' interests against those of the others who are affected by the company's actions. Much has been left to the discretion of the companies' boards.

It would be enormously helpful, therefore, to know what social purposes these companies have been embracing. The law gives boards tremendous discretion in choosing and implementing PBCs' and BCs' social goals. Are they using that discretion to select goals that most would agree are beneficial to society? Or are they choosing goals that—like Veeva's—seem indistinguishable from those a traditional corporation would articulate?

## What Specific Public Benefits Have Delaware PBCs Adopted?

To answer these questions, I conducted an empirical study with the help of a research assistant, Kristen Abajian. We examined a sample of over five hundred Delaware PBCs, chosen alphabetically from a list of all Delaware PBCs generously furnished by the Delaware Secretary of State's Office. We chose to look at Delaware PBCs rather than another state's BCs for both conceptual and practical reasons. Delaware is the most important state for corporate law, and so we expect a disproportionate share of the largest and most substantial social companies to choose Delaware as their state of incorporation. We also chose Delaware because it—unlike many other states—tracks PBCs separately from traditional corporations. For most states, it is essentially impossible to obtain a comprehensive list of the state's BCs (or even to discover whether a particular corporation filed as a BC or a traditional corporation by looking at the state's corporate filings website). Delaware, in contrast, has done an admirable job of cataloging PBCs as a separate type of entity, and the state's Secretary of State's Office kindly provided us with a comprehensive list of Delaware PBCs.

Once we had our sample, Kristen searched the PBCs' websites to see what the companies stated was their specific public benefit. A number of these PBCs either had no web presence at all or did not state clearly what their specific public benefit was. After eliminating these from our sample, we were left with 298 PBCs. We then cataloged the sample based on the type of specific public benefit each company had adopted. Table 6.1 shows our results, listed in order of frequency.

The largest category by far was the environment. Fifty of the companies (16.78 percent) stated a purpose of helping the environment in some way. We found this result highly encouraging. Helping the environment is likely to prove a relatively uncontroversial fulfillment of the goals of the PBC form. Although global warming remains a hot-button issue politically and views on the environment still differ by party affiliation, a recent poll by the Pew Research Center found that 67 percent of respondents thought the federal government was doing too little to combat climate change, and similar percentages also thought the federal government was not doing enough to protect water and air quality.[18]

Health was the next most popular category of specific public benefit,

TABLE 1. **PBC Purposes in Delaware**

| Category | Number | Percent |
|---|---|---|
| Environment | 50 | 16.78 |
| Health | 43 | 14.43 |
| Technology | 39 | 13.09 |
| Education | 31 | 10.40 |
| Business | 24 | 8.05 |
| Art | 13 | 4.36 |
| Food/Beverage | 12 | 4.03 |
| Agriculture | 11 | 3.69 |
| Finance | 11 | 3.69 |
| Labor | 11 | 3.69 |
| Informational | 10 | 3.36 |
| Merchandising | 9 | 3.02 |
| Gender | 7 | 2.35 |
| Children | 6 | 2.01 |
| Politics | 5 | 1.68 |
| Economic | 4 | 1.34 |
| Legal | 4 | 1.34 |
| Animals | 3 | 1.01 |
| Entertainment | 3 | 1.01 |
| Religion | 2 | 0.67 |
| Total | 298 | 100.00 |

with forty-three companies (14.43 percent) listing health care or the promotion of health as their company's social purpose. Although one might imagine particular health-related goals as being controversial—abortion comes to mind—most target goals that just about everyone would find beneficial. For example, Aldatu Biosciences works to develop better tools to diagnose diseases.[19] Drip Drop Hydration has developed an oral rehydration solution that tastes good, making it easier to administer to children (and even adults).[20] And Chiesi USA. aims to develop cures to diseases while operating in a socially and environmentally responsible manner.[21] Few people would find these aims objectionable. (Whether these companies execute on these aims effectively is a separate question entirely, but our focus in this chapter is on the companies' purpose, not on the enforcement of that purpose. We cover enforcement in Chapter 5.)

Third on the list, however, is technology, with thirty-nine companies (13.09 percent), and fifth is business, with twenty-four (8.05 percent). At least at first glance, these seem like purposes that a traditional corporation could adopt without changing anything about the way it runs its business. At least some of the technology companies, however, do seem aimed at prosocial goals. 42 Strategies, for example, is a digital strategy and consulting firm, but its stated purpose is to help social-mission-driven organizations maximize their impact.[22] In this way, the company has incorporated a social mission into its business model. Similarly, in the business category, Charity Charge issues a credit card to individuals who, instead of earning airline miles or other reward points, earn 1 percent cash back as a donation to any nonprofit of the user's choice.[23] Charity Charge is a credit card company, but its business model also helps raise money for charity, which seems as clearly worthy a purpose as one could imagine.

Acid Zebra, in contrast, is a technology company whose business model seems to have little that is recognizable as attempting to solve some pressing social problem. It empowers its customers to engage live audiences at marketing events with gamification.[24] Nothing on its website suggests that it serves customers who are particularly engaged in social missions. In fact, its website does not seem to mention its PBC status at all (which at least suggests it is not engaged in purpose washing).

Still, even PBCs such as Acid Zebra, whose business model is not tied to a social mission, may be run in a way that is meaningfully better for the community than traditional corporations are. It may have more generous policies for employees, may engage in greater efforts to reduce its carbon footprint, and may even donate a portion of its profits to charity. For example, Inc. Now helps companies of all types incorporate in Delaware. This is a business model that is not inherently mission driven, but the company donates up to 5 percent of its profits to charity.[25] Still, we have to acknowledge that companies may take none of these progressive steps and still legally claim PBC or BC status.

Most of the other popular purpose categories seem more in line with the ideals behind the PBC/BC movement. After environment, health, and technology, the next most popular category was education, which seems unambiguously appropriate for a social enterprise form. Then, after business, we have art, food and beverage, and agriculture. The arts are a traditional charitable purpose for nonprofit organizations. The food and beverage companies tend to focus on producing healthier products or finding more environmentally sustainable methods of food production and reduction of food waste.[26] Agriculture PBCs similarly aim to reduce the impact of food production on the environment by reducing the inputs required (land, fertilizer, water) or bringing production closer to consumption centers through urban farming.[27] There are also PBCs devoted to improving gender equity,[28] training workers and bringing underrepresented groups into the labor force,[29] teaching Ugandans how to install solar power,[30] and finding lost pets.[31]

In other words, many PBCs are doing exactly the kinds of things we probably imagine when we think about a different sort of capitalism, one where companies harness the power of markets to solve social problems. But there are also some that seem, at least on the surface, to operate in just the same way that traditional corporations do. Self-selection does a lot of work to ensure that most of the companies that select PBC or BC status are trying to run their companies in meaningfully better ways than traditional corporations do. Companies that are not sincere in their desire to experiment with a new model have mostly stayed away. But the statutes that govern the new forms are so broad in their definition of permissible purposes that they do not effectively bar less sincere companies from also choosing one of the new forms of business organization.

### Should the Law Have a Stricter Definition of Public Purpose?

The lack of an efficacious legal barrier to prevent companies that only seek profit from becoming BCs or PBCs seems deeply troubling. Critics may reasonably argue that if these new forms are to have meaning, the law should define permissible purposes in a way that tracks the movement's prosocial goals. A company whose only aim is to sell its products to as many people as possible at as large a profit as possible should not be able to incorporate as a PBC or BC. The statutes' failure to define purpose narrowly enough to exclude traditional, profit-maximizing companies could present a fatal flaw in this bold experiment.

Perhaps, though, the breadth of the social purpose definition in the Delaware PBC statute and the Model Act need not present as serious a problem as first appears. One way to think about this issue is to consider the analogous space of nonprofit organizations. More specifically, we should examine how the federal government has regulated § 501(c)(3) organizations, so called because the statute that governs them is § 501(c)(3) of the Internal Revenue Code.

These companies not only pay no taxes, but donations made to them are tax deductible to the donor. That is, if a donor gives $10,000 to one of these organizations, the donor's taxable income is reduced by the amount of the gift, $10,000. This can result in substantial tax savings to donors. For a donor whose marginal federal tax rate—the taxes paid on the last dollar earned—is 32 percent, that $10,000 donation would save the donor $3,200 in taxes. The gift's recipient gains the full amount of the $10,000 gift, but the gift costs the donor only $6,800 in forgone after-tax income. The rule thus makes donations to qualifying organizations much cheaper, with the amount of the discount changing based on the donor's marginal income tax rate. (One criticism of § 501(c)(3) is that wealthy donors enjoy a steeper discount than poorer donors because they have a higher marginal tax rate.) The benefit can be even greater for donors who live in states with state income taxes, since most such states also permit gifts to § 501(c)(3) organizations to be deducted from the state's measure of taxable income. In a state with a 10 percent marginal tax rate, for example, our same donor would effectively pay only $5,800 out of after-tax income to make a gift of $10,000.

Where does the extra money come from? How can a taxpayer make a $10,000 gift while paying only a little over half that amount?

The balance of the money comes from the government branches that grant the tax deduction. That is, in our example, $3,200 will come from the federal government, and $1,000 will come from the state government. In both cases, the government gives up tax income it would otherwise have received if it had not permitted this type of income deduction. This law therefore in effect gives individual donors the power to dictate federal (and sometimes state) spending in favor of any organization that qualifies for § 501(c)(3) treatment. By donating money to a qualifying organization, the donor is forcing the government to support the organization as well in the form of tax receipts it would have collected if not for the gift.

The most persuasive rationale given for this charitable deduction rule is that the organizations that benefit from it provide valuable services to the public that the government would otherwise have to supply. An organization that feeds the hungry, for example, reduces the need for the government to provide food through social welfare programs. Moreover, the rule does this in a way that is much cheaper than if the government operated the organization (and paid for it) directly. For the government to provide $10,000 worth of social services itself would cost the government the full $10,000. But when some other organization provides that same $10,000 worth of social services, it costs the government only the amount of the forgone tax receipts, which in our example is $3,200. The charitable deduction rule thus presents the potential for a win-win situation: the government pays much less to generate social services while charitable organizations can raise money more easily by providing a tax deduction that makes donations cheaper.

Because § 501(c)(3) gives ordinary taxpayers the power to direct federal spending, the rules that define which organizations qualify for this generous treatment are incredibly important. Spending is one of the key ways that governments express their political values. If the qualification rules do not reflect the government's policy choices, ordinary citizens will have the power to force the government to spend money in ways it opposes. We should therefore expect the § 501(c)(3) qualification rules to be quite political and to change sharply with every shift of administration, just as other forms of government spending often do.

Surprisingly, the rules look nothing like what we might expect; on the contrary, they are quite apolitical and stable. Here is the statute's text defining the category of organizations eligible for tax-deductible donations:

> Corporations, and any community chest, fund, or foundation, organized and operated exclusively for religious, charitable, scientific, literary, or educational purposes, or to foster national or international amateur sports competition (but only if no part of its activities involve the provision of athletic facilities

or equipment), or for the prevention of cruelty to children or animals, no part of the net earnings of which inures to the benefit of any private shareholder or individual, no substantial part of the activities of which is carrying on propaganda, or otherwise attempting, to influence legislation . . . and which does not participate in, or intervene in . . . any political campaign on behalf of (or in opposition to) any candidate for public office.[32]

The list of included purposes seems in keeping with the underlying rationale for granting the tax deduction, at least for the most part. Religious organizations are included, as are charities and scientific and educational organizations. Each of these could—at least sometimes—be seen as providing services that supplement or replace government programs. Religious organizations often help the poor, who would otherwise require governmental assistance. They also build communities that help raise children and generally advocate moral, law-abiding behavior, which may reduce the strain on the government's law enforcement resources. Charities also help those in need, again reducing the need for governmental social welfare programs. The government often sponsors scientific research, especially for medicine and defense purposes, and education is a core government function. Amateur sports seem like an odd fit; the government rarely sponsors sports, whether amateur or professional. But preventing cruelty to children and animals again seems in line with what governments generally do.

These categories are remarkably politically neutral. A religious organization could preach that women have the right to bodily integrity, and that this right includes a God-given right to an abortion. Alternatively, a religious organization could teach that God has decreed that life begins at conception and that abortion is murder. Either way, the organization's donors would be entitled to a tax deduction. Similarly, an educational institution could state that the best way for a government to interact with the economy is to take a hands-off approach, or it could advocate that governments regulate markets heavily. The political beliefs of an institution have almost no bearing on its ability to obtain § 501(c)(3) status.

There are some limits to the rule's political neutrality. Organizations whose purpose is against public policy will not qualify. The definition of public policy inevitably overlaps with politics at least to a degree. For example, Bob Jones University had its § 501(c)(3) status revoked in 1976 because the courts found the university was using racially discriminatory admissions policies.[33] The case involved a conflict between religious freedom on the one hand (Bob Jones University claimed that its faith banned interracial dating and marriage) and civil rights on the other. There were clearly strong political implications, yet the courts stepped in to draw a line in that instance.

For the most part, though, the organizational categories that qualify for § 501(c)(3) treatment are—and have consistently remained—remarkably apolitical. For example, when the government has wrestled with the right of an educational institution to advocate for LGBTQIA+ rights and still qualify for § 501(c)(3) treatment, it has generally taken a permissive approach. The IRS issued a revenue ruling so holding as far back as 1978, when social attitudes on this issue were far less accepting than they are today.[34]

This remarkable forbearance by both parties is the reason that the § 501(c)(3) exemption has survived as long as it has. Had the exemption become a political football, being reshaped as the parties each took their turn at the government's helm, it would have been seen through a partisan lens. Members of the party in power might have viewed it favorably for a time, but when the other party rose to power and changed the rules, love for the exemption would quickly turn to hate. Only by keeping the categories as apolitical as possible has § 501(c)(3) remained popular with both parties.

The drafters of the PBC and BC statutes faced a similar dilemma. They could have imposed a particular political slant on the public benefit definitions, restricting PBC/BC status to companies that aligned with the drafters' political views, but that would have doomed the new forms. Had the public benefit definitions aligned closely with Republican values, for example, Democratic state legislatures would never have approved them. Moreover, customers, investors, employees, and other corporate constituents would likely have adopted a view of the new forms that lined up with their politics, with Republicans favoring them and Democrats avoiding them. The converse would be true if the statutes' drafters had embraced Democratic values in defining what counts as a public benefit.

In order to gain widespread bipartisan support for the new forms, the statutes' drafters *had* to draw the lines broadly, in a way that was clearly neutral politically. The new forms' remarkable popularity, with both blue states and red states passing enabling legislation in overwhelming numbers, is due to the drafters' success at this task. In other words, even though the breadth of the definition of the public good raises difficult challenges in branding the BC and PBC forms and in avoiding purpose washing, that breadth is a key feature of the statutory framework, not a bug. Without it, the new forms would have stood little chance of passage in many states, much less of achieving widespread acceptance among the entrepreneurship and investment communities.

This still leaves us with something of an identity dilemma for BCs and PBCs. Because the statutes are so permissive in permitting companies to declare how they will be better than traditional corporations, there is a real risk that at least some BCs and PBCs will choose not to be. This risk may be aggravated by a recent, well-intentioned move to persuade major traditional corporations to convert to BC or PBC status.

In 2020, a nonprofit organization, The Shareholder Commons, sponsored shareholder proposals in traditional companies such as ExxonMobil and Wells Fargo, urging them to convert to BCs or PBCs. (The Shareholder Commons was founded and is run by Rick Alexander, who was deeply involved in drafting the PBC statute in Delaware and worked with B Lab for many years.) Most of these companies were not historically associated with progressive capitalism, outside of the traditional donations of a small percentage of their profits to charity and perhaps some minor environmental programs. (Even oil extraction companies like ExxonMobil have such programs that they trumpet on their websites.[35])

If a company like ExxonMobil converted to a PBC, what would its specific public benefit be? Perhaps it would follow Veeva's example and adopt the specific public benefits of helping its customers economically and providing high-quality jobs. As we have already discussed, Delaware counts helping people or entities economically as a "specific public benefit." Providing high-quality jobs to ExxonMobil's employees would presumably count as producing a positive economic effect on a category of people, those who work for ExxonMobil. These two public benefits would seem to qualify for ExxonMobil under Delaware law, just as they do for Veeva. Yet neither of these specific public benefits would seem to crimp ExxonMobil's quest for profits or induce it to behave any differently than it has historically.

ExxonMobil would also have to comply with Delaware's balancing requirement, though. That requirement mandates that PBCs balance the pursuit of profits against the impact of their actions on those materially affected by them. This should be read to include a company's employees, customers, and suppliers, as well as—most important for ExxonMobil—the environment. The balancing requirement, if taken seriously, could require ExxonMobil to make quite different choices than it has in the past.

The utility of requiring companies with troubling pasts to convert to PBCs or BCs as a method of curbing their bad behavior will largely turn, then, on how seriously their boards of directors take the balancing mandate. Perhaps organizations like The Shareholder Commons are right to push for conversion as a remedy for these companies' problematic behavior. It is certainly possible that public company directors, accustomed as they are to complying with securities rules, substantive laws that regulate their industries, and state governance laws, will take the balancing mandate seriously as they make corporate decisions. It is also possible that they will simply create a paper record of technical compliance while making the same decisions they would have made under the laws governing traditional corporations.

Much of what we can expect from any such shift will depend on how the mandate is enforced, a topic covered in Chapter 5. But we must recognize that there is a substantial risk that forcing corporations with poor social track records to convert to BCs or PBCs will dilute the meaning of the new forms by grafting them onto hostile corporate cultures that will seek to subvert the rules. Whether this is a risk worth taking remains to be seen.

This first round of shareholder resolutions attracted very little support. Over time, as BCs and PBCs become better known and gain credibility, that may change. An ExxonMobil or Wells Fargo PBC will likely represent a sea change for the movement. The question is whether the change will represent a catalyst that will transform capitalism for the better or a Trojan horse that will gut the new forms' meaning and effectiveness.

———

In this chapter, we discussed the legal requirements for BCs and PBCs to pursue some public purpose, whether general or specific. We learned that the law imposes very few restrictions on how BCs and PBCs define their public purposes. We considered the costs and benefits of imposing a narrower definition, recognizing the risk on the one hand of BCs and PBCs appearing indistinguishable from traditional corporations, but also recognizing on the other hand that a narrower definition would inevitably court political controversy. The BC and PBC statutes err on the side of inclusiveness to avoid the inherently political line-drawing process of which public purposes should qualify, much as the § 501(c)(3) rules do for charities that can receive tax-deductible contributions. In the next chapter, we discuss another reason to be concerned about purpose washing in BCs and PBCs: the weakness of the legal mechanisms designed to enforce these entities' social purpose.

# FIVE

## PURPOSE ENFORCEMENT MECHANISMS

In an apparent attempt to capitalize on the Black Lives Matter movement, in 2017 Pepsi released a national commercial featuring a diverse group of young, attractive people marching together in the street. The protesters held signs with peace symbols and the phrase, "join the conversation." The protesters eventually reached a line of stern police officers, at which point model Kendall Jenner handed a can of Pepsi to one of the officers, causing the protesters to erupt in congratulatory celebration while the officer smiled warmly.[1]

The commercial unleashed a storm of criticism arguing that Pepsi was minimizing the very real police violence actual civil rights protesters experienced. Bernice King, the daughter of Martin Luther King Jr. and Coretta Scott King, tweeted a photo of her father being pushed by a police officer at a protest with the message, "If only Daddy would have known about the power of #Pepsi."[2] Many others posted similar comments decrying the nonsensical message that a soda would bridge America's racial divide.[3] Pepsi quickly apologized and pulled the ad.[4]

Pepsi seems to have been trying to portray itself as a force for unity in a deeply divided culture, on the side of both protesters and the police. Perhaps the message was, "As long as we all enjoy Pepsi, nothing can be too wrong in our society." The ad was, to say the least, tone deaf, not to mention horribly ineffective. Instead of aligning popular perception of Pepsi's products with a spirit of inclusion and youth culture, the ad displayed just how out of touch the Pepsi executives were. In presenting a thoroughly inauthentic claim to supporting a social movement, Pepsi damaged its brand instead of boosting it.

The Pepsi ad demonstrates some of the dangers of purpose washing. Companies may be tempted to purpose-wash in order to gain the benefits that important audiences grant to companies that they believe behave better in meaningful ways than ordinary corporations do. While the story of the Pepsi commercial highlights the dangers of purpose washing, other companies might be more successful than Pepsi was in falsely cloaking themselves as champions of a cause.

Companies can expect to see some pecuniary benefit from positioning themselves as positive social forces. Customers may prefer to buy such companies' products and services, employees may prefer to work for such companies, and investors may prefer to support them, for the reasons we discuss in Chapters 6 and 7. Research strongly supports the thesis that the market's perception that a company acts with social purpose can improve such a company's financial results. Consumer surveys indicate that a strong majority prefer to purchase from companies that espouse a social purpose. For example, a study by Porter/Novelli in 2021 showed that 71 percent of respondents would buy from a purpose-driven company over a competitor when cost and quality are equal.[5] That same study also found that employees were 78 percent more likely to want to work for purpose-driven companies.[6] A 2022 study by Edelman similarly found that 69 percent of employees expected their companies to reflect their values.[7] And an Accenture study found that 62 percent of consumers thought companies should take a stand on issues such as the environment and workplace equity.[8] When these consumers were disappointed in a company's social action, 42 percent of them abandoned the brand, with half of these consumers never returning.[9] A 2021 McKinsey study found that companies that infused social purpose into their operations enjoyed much faster revenue growth rates than those that did not.[10]

Authentic purpose-driven brands, then, enjoy a significant edge in the marketplace. Social purpose is often quite expensive, though, requiring companies to invest in greener manufacturing, for example, or donations to charitable causes. Profit-maximizing companies may therefore strive to seize the advantages of *appearing* purpose-driven without bearing the costs of actually pursuing a social purpose.

Survey data suggest this danger is very real, with one study finding that while 86 percent of companies had adopted a statement of purpose, 83 percent had not considered the implications of that purpose for its operations.[11] Also, most public company boards structure their executive compensation plans under the theory that tying executive pay to important metrics of corporate success will motivate executives to produce that success. While I have serious concerns about that theory, there is little doubt that it drives most executive compensation decisions.[12] Corporate boards that want their companies to take a social purpose seriously would therefore presumably tie executive compensation to measures of the relevant social purpose. A company that wanted to reduce its carbon footprint, for example, might pay its CEO a bonus based on how well the company cut its emissions.

While many companies do pay their executives in part based on the companies' performance along environmental, social, or governance (ESG) measures, the pay that depends on ESG is a drop in the bucket compared to the amount that depends on the performance of the company's stock price.[13] One study examined executive pay at thirteen companies that had supplied board members to the Business Roundtable between 2019, when the Business Roundtable began endorsing stakeholder governance, and 2021. Presumably these companies supported the Roundtable's endorsement and would have enshrined their commitment to stakeholders other than shareholders by tying executive pay to these other groups' welfare. At those thirteen companies, pay tied to a company's ESG performance was typically about two tenths of a percent of the value of pay tied to the company's stock price.[14] This huge discrepancy in the amount of pay that depends on ESG compared to the amount that depends on stock prices may indicate that boards typically care much more about financial performance than social performance.

Nevertheless, some have argued that since good ESG performance is supposed to drive better financial performance, tying pay to ESG performance is redundant. If executive pay is tied to long-term profitability, then a wise and self-interested executive team will focus on ESG as a means of increasing profits.[15] There is no need for ESG-specific performance pay. As long as executive pay depends on the company's long-term financial health, executives will work to improve their companies' ESG performance as an efficient method of improving profitability.

Regardless of how prevalent purpose washing is among traditional corporations, it is clearly vital to prevent it among BCs and PBCs. The central rationale for these entities is that their governance structures will ensure they pursue broader societal goals in addition to pursuing profits. If their governance structures fail at this central task, we might well question whether there is any reason to adopt these new entities.

Two types of constraints on the choices of the directors of PBCs and BCs might help ensure these entities pursue their social missions: mechanisms within the PBC and BC statutes (public mechanisms) and mechanisms the companies might adopt with a bylaw or charter provision (private mechanisms).

## Public Mechanisms

The Model Act and the Delaware PBC statute take similar approaches to providing tools to ensure that BCs and PBCs provide a meaningful social benefit. Both statutes permit shareholders to sue to enforce the board's duty to balance the company's social mission against its quest for profits, and both also require disclosure of the company's progress in advancing its social mission.

### *Benefit Enforcement Proceedings*

#### HOW THEY WORK

The Model Act permits shareholders who own at least 2 percent of a class of the BC's stock (or at least 5 percent of the equity of the BC's parent company, if there is one) to bring a benefit enforcement proceeding for any failure of the BC to create a general public benefit. Such shareholders may also sue to enforce any specific public benefit the BC has included in its corporate charter as part of its purpose or to remedy any violation of a duty established by the Model Act.[16]

The BC itself may also bring a benefit enforcement proceeding. But since these suits are brought against the directors and the directors control the benefit corporation, we should not expect to see many such suits.[17] Few directors would agree to sue themselves for their own failure to fulfill their duties! In some states, a single director may also bring one of these suits, but we should expect to see these only when all sense of teamwork and common purpose has broken down.[18]

Similarly, under Delaware law, a shareholder owning at least 2 percent of the company's outstanding shares (or, if the PBC is publicly traded, the lesser of 2 percent or $2 million worth of stock) may bring suit to enforce the directors' balancing duty.[19] Remember that in Delaware PBCs, directors must balance the pursuit of profits against the best interests of those materially affected by the PBC's activities and the specific public benefit the PBC has adopted.[20]

When a shareholder brings a suit for violation of the directors' balancing duties under Delaware law, the suit must be brought derivatively. The same is likely true when a shareholder brings a benefit enforcement proceeding under the Model Act.[21] As noted previously, a derivative suit is based on a claim that belongs to the corporation, not to the individual shareholders. Since boards of directors are entrusted with control of the corporation, the directors would normally have the power to decide whether the corporation should bring an action based on a claim that belongs to the corporation. When a shareholder wants to bring a claim that belongs to the corporation, he or she must therefore first make a demand on the board, asking the directors to cause the corporation to bring the claim. The directors' decision in response to any such demand will be protected by the business judgment rule. Since the directors are generally themselves the defendants in these actions, they are highly unlikely to agree to have the corporation bring suit against themselves.

To escape the directors' conflict of interest, a shareholder who wants to bring a derivative claim must allege that there is no point in making a demand on the board because any such demand would be futile. The court will then evaluate the truth of the shareholder's claim of futility. In Delaware, the court will apply the test it recently adopted in *Zuckerberg*. This test examines whether the board can be trusted to decide whether the corporation should bring the suit based on whether the directors received a personal benefit from the alleged misconduct at issue in the suit; whether the directors face a substantial likelihood of liability in the suit; and whether their judgment would be materially influenced by their relationship with someone who either received a personal benefit from the alleged misconduct or faces a substantial risk of liability in the suit.[22] Similar rules apply in other states.[23] The other rules that apply to derivative suits would also apply to these actions, such as the continuous ownership rule and the possibility of a motion to dismiss by an independent litigation committee of the board.

## STRENGTHS

The threat of a lawsuit is a time-tested method of shaping behavior. The legal system relies heavily on the deterrent effect of litigation to prevent fraud, ensure products are safe, prevent negligence, and pursue a host of other important social policies. It seems natural, then, to rely on litigation to enforce the board's balancing requirement as well. Directors who fear personal liability have an incentive to take care to balance carefully and document that they have done so.

Purpose-driven investors may be particularly likely to launch suits to enforce boards' obligations to pursue a social purpose, as well as profit. As we will discuss in Chapter 7, a large and growing segment of investment capital is earmarked for firms that have a social purpose. Some of these investors choose social-purpose companies as investment targets because they believe that companies run with purpose are more likely to be profitable. Others regard the purpose itself as a worthy goal, even if they must sacrifice a degree of return to achieve it. Both groups might be motivated to correct a board that steered the company only toward profit and ignored its social purpose.

Lawsuits can be effective deterrents not only because the potential defendants fear financial liability, but also because they fear embarrassment. Lawsuits are public, and suits that allege hypocrisy seem particularly likely to attract the attention of the press and achieve viral status on social media. The directors of a social-purpose corporation such as a BC or PBC likely derive some benefit, psychological and reputational, from being associated with a company with a social purpose.

In addition, these directors should be mindful of the tangible advantages the company may enjoy from having a mission-based brand. All of these benefits, to both the directors individually and the company more broadly, can be lost through a lawsuit that alleges the company's claimed social purpose is inauthentic marketing that masks a purely profit-seeking corporate culture. The threat of such a suit may be sufficient to bring recalcitrant directors back into line and revive the company's social purpose.

When a BC or PBC is publicly traded, the shareholder ownership requirement to qualify to sue may become difficult to satisfy. On the other hand, an enterprising plaintiffs' lawyer may be able to gather sufficient shareholders together to meet the requirement, and the greater public profile of a publicly traded entity may magnify the publicity impact of the suit. But we will hold off on discussing publicly traded BCs and PBCs until Chapter 9.

### WEAKNESSES

While the lawsuits both Delaware and the Model Act use to enforce their balancing requirements have the potential to shape directors' behavior and push them to take social concerns as seriously as they take the pursuit of profits, these suits suffer from material weaknesses that may dilute their impact, including the limitation on who can bring these actions, the damage limitations, and the challenging legal standard they will apply that makes it hard for reform-minded shareholders to win them.

In Delaware and under the Model Act, only shareholders are permitted to bring suit to enforce directors' balancing duties. In fact, only shareholders who own quite a bit of stock are permitted to do so. If the BC or PBC is small, the 2 percent requirement may not be difficult to meet. Often small companies have only a few shareholders who each own a substantial percentage of the company, considerably more than the 2 percent minimum. Shareholders in private companies may also be more capable of monitoring the company's social performance if that matters to them.

For public companies, though, the 2 percent requirement will require considerably greater resources to qualify. Eyeglass manufacturer Warby Parker, for example, has a market capitalization as of this writing of approximately $2.8 billion.[24] In order to have what lawyers call "standing" to sue the directors for failing to balance profit against purpose appropriately, a shareholder would have to own $56 million of Warby Parker stock if the 2 percent rule applied. Fortunately for those who might want to bring such a suit, Warby Parker is incorporated in Delaware, which imposes a $2 million cap on the eligibility requirement. The Model Act has no such cap, so if Warby Parker were instead incorporated in, say, New Mexico, only shareholders who owned at least $56 million in stock would have standing to enforce the directors' balancing requirement.[25]

Note that some states, such as California, have no minimum threshold for share ownership. In these states, any shareholder—even one who owns a single share—has standing to bring a benefit enforcement proceeding.[26]

The greater weakness when it comes to standing, though, is not the amount of stock a plaintiff must own but the fact that only shareholders may sue. (Again, the company itself, controlled by the board of directors, can sue the board, but the directors seem unlikely to choose to sue themselves.) Shareholders—especially large shareholders—will often value profit over the company's social purpose. There are socially motivated shareholders who are willing to sacrifice financial returns for other social benefits, and these "profit-plus" investors may care enough about a company's social purpose to sue when the company veers too far to the profit side. But more shareholders will likely cheer the board for choosing profit over purpose. Even profit-plus shareholders who want to encourage companies to pursue a social purpose may lack the means to monitor this dimension of companies' performance very easily. As we will discuss in Chapter 9, Securities and Exchange Commission (SEC) disclosures may not contain much data on companies' social performance, and, as we will discuss shortly, the purpose disclosures the BC and PBC statutes require tend to be underwhelming in practice.

The people who seem much more likely to sue boards to ensure they take the company's social purpose seriously are the beneficiaries of the company's avowed public benefit, or public interest organizations who represent those beneficiaries. For example, if a Delaware PBC chooses building low-income housing as its specific public benefit, groups representing the unhoused would have a strong motive to monitor the PBC's performance and take action if it fails to live up to its stated goals. Neither these groups nor the unhoused themselves, however, have standing to sue the PBC under either Delaware law or the Model Act. In fact, both the Act and Delaware law explicitly state that the directors of a BC or PBC have no fiduciary duty to the beneficiaries of a BC's or PBC's public benefit, meaning that the beneficiaries have no standing to sue the directors for failure to provide a public benefit.[27]

Denying standing to the people most likely to bring suit makes it far less likely that we will see many enforcement actions. Events seem to be bearing out that prediction. As of this writing, there is not a single published court opinion deciding a benefit enforcement proceeding. Without a motivated plaintiff, the theoretical availability of suits to enforce directors' balancing duty will do little to ensure that BCs and PBCs pay at least some attention to their social goals.

The second problem with these suits is that in states that adopted the Model Act, no damages are available unless the directors had a conflict of interest in making the decision at issue. The Model Act protects BC directors from personal liability for breach of their balancing duty as long as they were not personally interested in the decision, meaning that they had some conflicting personal financial interest in the action the corporation took.[28] Although a plaintiff could still secure a court order forcing the board to change bad behavior (something lawyers call an "injunction"), the directors' immunity from personal financial liability deals a major blow to any deterrent effect these suits may have.

Damages also play a critical role in motivating lawyers to take these cases, since the lawyers are often paid a portion of the recovery in derivative suits. Shareholders are rarely the true motive force behind derivative suits. Few shareholders own enough of a company's stock to make it worthwhile for them to shoulder the hefty expenses of a lawsuit themselves, even if the suit is likely to increase the company's value substantially. Instead, there is a type of law firm that looks for actionable corporate conduct and then finds shareholders to serve as the named plaintiff. The shareholder plaintiff has very little real role in these suits and is generally not responsible for paying the lawyer's fees. Instead, the lawyer is paid only if the suit is successful.

Unlike most lawyer-client arrangements, where the lawyer negotiates a fee with the client, it is the court that determines the amount the lawyer will be paid in derivative suits. Courts often calculate the lawyer's fee based on a percentage of the amount recovered in the suit. Suits with large potential damage awards therefore are more likely to attract substantial attention from lawyers, while those without may languish even if they are meritorious. Courts can pay lawyers using something called the lodestar method, which is akin to an hourly fee, when the suit, though successful in forcing a change in corporate behavior, does not result in a large damages award.[29]

Lawyers may be less willing to take such cases, though. It may be harder to persuade a judge that a large fee is warranted when the corporation did not recover any money.

Delaware, however, does not insulate the directors from personal liability for failing to fulfill their balancing duties, making these suits more feasible. Many states that adopted a version of the Model Act have also opted against insulating directors this way, though some of them do protect the BC itself from liability for failing to balance.[30]

Before we start congratulating these states, though, we should recognize that states often have provisions that allow both traditional corporations and BCs and PBCs to opt into protecting their directors from personal liability for violating the duty of care. Remember that the duty of care requires that directors act as reasonably prudent people would when making business decisions for the company. Delaware has such an exculpatory provision.[31] These provisions do not automatically protect directors from personal liability, but they empower corporations to adopt a provision in the articles of incorporation that does so. Many publicly traded corporations registered in Delaware have such provisions. BCs and PBCs that adopt such provisions provide their directors with liability protection similar to that offered by the Model Act. Without the threat or promise of personal liability for directors, lawyers seem less likely to bring these suits, and directors have less need to fear them.

The final flaw with these suits to enforce directors' balancing duty is that the standard of liability is very difficult for shareholders to meet. Even if a shareholder can be found with sufficient stock who is willing to bring suit, and even if the BC or PBC is incorporated in a state that does not insulate directors from personal liability, and even if the particular BC or PBC has not chosen to protect its directors from personal liability with a provision in the company's articles of incorporation, shareholders are still unlikely to win these suits if their only claim is that the directors breached their duty of care.

The standard of liability for these suits will generally be the business judgment rule.[32] Under this rule, the complaining shareholders have the burden of overcoming the presumption that the board made an informed, disinterested decision in good faith. If the shareholders fail to meet this burden, the court will evaluate the board's decision under the extremely deferential waste/rationality test.[33] This test is notoriously hard for the shareholders to meet. Directors who can document that they at least paid lip service to balancing social purpose against profit will generally be safe from liability as long as they did not act in bad faith or have a personal interest in the transaction at issue.

In sum, while a lawsuit is the traditional way to enforce a duty, it seems unlikely to prove very effective in enforcing directors' balancing duty. The parties with standing to bring these suits seem unlikely to want to do so. When they do, they will often be unable to collect damages from the defendant directors, either because the state of incorporation protects directors from personal financial liability entirely in suits over directors' alleged breach of their duty of care in balancing profit against purpose or because the standard of liability is too difficult to meet. We need some other mechanism to prevent purpose washing.

### Benefit Reports
#### HOW THEY WORK

Both the Model Act and Delaware law require BCs and PBCs to report periodically on how well the company is performing its social purpose. The Model Act requires BCs to report annually. These reports must include a description of how the company pursued the general public benefit and any specific public benefit the company has adopted, as well as how successful the company was in creating those benefits. The reports must also assess the company's overall social and environmental performance against a standard created by a third party, not the company itself. The report must explain why the company chose the third-party standard it selected. Finally, if the company decided to appoint a benefit director or officer, the report must disclose those people's names and addresses and must include the benefit director's evaluation of the company's social performance.[34]

Delaware requires similar disclosure, but less often. Delaware PBCs need only report on their social performance every other year. Also, although Delaware does require PBCs to explain the standards the board has adopted to measure the company's social performance, those standards do not have to be promulgated by a third party. Finally, Delaware PBCs must issue the benefit report only to the company's shareholders. In contrast, the Model Act also requires BCs to post the benefit report on the company's website, assuming it has one, in addition to sending the benefit report to the company's shareholders.[35]

STRENGTHS

Disclosure can be an incredibly effective tool to shape behavior. As US Supreme Court Justice Louis Brandeis wrote, "Publicity is justly commended as a remedy for social and industrial diseases. Sunlight is said to be the best of disinfectants; electric light the most efficient policeman."[36] Disclosure has the potential to be particularly effective in encouraging BCs and PBCs to behave as exceptional corporate citizens, since most of the pecuniary benefits of these forms are tied into public perceptions that these companies are more benevolent than most others.[37] Customers' willingness to favor the products and services these companies provide, for example, is rooted in customers' belief that these entities will treat their workers well, minimize their impact on the environment, and generally behave responsibly in addition to working meaningfully toward any other social goal stated in their bylaws or charter. Forcing companies to evaluate and then disclose their social impact should enhance these benefits for companies that live up to this promise. Disclosure should also punish those companies that instead engage in purpose washing by exposing their failure to act as true social enterprises.

The existence and widespread dissemination of the public benefit reports should allow the media to help police BCs and PBCs. Stories of corporate hypocrisy can attract a great deal of attention, so the popular press and bloggers should have a strong motivation to examine these reports and highlight companies that seek profit without regard to how their activities damage their workers, the environment, their customers, their suppliers, or their communities.

The Model Act's requirement of a third-party standard should make these reports more credible. I hope that one or two standards will gain widespread acceptance, so that companies can easily be compared based on their social performance. Although Delaware does not require PBCs to use a third-party standard, they may feel pressured to do so if most other social entities do. Publicly traded companies may ultimately be compelled to do so by the SEC, but we will wait until Chapter 9 to discuss how being publicly traded may have an impact on BCs and PBCs.

WEAKNESSES

Although disclosure shows great promise as a method of encouraging BCs and PBCs to take their social performance seriously, there are also two causes for concern that the benefit report requirements may not be helping to guard against purpose washing very effectively. The first of these is that the rules that govern these reports' content are quite loose, and the second is that states are not adequately enforcing the rules that do exist.

We can best understand the problem with the existing rules by comparing them to the disclosure rules set by the SEC for all publicly traded companies. Those rules are vast and extremely detailed. Regulation S-K, for example, which tells companies what information they must include in their annual report to shareholders, runs on for hundreds of pages and goes into incredible detail on subjects as diverse as mine safety and executive compensation.[38]

In contrast, neither the Model Act nor Delaware provides much guidance on what companies should say in these reports. The Model Act requires a narrative description of the company's efforts to provide social benefits and the company's success in doing so. It also requires that BCs select some third-party standard; provides some general requirements for the creator of this standard; and mandates that the standard measure benefits to employees, customers, the community, and the environment.[39] Beyond those broad guidelines, though, the Act imposes few requirements on the benefit report. Delaware's statute is even more permissive, requiring only that PBCs disclose their social goals, the standards they have adopted to measure achievement of those goals, objective facts regarding that achievement, and an assessment of the extent to which they have met their goals.[40]

Both the Model Act and the Delaware statute, then, grant enormous latitude to BCs and PBCs to shape their benefit reports. Companies could choose to model their benefit reports on federal securities disclosure and provide enormously detailed information, perhaps even audited by an independent third party. On the other extreme, companies could craft the benefit report as a marketing brochure, providing only a page or two of glossy images and bold charts proclaiming their wonderful contributions to the world.

Worse, BCs and PBCs might choose not to produce a benefit report at all. Although these new forms have proven wildly popular with state legislatures of both political parties, most states have passed enabling legislation without also authorizing more money for secretaries of state offices to oversee the new BCs and PBCs. As a result, most secretaries of state offices are not even tracking BCs and PBCs as separate entities. Instead, they are recording them as for-profit corporations with no distinction from traditional corporations. (Fortunately for researchers, Delaware is at least tracking PBCs as a separate entity type in its database.) Most state governments—even in Delaware—are not supervising benefit reports. Not only are states failing to insist on a measure of quality for these reports, most are not imposing penalties on BCs or PBCs that neglect to produce them, with Minnesota as the notable exception.[41] The vast majority of BCs and PBCs are taking full advantage of this regulatory lapse. One early study found that fewer than 10 percent of BCs and PBCs were producing benefit reports, and a more recent study confirmed this result.[42] That more recent study demonstrated the importance of penalties for failing to file a benefit report, finding that in Minnesota, where the secretary of state is required to revoke the status of BCs that fail to file a benefit report,[43] there is a perfect compliance rate.[44] Disclosure can shape behavior only when the disclosure actually takes place. Without enforcement of this requirement, the benefit requirement is unlikely to provide much of a bulwark against purpose washing. Minnesota's example indicates that effective enforcement by the secretary of state's office can dramatically improve compliance. Perhaps Minnesota's success will inspire other states to follow its lead in this regard.

## Private Mechanisms

The two statutory protections against purpose washing leave much to be desired. Neither lawsuits to enforce boards' balancing duty nor the disclosure requirements seem likely to prevent purpose washing. BCs and PBCs that want to signal their sincere commitment to social enterprise should therefore seek out contractual arrangements that will provide a more robust assurance of prosocial behavior. Many such arrangements are possible, limited only by the creativity of the entrepreneurs and their lawyers.

Below I sketch out a few of these that seem most likely to be helpful, but this is not intended to be—indeed, could not possibly be—an exhaustive list. The private arrangements that appear most useful to me are third-party certification, governance by or at least including a nonprofit organization, and provisions that mandate particular types of trade-offs between profit and purpose of the type I propose in Chapter 8. Because the Model Act mentions it, I also discuss a mechanism I suspect will be less helpful: the option to appoint a benefit director or benefit officer.

### Third-Party Certification
#### HOW IT WORKS

Companies seeking third-party certification of their environmental responsibility, benevolent treatment of their workers and customers, conscientious communal citizenship, and sound governance practices typically turn to B Lab, the[45] nonprofit corporation that certifies companies as "meeting high standards of verified performance, accountability, and transparency on factors from employee benefits and charitable giving to supply chain practices and input materials."[46] Companies that wish to qualify for B Corp status must take the B Impact Assessment (BIA). The highest possible score on this self-assessment is 200 points, and companies must score at least 80 points to qualify for certification.[47] The BIA asks companies about their practices across five areas: governance, workers, community, the environment, and customers.[48]

The BIA itself is free, and B Lab states that over 150,000 companies have used it.[49] Companies that score over 80 on the BIA and want to achieve certification must go through several additional steps. Most relevant for our purposes, they must either convert to a BC or PBC form (if their state permits) or amend their corporate charter to accomplish the same legal changes that converting would bring (if their state has not yet authorized either form).[50] Companies wishing to certify must also go through a verification process with B Lab and pay an annual fee that varies with the company's size. The verification process also varies with the company's size, with the most stringent process reserved for publicly traded corporations and their subsidiaries.[51] Once B Lab has certified a company, the company must go through a recertification process every three years to remain certified.

#### STRENGTHS

Many companies make grand claims about how careful a steward they are of the environment, how well they treat their employees, or how concerned they are with their customers' welfare. These claims are sometimes based on sound evidence but all too often are exaggerated. Companies whose social commitments *are* sincere face a credibility problem: How can they persuade their target audiences that their claims are truthful when so many other companies' claims are false, or at least overstated?

One solution to this problem is to seek certification by a trusted third party. B Lab is a nonprofit corporation whose stated goal is to " [transform] the global economy to benefit all people, communities, and the planet."[52] It has a growing reputation as a reliable evaluator, with its logo appearing on more and more products each year.

B Lab's positive reputation is largely deserved. The BIA is not only carefully thought out and quite comprehensive, but B Lab has taken pains to ensure that the organization that created and continues to modify the BIA— the Standards Advisory Council—is independent of B Lab itself. Only one of the twelve members of the Standards Advisory Council is employed by B Lab.[53] B Lab also verifies at least some companies' claims before granting certification and reexamines companies every three years to ensure that their social and environmental practices have not deteriorated.[54] Increasing numbers of companies find B Lab's logo to be a valuable branding tool.

### WEAKNESSES

Although B Lab certification has much to recommend it, there are also some significant weaknesses. The certification process relies heavily on companies' self-reporting, with only light auditing by B Lab. Also, the point system, while communicating an admirably straightforward message with a single score, hides enormous complexity and problematic scoring mechanisms. Finally, although B Lab's brand is expanding, it is still far from a household name.

The BIA is a self-reporting mechanism. Companies answer the questionnaire themselves based on their own internal information. B Lab does engage in some verification of their answers and does ask for some supportive documentation. It is unclear, however, how extensive this verification process is. B Lab refers to its process as "verification," not "auditing," which suggests that B Lab's supervision is less than comprehensive. And in fact, B Lab asks for supportive documentation for only six to eight randomly selected questions, a far cry from a thorough audit.[55] Companies still have considerable latitude to get away with exaggerating their good acts.

Also, the point system's apparent simplicity masks enormous complexity beneath the surface. The BIA is not the same for every company. Companies receive different questions based on their size, their industry, and their home country's level of economic development.[56]

Tailoring the questionnaire is not only sensible but necessary. For example, use of pesticides is highly relevant to an agricultural company's environmental performance but entirely irrelevant for a consumer products company. Nevertheless, tailoring makes it difficult or impossible to compare companies that fall into different categories.

This comparison problem is aggravated by the fact that even when companies in different categories are asked the same question, the same answer may garner different numbers of points.[57] The same policies are rewarded differently across categories, with no explanation for why. This is a material issue, since the BIA offers some seventy-two company categories.[58] A score of 85 for a publicly traded manufacturing company may mean something very different from an 85 for a privately held services company.

Another issue in interpreting the BIA scores stems from the impact of scale. A five-person company that scores 120 on the BIA likely has a much lower impact on the world than a national company with a score of 80, yet the score itself seems to indicate that the small company contributes more. The score does not convey any sense of total impact.[59]

Relatedly, the BIA does not subtract points; it only adds them. A company that has a wonderful maternity leave policy and is a careful steward of the environment might score quite well despite paying below a living wage. B Lab has imposed some safeguards to prevent companies with particularly egregious behaviors from achieving certification, but more minor negative behaviors can escape penalty.[60]

The final, but perhaps most troubling, issue with the scoring system is its philosophical incomprehensibility. The BIA uses one metric—points—to score companies across five categories of behavior: governance, workers, community, the environment, and customers.[61] But how does the BIA determine equivalence among these very different categories? How much carbon reduction equates to housing one homeless person? These are fundamentally different activities; they cannot be measured on the same scale. Yet that is precisely what the BIA attempts to do. This effort to provide a simple metric of a company's social impact is admirable but difficult to justify logically.[62]

The last weakness of B Lab's certification lies in its own branding efforts. B Lab has worked hard to publicize its work. Countless media stories have mentioned the company, especially with the remarkable increase in the number of publicly traded public benefit corporations that occurred in 2021. Nevertheless, as an experiment, try asking people outside the social enterprise industry if they have heard of B Lab. Most likely have not, at least as of this writing. Perhaps that will change by the time this book is published; I very much hope it will. As of now, though, the primary branding benefit of certification seems lost if the target audience is not familiar with the certifier's own brand.

B Lab's certification process does bring intrinsic benefits, encouraging companies to self-assess and strive for improvement across a host of important and socially valuable metrics. But if the primary goal of certification is to enhance a company's credibility for its prosocial claims, B Lab still has some work to do.

*Nonprofit Governance*

HOW IT WORKS

Money sometimes tempts people to do terrible things. Taking away the possibility of earning enormous sums of money can conversely lead to greater virtue. This is the core idea behind the nonprofit corporation, the business form that most significant charities take. (Confusingly, California calls these legal forms "nonprofit public benefit corporations."[63])

Unlike BCs and PBCs, nonprofit corporations are not designed to earn money to return to their shareholders. On the contrary, they are bound by the nondistribution constraint that prohibits them from doing so. This constraint bars nonprofit corporations from paying out their net revenue to their owners or employees.[64] Since a nonprofit corporation's managers cannot profit from the organization's financial success, they are presumably less tempted to drive the organization to increase its profits at any cost. Instead, the nonprofit's managers may consider the welfare of the organization's intended beneficiaries and perhaps the broader society when deciding how the organization will act. As a result, nonprofit corporations often inspire greater trust than for-profit corporations, perhaps deservedly. Nonprofits often may feel intense pressure to raise money to fulfill their social mission, but that pressure is ultimately mission driven, which is quite different from the profit motive that may shape behavior in a for-profit business.

One way for a BC or PBC to boost its credibility as a social welfare producer may be to harness the reputation of a nonprofit corporation by authorizing the nonprofit corporation to supervise the BC or PBC's provision of public benefits. The power to supervise could come in a variety of forms. A minimalist mechanism could have the nonprofit corporation appoint a minority of the directors of the board of the BC or PBC or grant the nonprofit corporation information rights. Either step would allow the nonprofit to publicize any significant deviation from the company's social purpose. A more robust design could incorporate a dual board structure, with the nonprofit serving as a supervisory board with authority to veto decisions that fail to implement the company's social purpose adequately. The nonprofit could even be empowered to appoint a majority of the company's directors, giving the nonprofit legal control over every aspect of the company's operations.

Professor Emilie Aguirre has proposed a version of this idea.[65] She has argued that BCs and PBCs that go public, become acquired, or exceed a certain size should be required by statute to have boards that are evenly divided between shareholder representatives and directors chosen to represent other interests, such as the employees and the company's specific public benefit. Her proposal is for an amendment to state law to mandate this board structure rather than for a purely voluntary private ordering solution, as I am proposing. She also has a particular balance of power in mind, with shareholders controlling exactly half the board, while I envision companies choosing from a basket of options limited only by their own creativity and good judgment. Nevertheless, her proposed statutory reform represents one possible governance structure companies could choose to adopt voluntarily even without a change in law.[66]

## STRENGTHS

The nonprofit charity should ensure the BC or PBC remains dedicated to its social purpose, especially if the nonprofit is devoted to that same purpose. For example, if the Sierra Club, a prominent environmental organization, were given the authority to appoint a majority of Patagonia's board, it could ensure that Patagonia continued to act in accordance with its environmental values. The more power the charity has over the BC or PBC, the greater the assurance stakeholders should feel that the social purpose will receive adequate attention.

In addition, the nonprofit charity should provide greater credibility to the BC or PBC. In large part because of the nondistribution constraint, nonprofit corporations tend to have more credibility when they claim to pursue a social purpose. If a nonprofit corporation is in control of a BC or PBC's operations, then its credibility should transfer to the BC or PBC it is managing.

This possibility recently became more than just theoretical. The Chouinard family that owns Patagonia, the outdoor clothing company, announced in 2022 that it was transferring Patagonia's ownership to a nonprofit organization and control to a trust.[67] They chose to donate their stock rather than sell it in order to ensure that the company's profits going forward—which amounted to something like $100 million per year—would be devoted to fighting climate change and protecting undeveloped land.[68]

Patagonia has two classes of stock: voting and nonvoting. The voting stock consists of about 2 percent of the total number of outstanding shares. The family transferred the voting stock into a trust that will be run by the family and some of its advisers. Since the trust owns all the voting stock, it will have complete control over Patagonia. The family donated the remaining 98 percent of Patagonia's shares (all nonvoting) to a nonprofit organization, the Holdfast Collective, a § 501(c)(4) organization. That status allows the Holdfast Collective to make political donations, but the trade-off for this ability is a very sharp financial penalty for the Chouinard family: they did not receive a tax deduction for their enormous stock contribution. The Holdfast Collective will receive Patagonia's profits from now on and will spend the money pursuing environmental initiatives.[69] The Chouinard family gave up a vast amount of wealth in this transaction, but the net result should be a company that retains their strong environmental purpose for the foreseeable future.

WEAKNESSES

Providing a nonprofit charity power over a profit-seeking BC or PBC presents at least four potential problems. The first is that a charity may focus

too much on the company's social purpose and neglect the quest for profits. Charities may overemphasize the company's charitable purpose because
their own cultures are focused only on providing social good or because they
lack the expertise to run a profit-seeking enterprise. Investors may shun
companies that adopt these arrangements, and these companies may struggle
to survive without a management team that has a strong profit motive.

The second, related, problem is that the founders must generally give up
control for this mechanism to work. Founders understandably may prove
reluctant to cede control over the companies they built. The Chouinard
family is not entirely unique in this regard, but they are certainly rare.[70]

The third issue is in a sense the opposite problem: even charities may
succumb to the quest for profits. One BC that implemented a structure like
this is Impact Makers, a Virginia benefit corporation that provides business
and technology consulting services.[71] All of Impact Maker's voting shares
are owned by a nonstock corporation, IM Holdings Inc. (IMH), whose
purpose is to appoint directors of Impact Makers that will ensure that
the corporation fulfills its charitable pledge to donate much of its profits
to charity.[72] In addition, Michael Pirron, Impact Makers' founder and the
driving force behind its social mission, had a permanent seat on the IMH
board of directors and was appointed senior director at Impact Maker, a
position that gave him a veto right over decisions to pay dividends, issue new
shares, and award employees stock options.[73]

Despite all these layers of protection, litigation resulted between Pirron
and the other IMH directors. The cause of the litigation was allegedly that
the other directors attempted to pay themselves salaries at the expense of
Impact Makers' charitable partners and also attempted to sell the company
to a group of Impact Makers' executives at below-market value.[74] When
Pirron blocked these moves, the directors allegedly attempted to fire him as
CEO and force him to resign as permanent director.[75]

The case was ultimately settled, with Pirron returning as permanent director,[76] but the litigation demonstrates that even fairly robust governance
arrangements may fail when those in charge want to circumvent the company's social purpose. Despite this cautionary story, granting control to a
charity that is also the beneficiary of the BC or PBC's social purpose should
generally provide substantial protection to the company's social purpose
and also grant the company's social goals meaningful credibility.

Finally, the fourth problem is that owning a profit-seeking entity may create tax issues for the charitable nonprofit corporation. There are a number of potential issues here, the details of which are beyond the scope of this book. Merely by way of example, though, one issue is that if the charity pays insiders too much, it may run afoul of federal tax rules that prohibit excess benefit transactions.[77]

### Mandatory Trade-Offs

#### HOW IT WORKS

As we will discuss in Chapter 8, BCs and PBCs could choose to embed a balancing strategy into their corporate charters. The charter provision would require the boards to follow the strategy when deciding the degree to which the companies should give up profits in exchange for providing greater social benefits. Companies could then publicize their trade-off formula to encourage those investors, customers, and employees who thought it was worth rewarding to do so. (Chapter 8 describes a few possible balancing techniques, including minimum thresholds, trade-off ratios, and maximizing subject to constraints.)

Professors Dana Brakman Reiser and Steven A. Dean advanced a version of this idea, though theirs came in the form of a proposed new form of business organization, the mission-protected hybrid (MPH).[78] The MPH would be required to prioritize a social mission over profit by devoting a preponderance of its expenditures to its mission. That prioritization would be enforced by state government officials, who would deprive companies of their MPH status if they failed to comply.[79] Requiring a preponderance of expenditures to be devoted to a social mission is certainly one possible formula BCs and PBCs could adopt, but there are plenty of others, as we will explore in Chapter 8. Balancing formulas can represent any trade-off between profit and purpose that companies choose.

Much closer to my idea is Professor Emily Winston's proposal for public benefit plans (PBPs).[80] She proposed that BCs and PBCs find a representative of their social mission and then bargain with that representative to create a plan for pursuing the social mission. Winston argued for a change in the statutes so that failing to create a PBP would result in loss of a company's BC or PBC status. While I am not arguing for a mandatory scheme, Winston's proposal to bring in a representative who can advocate for the

social purpose is a good one, analogous to involving a charitable organization in governance.[81] I appreciate the flexibility that her proposal retains,
permitting BCs and PBCs to pursue profit and purpose in a way that they
choose while providing transparency—by requiring companies to file their
PBPs with the state—and some accountability, perhaps by allowing the representative of the social purpose to sue for breach of contract should the BC
or PBC fail to comply with the agreement.

### STRENGTHS

Placing a balancing strategy into the corporation's charter could help
prevent purpose washing by mandating a degree of social benefit. For example, minimum thresholds requires a BC or PBC to set a minimum threshold
for profitability and social good production. If the company is failing to
meet its goal for either profit or social good production, it must adjust its
strategy to sacrifice the more successful dimension until both aspects are
above the floors the board has set.[82]

A balancing provision in the corporate charter would make purpose
washing much less likely. The charter provision would be mandatory. If the
board ignored this requirement, a shareholder could launch a derivative suit
to force the board to comply. The charter provision would also provide some
degree of transparency, especially for publicly traded corporations.

The charter provision could be strengthened by giving some equity to
a charity with an incentive to enforce the provision or by adding a charter provision that grants a charity the right to sue to enforce the balancing
term, similar to Winston's proposal for a binding contract.[83] This tactic
would have many of the benefits of granting control to a charity without the
commensurate problems of most charities' lack of experience in managing
for-profit businesses.

### WEAKNESSES

Charter provisions that mandate a particular balancing strategy have
two primary weaknesses. First, they are inflexible. Because they are mandatory, they leave the board little latitude to depart from the original plan.
If unforeseen conditions arise that make a departure advisable, the board
could not change strategies without an amendment to the charter, which
would require the approval of both the board and the shareholders. One

solution is to ensure that these balancing strategies appear in bylaws, which can be changed by the board alone, rather than charter provisions, which require both shareholder and board approval for any amendments. That solution comes at a cost to the strategy's credibility, however, for precisely the reason that the board can easily change it.

Second, charter provisions can generally be enforced only by the directors themselves or by the shareholders in a derivative suit. If neither group felt it was in their interest to enforce the provision, the company could ignore it without legal ramifications. To the extent the provision was publicly known, ignoring it could cause reputational harm, though, to both the company and the board. Again, the balancing provision could be strengthened by granting a charity the right to enforce it.

### Benefit Directors and Officers

#### HOW IT WORKS

The Model Act permits BCs to designate a director as the benefit director.[84] In addition to the typical duties that directors must fulfill, the benefit director has the additional task of preparing an annual compliance statement. This statement must provide the director's conclusions and supporting reasoning on two issues: whether the BC acted to further the general public benefit and any specific public benefit the BC has adopted and whether the directors fulfilled their balancing duties.[85]

The Model Act also permits BCs to designate a benefit officer.[86] The primary purpose of this officer is to prepare the company's annual benefit report, but this person can also be assigned other duties related to the BC's general or specific public benefit.[87]

Delaware's PBC statute does not provide for either a benefit officer or a director. Delaware law is sufficiently flexible, though, that a PBC that wanted to create either position could do so by passing a bylaw or placing a provision in the corporation's charter.

#### STRENGTHS

Designating a benefit director increases the probability that at least one member of the board of directors is focused on ensuring that the company takes its social obligations seriously. Taking on a role can help promote behaviors consistent with that role.[88] A director assigned to care about the company's social mission may therefore act more aggressively to protect that mission, even in the absence of a preexisting dedication to the cause. The other directors may also behave differently, knowing that they will have to justify each decision to the benefit director. The presence of at least one strong voice advocating for the company's social mission has the potential to influence the entire decision dynamic and make pro-mission decisions more likely.

Also, under the Model Act's rules, the benefit director will enhance disclosure about the company's success in fulfilling its social mission. In addition to the benefit report that all BCs must produce each year, the benefit director will produce a separate report summarizing the benefit director's views on the company's progress in accomplishing its social goals. While the benefit report may reflect the views of the entire board, the benefit director has complete control over this separate report, giving him or her some leverage over the rest of the board in arguing for greater adherence to the company's social mission. If the board neglects the social mission, the benefit director has the power to publicize the board's failure.

The benefit officer prepares the benefit report and might therefore have a similar power to the benefit director's to threaten to embarrass the directors and the company if the board refuses to pursue the company's social mission sufficiently.

### WEAKNESSES

Allocating the task of pursuing the company's social purpose to a single director may have the perverse effect of giving the other directors implicit permission to ignore the company's social goals. Worse, the benefit director may become marginalized, a Cassandra who is routinely ignored.

The benefit director might also become coopted. Rather than face continued resistance from the other directors, a benefit director on a board that otherwise cares only about profit may go along with the majority and pay only lip service toward advocating for more social involvement.

The benefit officer seems quite a bit less useful than the benefit director. This officer presumably would not sit on the board and therefore would not have the same opportunity to persuade the directors to pursue the company's social purpose aggressively. The benefit officer also does not produce a separate report. He or she is entrusted with preparing the company's benefit

report, and so might have a similar power to the benefit director's in publicizing the company's lapses. But the power to prepare the report may not equate
to the power to decide the report's final text. If the board has final control
over the benefit report, then the benefit officer's power would be very limited.

### BC/PBC by Charter Provision?

In this section, we have been discussing methods of bolstering the credibility of the social mission of BCs and PBCs through private ordering.
Our thesis has been that the BC and PBC statutes do not provide adequate
enforcement tools to ensure that these entities actively pursue their social
goals. We have therefore explored how BCs and PBCs that wish to improve
their credibility as companies that act better, in some meaningful way, than
traditional corporations can set up private ordering arrangements that help
make their social commitments more binding and durable.

While not precisely on point, it might be worthwhile to take a brief
detour to talk about a related private ordering topic: Could a traditional
corporation transform itself into a BC or PBC without an enabling statute
by adopting charter provisions that mimic the BC or PBC statutes? A few
states have not yet passed legislation that empowers companies to become
BCs or PBCs. Can companies that wish to register in those states use private ordering to contract around shareholder primacy and commit themselves to social goals alongside profit seeking?

Unfortunately, the best answer we can give to this question is "maybe."
A majority of states have passed constituency statutes that empower traditional corporations to consider other constituencies such as employees and
communities when setting corporate policy.[89] Sometimes these statutes are
limited to the hostile takeover context, since the reason legislatures passed
these statutes was to protect their corporations from being taken over
against the will of their boards of directors. Usually, though, the statutes
are written more broadly. In states that have a constituency statute, then,
a corporation could likely add a provision to its charter disavowing shareholder primacy and adopting a rule permitting or requiring it to take interests other than profit into account when making decisions. Which interests
could be included would depend on the language of the particular constituency statute—the environment seems particularly likely to be excluded,
since it is not one of the factors generally listed in the statutes—but cor-

porations in such states could likely go some distance toward de facto BC/PBC status this way. In states without a constituency statute, though, the shareholder primacy rule might prevent corporations from taking this step.

Courts have generally enforced constituency statutes to grant directors greater discretion in making corporate decisions.[90] To my knowledge, though, the legality of using a constituency statute combined with charter amendments to transform a traditional corporation into a BC or PBC in a state that lacks a BC or PBC statute has never been tested in either states with constituency statutes or in states without them. The best we can do, then, is speculate on this point. Frederick Alexander, a noted authority on corporate law and BCs and PBCs, has argued that in states without a constituency statute, such an attempt would likely fail.[91] He also argued that it would be unwise to attempt the experiment even in states with a constituency statute.[92] Alexander does think it might be possible to transform a traditional limited liability company—a business form with more flexible governance rules than corporations have—into something like a BC or PBC, but still argues that BCs and PBCs are the better option for socially minded businesses.[93] Since forty states have passed some type of benefit corporation legislation—including Georgia and Alabama just a year ago as of this writing—the window for testing this method is rapidly closing.[94] If any readers decide to take the plunge, please let me know how it turns out.

————

In a book dedicated to explaining an exciting new legal mechanism to help companies pursue both profit and purpose, this chapter has a rather dispiriting message: the BC and PBC statutes do not contain good enforcement tools to ensure these companies pursue a social purpose. The statutory mechanisms—the balancing and disclosure requirements—are unlikely to prove effective deterrents against purpose washing. Fortunately, there are private ordering arrangements that might do a better job, but even these could conceivably be circumvented if those in power are sufficiently determined to pursue profit to the exclusion of purpose.

Nevertheless, I wrote this book because I think BCs and PBCs can be important tools to help companies pursue both profit *and* purpose. Although the statutory mechanisms are imperfect enforcement tools for social purpose, they are excellent *reinforcement* tools. Companies with cultures that are sincerely devoted to pursuing a social purpose will find that the new legal forms not only empower boards to sacrifice profit for purpose when they choose to do so but also help companies reflect on the social cost of each decision. Boards that take their balancing duties seriously will consider all the costs and benefits of each decision, not just the impact of the decision on the company's profitability. And companies that also take their disclosure obligations seriously will find that they offer an annual opportunity to reflect back on the prior year's decisions and how to improve them. Similarly, the various private ordering options can help companies balance profit and purpose appropriately by encouraging deeper self-evaluation with the help of an outside expert, bringing in dedicated people immune from profit pressures to weigh in on decisions, and committing to a particular method of balancing profit and purpose that is transparent, credible, and measurable.

Moreover, the commitment to the BC or PBC form has value in creating a culture that values purpose as well as profit. That culture itself has tremendous power. Companies that start with a sincere desire to pursue a social purpose alongside profit will likely recruit employees who share that desire and attract investors and customers who cherish the company's commitment to purpose. Those three groups—employees, investors, and customers—can play a critical role in holding the company to its purpose commitments. The combination of corporate culture and a purpose-driven marketing strategy can produce tremendous momentum that is hard to overcome.[95] A company's status as a BC or PBC helps reinforce a purpose-driven culture by sending a message to important constituencies like employees, investors, and customers and by providing legal mechanisms that reinforce the company's commitment to social purpose.

In the next chapter, we analyze whether this mix of risks and potential advantages adds up to a recommendation for or against these new forms for entrepreneurs. Given the weaknesses in the definition of purpose and the enforcement mechanisms, why would an entrepreneur choose one of the new hybrid forms?

# SIX

# *SHOULD ENTREPRENEURS CHOOSE A HYBRID FORM?*

Yvon Chouinard discovered rock climbing in high school. He began by rappelling down California cliffs looking for hawks' nests, then progressed to climbing mountains in Wyoming's Teton Range. He tried college briefly, but it did not stick; he far preferred dangling from great heights, suspended by nothing more than a piece of iron wedged into a rock. Offended by the permanence of those iron pitons on whose stability his life depended, Chouinard began making his own reusable version out of steel.[1]

So began the company that eventually became Patagonia, the world-famous outdoor clothing and equipment seller. The business started out of a desire to preserve the wilderness, and Patagonia kept that core motivation as it grew. Chouinard sells products to help people comfortably enjoy the outdoors, hoping that once they love the wilderness, they will fight to protect it. He has helped finance groups devoted to that end, giving 1 percent of Patagonia's sales to environmental organizations. And he has striven to ensure his products embody environmental responsibility, manufacturing fleece from recycled plastic bottles and base layers from recycled polyester.[2] Patagonia even launched an advertising campaign whose slogan was "Don't Buy This Jacket." The campaign admonished customers to buy only what they truly needed, since even Patagonia's famously green products imposed a punishing environmental toll.[3]

Lemonade, Inc. is as unusual an insurance company as Patagonia is a retailer. Lemonade issues insurance policies to cover renters and home-owners, which seems a prosaic enough business. But its two founders are unusual: neither comes from the insurance world. Daniel Schreiber is a British-trained Israeli lawyer turned tech executive, whose job immediately before cofounding Lemonade was running Powermat, an Israeli company that manufactures wireless phone chargers. Shai Wininger is a coder and serial tech entrepreneur. His most successful prior enterprise was Fiverr, an online marketplace for freelancers, also based in Israel. Neither had even a whiff of insurance experience before founding Lemonade.[4]

Schreiber and Wininger aim to disrupt the insurance market by inspir-ing greater trust than traditional insurers enjoy while charging lower pre-miums and paying claims faster. To accomplish all these goals, Lemonade groups its customers into pools organized by the customers' chosen charity. At the end of each year, Lemonade analyzes how much each pool brought in to the company in premiums, subtracts its fixed fee, reinsurance costs, and some other expenses, and then donates the remaining funds to the group's chosen charity. Lemonade says that donations can amount to as much as 40 percent of a customer's premium. It donated over $600,000 to charity in 2019 with this Giveback program, or about 1 percent of its revenues that year, despite losing over $100 million overall, and donated over $2.3 million in 2021.[5]

Lemonade's fixed fee model eliminates the profit incentive traditional insurers have to deny claims. While traditional insurers keep any excess of premiums over payouts as profits, Lemonade keeps only its fixed fee regard-less of the size of any premium excess. It also employs advanced artificial intelligence algorithms that permit it to determine payouts in a large per-centage of cases without any human involvement, vastly increasing speed and reducing costs. And the fact that the surplus funds go to charity should help cut down on fraud by its customers, since criminals are robbing a char-ity, not a faceless insurance company.[6]

Patagonia and Lemonade have purpose built into their business models at a fundamental level. Customers buy from Patagonia in part for their products' quality, but also in part because they know Patagonia shares their commitment to the environment. Lemonade's customers like Lemonade's low prices, but they also value Lemonade's trustworthiness, a credibility that comes in large part from Lemonade's commitment to donate a substantial portion of its revenues to charity.

Patagonia is registered as a California BC. Lemonade is registered as a Delaware PBC. Why did they choose these forms over a traditional corporation or other standard business forms such as a limited liability company (LLC)? Did they make the right decisions, or should they have stuck with a traditional corporation or LLC?

### The Negative Case: Are Hybrid Forms Bad for Entrepreneurs?

For a number of reasons, the choice of a BC may have been a mistake, even if the companies' cultures and business models seem a good fit for one of the new hybrid forms. BCs and PBCs may sometimes sacrifice profit to pursue their social purpose, and this is a trade-off some entrepreneurs may be unwilling to make. BCs and PBCs have more complex governance requirements, especially the mandate to balance other goals against the drive for profits. They may face greater liability risks for failing to meet this balance requirement. They have greater disclosure obligations as well, which may also result in potential liability exposure. At least for a time, transaction costs may prove higher for BCs and PBCs simply because these are new business types and lawyers and investment bankers have not yet learned the governing rules or developed applicable forms. The costs of incorporating or converting, governing, and buying or selling these new entities may turn out to be higher for a time until everyone catches up on the new rules. And the very act of converting—for companies that initially incorporated in a traditional form—may prove a daunting process because it requires shareholder approval.[7] We explore each of these challenges in this chapter.

This chapter focuses on entrepreneurs' initial decision concerning the legal form when they found a company. It is also possible, as we discovered in Chapter 3, for companies to convert to a BC or PBC despite having originated as a traditional corporation. Such conversions, however, require shareholder approval. At the start of a company's life, the shareholders are often synonymous with the founders. Early on, then, it would still be the founders who made the conversion decision. Once the company takes on outside investors, though, the shareholders become a mixed group of the founders and early employees, on the one hand, and outside investors, on the other. At that point, the company is likely to need the investors' consent to switch over to a BC or PBC, which places the decision into the realm of Chapter 7, which covers investors' interests. For that reason, in this chapter, we assume the decision is being made at the outset by the founders, while in the next chapter, we ask about investors' willingness to invest in existing hybrid companies and their parallel willingness to consent to a company's conversion to a BC or PBC.

### A Cautionary Tale: The Honest Company

The Honest Company is a perfect example of a company that seems well suited to be a BC or PBC yet has remained a traditional corporation.[8] Understanding why The Honest Company has declined to become a BC or PBC may shed some light on the challenges facing advocates of these new forms.

The Honest Company was cofounded by actor Jessica Alba, who landed her first major acting role on the television series *Dark Angel*, which premiered in 2000. The director, James Cameron, chose her out of the thousand-odd actresses who auditioned for him in large part because of her "punk attitude." [9] Cameron recalled that Alba was a terrifically hard worker and that she "never backed down from a fight."[10]

*Dark Angel* took place in a dystopian (and then-future) Seattle of 2019 in which the United States had suffered a terrorist attack that knocked out all of the country's computers and communications equipment, destroying its economy and collapsing the social order. Alba played Max Guevara, the show's central character and the product of a government project to create genetically enhanced soldiers. Guevara had escaped the government lab that created her when she was nine years old and managed to elude the authorities while scrapping out a living as a bicycle messenger. Eventually Guevara joined forces with an underground journalist to expose governmental misdeeds.

Alba's character was strong both physically and mentally. Not only did her genetic enhancements give her superhuman strength and coordination, but her mental toughness enabled her to survive in an extremely hostile world. Guevara was typical of Alba's later role choices. Although she has starred in her share of romantic comedies, she has often played tougher characters such as the Invisible Woman, the superhero in Marvel's *Fantastic Four*, and a former Drug Enforcement Administration agent on the television show *L.A.'s Finest*. These roles seem highly appropriate for an actor who went on to cofound a billion-dollar corporation, The Honest Company.

Alba's interest in business began when she was pregnant with her first child. She had washed some baby clothes she had received as a gift in a detergent recommended by her mother, only to discover that the detergent made her break out in hives. She grew deeply concerned that her still-unborn child could have an even more serious allergic reaction and began researching to find a safer detergent.[11] She quickly discovered how difficult it was to judge a detergent's safety from the labeling, since manufacturers could label potentially harmful chemicals simply as "fragrance." She resolved to build a company that would provide safe and effective products that were also less harmful to the environment.[12] She joined with LegalZoom.com cofounder Brian Lee, PriceGrabber.com executive Sean Kane, and author Christopher Gavigan to form The Honest Company in 2012.[13]

The Honest Company's pledge to provide safe, environmentally friendly family products helped it grow rapidly at first. To boost its credibility as a prosocial brand, the company applied for and received certification as a B Corp by B Lab in its first year, at the end of 2012.[14] Within three years, the company had raised a $100 million investment round for just a small slice of the company's equity, valuing the company as a whole at $1.7 billion.[15] The company grew from $10 million in sales in its first year to $300 million in 2016.[16]

But beginning in 2016, the company's progress stumbled. The company faced a number of lawsuits, including one by the Organic Consumers Association alleging that the company's products were not really organic, as well as a class action accusing the company of misrepresenting the ingredients in some of its products.[17] The company also recalled its baby powder and baby wipes because of problems with both products, including numerous instances of mold found in its baby wipes. International consumer products giant Unilever expressed interest in buying the company that year but ultimately bought Seventh Generation—one of The Honest Company's primary competitors—instead. And the company suffered a down investment round, one that valued the company at far less than the $1.7 billion of the prior round. In fact, the 2016 round valued the company at under $1 billion, depriving it of its coveted "unicorn" status.[18]

At some point, The Honest Company decided not to convert to a BC or PBC and therefore gave up on its B Corp status. The company has not issued a public statement on this decision that I can find. In fact, its website still trumpets its achievement of B Corp certification in 2012.[19] The closest substitute to an official statement by the company seems to be an article B Lab published on its blog about Alba's cofounder, Christopher Gavigan. The article focused on Gavigan's subsequent venture, a producer of CBD-based personal care products called Prima. Gavigan chose the BC legal form for Prima (and also certified Prima as a B Corp with B Lab), explaining:

> Becoming a benefit corporation clearly identifies an honorable pathway for a brand's tone and manner, as well as giving meaningful, verifiable structure to an organizational and financial plan. . . . I firmly believe that a business's financial statements and operating structure are moral documents. They identify why you exist and what you care about: Do you care about others or yourself? Do you care about impact or profit?[20]

In discussing Gavigan's background and involvement with The Honest Company, the article mentioned that the company had obtained B Corp status early in its existence. Gavigan set forth the rationale for seeking to credential The Honest Company as a B Corp, stating:

> Like our contemporaries, we felt there was a moral imperative for businesses to act swiftly and with clear intent on environmental and social issues threatening humanity. . . . It was a club of commitment, and we absolutely wanted to do our part.[21]

Without quoting Gavigan directly, the article went on to explain why The Honest Company had not converted to BC or PBC status, and in fact had eventually given up its B Corp certification despite a commitment to B Lab's values. The article justified the move this way:

> Yet, because Honest was initially established as a C-corp, growth and governance dynamics made it difficult for the organization to make the shift to a public benefit corporation in Delaware (B Corps are required to become benefit corps or the equivalent offered in their state of incorporation to maintain certification). The company ultimately lost its B Corp certification.[22]

By "C-corp," the article likely meant a traditional corporation. The term *C-corp* actually refers to a federal tax status, not to a type of corporate governance form, but this is a common misuse of the term.[23] The article's view, then, appears to be that The Honest Company 's initial choice to incorporate in a traditional form was sticky and difficult to change later. The article provides no detail about why this might have been the case, or what "governance dynamics" interfered with the founders' presumed desire to convert to a BC or PBC form and preserve their B Corp certification with B Lab.

There are other examples of prominent companies that seemed bound for BC or PBC status that chose instead to relinquish their B Lab certification and remain in a traditional corporate form. This one should suffice, though, to illustrate the challenges that larger companies—whether publicly traded or backed by venture capital funding—may face when trying to select the BC or PBC legal form. Next, I discuss these challenges individually, using The Honest Company to illustrate how each challenge might discourage a company from adopting one of the hybrid forms.

### Purpose at Profit's Expense

One such challenge is the potential tension between pursuit of profit and the fulfillment of the company's social purpose. Purpose and profit will not always conflict; in fact, sometimes purpose can bolster profits. For example, The Honest Company 's commitment to community service likely helps persuade customers to buy its diapers rather than Pampers or Huggies. The company says it has donated over 25 million products to its nonprofit partners and that its employees have volunteered over eighteen thousand hours to nonprofit organizations that serve meals, clean beaches, and serve other important charitable needs.[24] Customers who want to support The Honest Company 's good works may choose to buy their diapers rather than Pampers, even if they believe Pampers' price is better than The Honest Company 's.

On the other hand, The Honest Company 's social purpose may sometimes conflict with its desire for profits. Giving away free diapers and wipes to the disadvantaged costs money that would otherwise go to the company's bottom line. Even if The Honest Company 's management cares only about profits and not at all about its social purpose—if its stated social purpose is designed only to boost its profits—it has to figure out how much genuine

good it must do along the social-purpose dimension to create brand loyalty among its customers. If the cost of doing this much good exceeds the
benefit in increased sales, it will abandon its social purpose. From a purely
profit-maximizing viewpoint, in fact, The Honest Company should prefer
to create the illusion that it is giving away a lot of free diapers to the poor
without actually doing so. If it could manage this trick, it would gain all the
marketing benefits of a prosocial brand without bearing any of the costs of
actually donating goods and services.

The Honest Company's decision to remain a traditional corporation, then, may have been motivated by a reluctance to reduce its freedom
of action in regard to scaling down its social-purpose expenditures. If it
became a BC or PBC, the law would impose a fiduciary duty on its board
of directors to balance profit and purpose as independent goals instead of
being able to consider purpose only as a means to achieving profits. With a
traditional structure, the board retains the unfettered ability to reduce or
eliminate its charitable donations, based purely on the board's view of how
best to maximize profits. Giving up this freedom and occasionally being
required to sacrifice profit for purpose may have seemed too steep a price to
pay for whatever measure of additional credibility for its social purpose—
and related branding advantages—might come with the commitment to BC
or PBC legal status.

### More Complex Governance

A related reason why some entrepreneurs might forgo BC or PBC status
and instead choose a traditional corporation or limited liability company
is that the hybrid forms make corporate governance more complex. In a
traditional corporation, the board's sole task is to maximize profits for the
company's shareholders.[25] But in a BC or PBC, the board must balance the
quest for profits against the company's social mission, giving appropriate
priority to both. This balancing requirement arguably makes the board's
task more difficult and complex.

Gavigan, The Honest Company cofounder, may have been referring to
this issue when he cited "governance dynamics" as a reason why the company gave up its B Corps status and chose to remain a traditional corporation rather than convert to a BC or PBC.[26] The Honest Company's board

might have rejected the BC and PBC forms to avoid taking on this added complexity.

### Potential Liability Risk

Entrepreneurs may also hesitate to convert to one of the hybrid forms out of fear of personal liability. Under both the Delaware statute for PBCs and the Model Act for BCs, shareholders have the right to launch a lawsuit against the directors for failing to balance profits against the company's social mission appropriately.[27] The details for these actions differ in the two statutes, but the basic idea for both is that the board of directors is theoretically accountable to the shareholders for its balancing decisions. If The Honest Company became a Delaware PBC and then decided to give away so many free diapers that it ceased to be profitable, its shareholders could sue the board. Conversely, if The Honest Company gave away only a dozen boxes of diapers a year, its shareholders could sue, demanding that it donate more. Since company founders commonly serve on the board, they may find themselves defendants in these suits.

I argued in Chapter 5 that these lawsuits are unlikely to prove very effective in disciplining directors in either direction; shareholders are likely to lose these suits whether they seek to make the directors pay greater attention to profitability or to the company's social mission. But even if ultimately unsuccessful, lawsuits are expensive, time-consuming, and unpleasant for the defendants. They may also damage a company's brand value by publicizing allegations that the company's public commitment to improve society is just marketing hype without real substance. Whether out of concern about liability or just to avoid the possibility of these suits, companies like The Honest Company might decide to forgo the new hybrid forms and stick with a traditional corporation or LLC.

### Greater Disclosure Obligations

Both BCs and PBCs also expand a company's disclosure obligations, which may deter some company founders from adopting these forms. These hybrid forms mandate that the company report periodically to its shareholders—and sometimes to wider constituencies—on the company's effectiveness in providing a social benefit.[28] For privately held companies, these disclosures need not be very burdensome. As we saw in Chapter 5, states are not enforcing these requirements for the most part, effectively making the reports voluntary. Once a company becomes publicly traded, however, any statement to the public could conceivably place it in jeopardy of liability under the federal securities laws for making a false or misleading disclosure.[29] In addition, for both public and private companies, these reports risk embarrassing the company and damaging the company's brand if they reveal that the company's marketing claims of providing meaningful social benefits are exaggerated.

If The Honest Company, for example, prepared and publicized such reports, the reports might reveal that its claims of ensuring that all its products contain only healthy and environmentally friendly ingredients are flawed, as some plaintiffs have suggested in suits against the company.[30] Remaining a traditional corporation did not prevent these suits, but disclosing any failures in a company report might have accelerated the suits and perhaps even encouraged additional claims.

### Legal Novelty

BCs and PBCs are new; they did not exist when most currently practicing lawyers and investment bankers went to graduate school or even when they were starting out in their professions. The first state to pass a BC statute was Maryland in 2010. Delaware passed its PBC statute in 2013. There are still relatively few BCs and PBCs, at least as far as can be determined. Although most states are not tracking these entities separately, making it difficult to determine precisely how many there are, Delaware, fortunately, is an exception. As of September 2019, nearly two thousand PBCs were registered in Delaware.[31] In comparison, there were nearly 1.5 million business entities of any kind registered in Delaware at the end of 2018. LLCs remain by far the most popular form of entity by volume, but over ninety thousand corporations registered in Delaware in 2018 and 2019.[32] Fewer than one thousand of these were PBCs.[33]

Not surprisingly, corporate lawyers remain much less familiar with these new forms than they are with traditional corporations and LLCs. The costs of hiring a lawyer to form a PBC or cause a PBC to engage in a transaction such as a merger with another entity are therefore likely to prove somewhat higher than for a traditional corporation. Transactional lawyers rely heavily on forms to reduce transactions' drafting costs. They begin each deal with a form from some past similar deal and then modify it to suit the particular needs of the transaction at hand. Using forms from prior deals is much cheaper than drafting each deal document from scratch. Because BCs and PBCs are relatively new, most lawyers have not yet confronted creating documents for them and do not yet have time-tested forms for BC or PBC transactions.

The newness of these hybrid entities not only makes transactions more expensive; it also makes them riskier. As of this writing, there are no reported court decisions involving the governance rules for BCs or PBCs.[34] Although the statutes for both forms seem reasonably clear, there are bound to be disputes over the meaning of some terms. Until courts have analyzed these statutes and issued binding public rulings, lawyers will remain concerned that they lack a reasonable basis to interpret the law for their clients. Lawyers may fear they cannot predict what a court will say the rules are for these new forms or draft appropriate forms that take the new rules into account. Over time, this concern should wane as lawyers become more familiar with hybrid forms and courts begin to issue opinions interpreting the new statutes.

### Conversion Requirements

Finally, companies that started as traditional corporations might hesitate to try to convert to BCs or PBCs because of the burdens involved in the conversion process. Traditional corporations that want to convert to a BC under the Model Act must secure the approval of a "minimum status vote" by the shareholders, which means that at least two-thirds of each class of the company's stock must vote to convert the company to a BC.[35] Traditional corporations that choose to convert to a Delaware PBC until recently also had to secure a two-thirds shareholder vote. In addition, shareholders who voted against converting the company to a PBC were entitled to appraisal rights—the right to force the company to buy their shares in cash at a fair price determined by the court—if the conversion went through despite their disapproval.[36]

Delaware loosened these rules in 2020, requiring only an absolute majority of the outstanding shares to approve a conversion and no longer granting dissenters appraisal rights.[37] Going forward, then, this may prove less of a concern, though even persuading an absolute majority of share-holders to convert to a PBC might prove challenging, depending on who the shareholders are.

One company that may illustrate the importance of this change in the law is eyeglass manufacturer Warby Parker, a Delaware PBC that is publicly traded on the New York Stock Exchange. Warby Parker employs a "buy one, give one" strategy, giving away one pair of glasses to the disadvantaged for every pair it sells, making it a natural fit for PBC status.[38]

For a number of years, though, Warby Parker remained organized as a traditional company and even gave up its B Corp certification because it refused to convert to a BC or PBC. At the time, Warby Parker stated that converting to a PBC "proved challenging given the size and stage of the company."[39] This statement might have been referring to the rigorous shareholder vote requirement and the appraisal rights for dissenters in such a vote that existed at the time under Delaware law. Warby Parker's investors might not have felt as passionately as the founders did about the company's mission to provide eyeglasses and eye care to those who could not afford it. They might have been more focused on the company's profit growth and been reluctant, for some or all of the reasons discussed above, to convert to a PBC. As long as the outside investors controlled over one-third of the votes, they had the power to block any conversion. Even if they had fewer votes than required, their threat to demand appraisal rights upon a conversion to a PBC might have served as an effective block, since the company might not have had the cash to buy out a large number of shares.

After the statute changed to make conversion easier, Warby Parker converted to become a Delaware PBC shortly before going public.[40] The company's change of heart on this issue may well have been motivated at least in part by the legal changes that made conversion easier.

### The Positive Case: Are Hybrid Forms Good for Entrepreneurs?

So far, this chapter has discussed why entrepreneurs might prefer to avoid these new forms. That analysis might seem to spell the end of the BC/PBC experiment. But the evidence is very much to the contrary: there are thousands of BCs and PBCs throughout the country as of this writing, including some large companies and even a number that are publicly traded. And the number of companies choosing one of these hybrid forms appears to be growing fairly quickly. There must, then, be reasons why entrepreneurs like these new forms, despite the many concerns the hybrid forms raise.

To explore this question properly, we first have to recognize that a traditional corporation or LLC is not the only alternative company founders may be considering for their mission-driven business. They may also be thinking about forming a nonprofit corporation. In this section, I start by discussing the reasons founders might like the idea of a BC or PBC instead of a traditional for-profit corporation, and then I explore why the hybrid forms might be preferred over a nonprofit.

There are at least four reasons why founders might like the idea of forming their business as a BC or PBC, even if they are primarily or exclusively focused on earning profits and are not willing to sacrifice profitability to fulfill a social mission: (1) hybrid forms may better attract customers than traditional corporations; (2) hybrid forms may better attract and retain employees than traditional corporations; (3) hybrid forms may better attract investors than traditional corporations; and (4) hybrid forms may include a type of protection from hostile takeovers knows as a "sweet pill." There is also a nonfinancial reason founders may prefer a hybrid form; they may want their form of business organization to express their ideals.

### Attract Customers

Founders may reasonably believe that customers will choose their products and services over those offered by their competitors—and perhaps even willingly pay more for them—if the company is perceived as caring about improving society in some meaningful way. A 2014 Nielsen study reported that over half of global online shoppers would willingly pay a premium for items furnished by producers committed to positive social and environmental policies.[41] Companies appear to be well aware of this trend; many advertise their products as being in some way good for the world. Patagonia markets both its strong commitment to creating environmentally friendly products and its generous treatment of its employees.[42] State Bags, a PBC that sells backpacks that retail for as much as $198 each,[43] celebrates its generous policy of donating backpacks full of school supplies to children in need.[44]

In a series of interviews I conducted with entrepreneurs who had founded BCs or PBCs, I heard this "attract customers" reason many times as an advantage of the hybrid business form. One company I heard this from was MF Fire, from its cofounder Taylor Myers.

MF Fire began with a school competition. Myers and his cofounder were students at the University of Maryland at the time, and the university hosted a competition to see which student team could build the most efficient wood-burning stove to provide residential heating. Most such stoves spew a great deal of particulate waste into the air that has been linked to cancer and respiratory ailments. The competitors' task was to design and build a wood-burning stove that would produce less smoke and particulate matter. Myers and his cofounder designed such a good stove that they decided to form a BC to produce and sell it. Myers told me they chose the BC form in part because they thought it would help attract customers to their product. Myers said, "Our gut feeling is that it would help to attract customers, and that's something that we are relying on as we're moving forward, something that we are trying to build into the way we get customers, that we're a company that is not just for profit that there is some social good associated with what we are doing."[45]

*Inspire Employees*

Just as customers are attracted to buying products and services from companies with an appealing social mission, employees tend to like the idea of working for companies that are meaningfully prosocial. This is particularly true of millennials. A recent international survey found that 87 percent of millennials thought that financial performance should not be the only measure of a company's success.[46] Millennials are far from unique, however. A 2022 survey of seven thousand employees found that 69 percent of respondents said that they strongly expected their employer to reflect their values, have a greater purpose, and address social problems.[47] A company's success often hinges on its employees, so attracting and retaining talent is critical to a company's future.[48] A company's ability to retain employees can be as important as its ability to attract them. Every time an employee leaves, the company loses roughly the equivalent of one-third of that employee's annual salary on lost productivity and funds spent hiring a replacement.[49]

Companies organized as BCs and PBCs have made a statement that they are committed to pursuing some social mission over and above the desire to earn profits. That statement can help in both attracting and retaining a talented workforce. A number of the BC and PBC founders I interviewed as part of a study cited this factor as an advantage of their hybrid status. Michael Pirron, the founder of Impact Makers, actually quantified the difference. Impact Makers is an information technology consulting firm that Pirron founded with just $50 and a laptop. It was originally organized as a nonstock corporation, but it soon converted to BC status. Pirron explained that most IT consulting firms have difficulty retaining their employees, who are in high demand. A typical IT firm would lose 20 to 25 percent of its workforce *every year*. Impact Makers, which at the time of our interview employed about one hundred people, lost only ten people in its first nine years, or something like 1 percent per year.[50]

### Entice Investors

A third potential advantage of hybrid status is the ability to attract investors who care about a company's social mission. Although the next chapter is devoted to this topic, it is worth giving it a quick mention now, since the appeal of these forms to investors may also bear on their attractiveness to entrepreneurs. Entrepreneurs who cannot persuade investors to back their firms will seldom succeed, after all.

Traditional investors, whose goal is solely to seek the highest return they can achieve for a given risk profile, may be interested in hybrid forms if the new forms can help the companies earn higher profits. We have just discussed two reasons why this might be the case, the potential of BCs and PBCs to attract customers and employees. In addition, the new forms might prove helpful in appealing to a different type of investor, one who cares about both the financial return of their investments and the social benefits generated by their portfolio companies—the social impact investor.

Both the Model Act and the Delaware PBC statute impose requirements that arguably make the prosocial claims of BCs and PBCs more credible (though we examined the weaknesses of these requirements in Chapter 5). Social impact investors therefore might be interested in companies that have organized themselves as BCs or PBCs.

Social impact investors may have a range of motives for targeting companies with an avowed social mission. Some investors, such as charitable foundations investing their endowment capital, may want to leverage their capital to pursue their social missions, in addition to earning returns that fund their missions more directly. These investors might be willing to sacrifice some financial return in exchange for the larger social return. Other investors might be interested in mission-driven companies out of a purely profit-motivated investment strategy, betting that prosocial companies may generate returns at a lower risk than traditional companies.

The amount of money at stake is likely significant. Estimates of the amount of money designated for social impact investing vary widely, but the figure is likely in the hundreds of billions of dollars, and perhaps even in the trillions.[51] Founders and shareholders of companies that seek outside investment might want to think about pursuing this pool of investment capital, and organizing as a BC or PBC could prove helpful in those efforts. So far, though, this possibility seems to remain an interesting potential rather than a concrete advantage for businesses that choose a hybrid form. In my empirical study of PBCs that have garnered investment from venture capital firms, the bulk of the investment came from sources that sought profit alone rather than from impact investors.[52]

### Sweet Pill

The final pecuniary reason company founders might choose a BC or PBC is the "sweet pill." The sweet pill takes its name from the more famous "poison pill," a device publicly traded corporations have often used to fend off hostile takeovers. In its most common form, the poison pill deters hostile takeovers by inflicting significant financial harm on the raider. If the raider buys more than a set percentage of the target's stock—the trigger—all of the target's shareholders except the raider gain the right to buy newly issued target stock at a steep discount. The other shareholders effectively take a significant portion of the raider's equity without adequate compensation, diluting the raider's stake and sharply reducing its value.

The sweet pill works entirely differently but may prove similarly efficacious in deterring raiders. One of a hostile raider's most potent weapons is the Delaware Supreme Court's *Revlon* case, which we covered in Chapter 2. When *Revlon* applies, the board loses its ability to turn down offers to purchase the company on the grounds that the board has a better plan to manage the business that will ultimately result in a higher share price. Instead, the directors become auctioneers and must sell the company to the highest bidder.

The *Revlon* doctrine is premised on the shareholder primacy principle that the board's duty is to maximize shareholders' return. The BC and PBC statutes require directors to *balance* the pursuit of profits and the pursuit of a social mission rather than maximize profits alone as in a traditional corporation. There is therefore a strong possibility that BCs and PBCs will be less vulnerable to the *Revlon* doctrine. Directors of hybrid entities can argue that they are within their rights to reject a hostile offer—even if *Revlon* would normally apply and even if the offer is clearly the highest bid—because the raider would abandon the company's social mission. In balancing profit and social mission, in other words, the board might reasonably conclude that it should accept a different offer, even if the bid is lower, because the favored buyer has committed to preserve the company's social mission. This is what is meant by the "sweet pill."

A number of entrepreneurs I have interviewed have mentioned this as a desirable advantage of BCs and PBCs. The cautionary tale they sometimes cite is that of Ben & Jerry's Homemade, Inc. Ben & Jerry's is a premium ice cream maker that is perhaps as famous for its progressive values as for its creative ice cream flavors. Ben Cohen, one of the company's two cofounders, offered to take the company private in 2000. The company's board liked the idea until two other buyers materialized. The board then initiated what amounted to an auction and sold the company to the highest bidder, international conglomerate Unilever.[53] Although the sale to Unilever included a number of provisions to ensure Unilever would retain Ben & Jerry's progressive management style, the company's cofounders expressed regret about the sale. Both Ben Cohen and Jerry Greenfield publicly stated that they would have preferred not to sell the company, but they believed the board was required to sell to the highest bidder.[54]

Cohen and Greenfield may well have been mistaken on that point under Vermont law,[55] but there are circumstances in which, particularly for companies registered in Delaware, their fears would be well founded. As we discussed in Chapter 2, the *Revlon* doctrine does sometimes require the target company's board to sell the company to the highest bidder. The sweet pill remains untested in court, but it seems likely to prove an efficacious response to *Revlon*, especially when the highest bidder refuses to commit to maintaining the target company's social mission.

*Express Ideals*

These first four rationales for founders to choose a hybrid form of business organization were rooted in some pecuniary advantage from the new forms. In other words, founders might want to choose a BC or PBC because those forms might help them earn more profits. There is another reason that founders might choose one of these new forms, although it has nothing to do with improving a company's bottom line. The founders may simply want their legal status to mirror their personal values. This rationale is an expressive function of the new forms.

In my interviews of BC and PBC founders, the expressive function was the most common—and most passionately expressed—reason the entrepreneurs gave for choosing a hybrid form of business organization.[56] They told me that even if the new forms did not generate any practical advantage over a traditional corporation, they felt so strongly about their social mission that they wanted it represented in the very legal structure of the business.

One of these founders was Chris Norton, of Crowdspending, which gathers consumers together to gain market power. The company then negotiates with suppliers of insurance, wireless service, and financial services to obtain better terms for the group. Crowdspending chooses one supplier of each service to provide all its customers: one insurer, one bank, one cell phone service provider. These companies then give back the money they would have spent on marketing to Crowdspending's customers, and Crowdspending then gives its customers a choice; they can keep the money or donate it to charity.[57] Norton explained Crowdspending's decision to form as a California BC this way: "To me it was about making a statement, that, you know, we were going to—this business is about mission maximization, you know, as opposed to profit maximization. Profit is a part of our mission, but it is not the only thing."[58]

*Hybrids over Nonprofits?*

Hearing the devotion to benefiting society from entrepreneurs like Norton, one might justifiably wonder if the real choice for these founders was not between a hybrid form and a traditional corporation, but rather between a hybrid form and a *nonprofit* corporation. Not surprisingly, some of the entrepreneurs I interviewed had considered a nonprofit as an alternative. They cited a variety of reasons for rejecting nonprofit status in favor of a BC or PBC. Note, however, that nonprofits do offer two powerful advantages over hybrid forms: freedom from taxation and, at least in some cases, the ability to offer donors a tax deduction for money contributed to the enterprise. BCs and PBCs do not, as of now at least, come with any tax benefits. Companies that plan to rely heavily on donations for funding should think seriously about the nonprofit form.

### Easier Compliance

One problem with nonprofits, some founders said, was the high costs of compliance with the governing statutes. This is especially true of nonprofits that wish to qualify for federal § 501(c)(3) status, which enables some nonprofits to secure tax-deductible contributions from donors. Such companies must be organized and operated entirely for one or more exempt purposes listed in the statute, such as education or charity. Also, none of their earnings may benefit any private shareholders or other owner. They must also avoid participating in any campaign activity for or against political candidates.[59]

### Stronger Governance

A second reason some entrepreneurs gave for avoiding nonprofit status was their experience that nonprofits suffered from weaker corporate governance than for-profit companies. They pointed out that nonprofit directors typically had no financial stake in the enterprise and might lose the motivation to help the cause that inspired them to join the board. It is also more difficult for a founder to retain control over a nonprofit than a for-profit entity, because control over the board is not driven by stock ownership. For example, Tayde Aburto, the founder of the Hispanic Chamber of E-Commerce, explained his decision to choose a hybrid form instead of a nonprofit corporation in part because of his governance concerns:

> We didn't want to incorporate as a nonprofit just because I also found out that a lot of Hispanic chambers that were in crisis at the time were because of poor boards of directors. And even though I knew I could have a good board . . . I was a little afraid that it could happen to our organization, something that had happened to a lot of nonprofits in the past. And that's when . . . good boards of directors for some reason stopped contributing to their organization, they take different paths. And that rotation of people throughout

the years, to some extent, drives some nonprofits organizations in the direction where their founder didn't want it to go.[60]

*Financial Advantages*

The third and perhaps most important reason some entrepreneurs shied away from the nonprofit form of business organization involved finances. Some company founders expressed concern that nonprofits were not as financially sustainable as for-profit entities. In part, the concern stemmed from the very nature of a nonprofit. Nonprofits are not permitted to distribute profits to their owners. As a result, as a practical matter, nonprofits cannot seek investors. The point of investing is to earn a financial return based on the company's earnings. Because nonprofits cannot provide that return, they cannot attract investors. Instead, nonprofits fund themselves by charging for their operations (think of a nonprofit hospital charging for medical services) and by seeking donations. Donations, however, sometimes come with significant restrictions, especially when they come from charitable foundations.

The same limitation on distributing profits also prevents nonprofits from rewarding their founders. They cannot pay out a portion of their revenues to the founders as a dividend. They also cannot reward their founders with a portion of the proceeds if the company is sold. Entrepreneurs who want to seek capital from investors or share in the financial rewards of the company's success should probably avoid the nonprofit corporation form.

———

This chapter has offered an analysis of the advantages and disadvantages of the BC and PBC forms from entrepreneurs' perspectives. Disadvantages include potentially having to sacrifice profit for social purpose, a more complex governance structure, possibly a greater liability risk, additional disclosure obligations, lingering legal uncertainty, and perhaps higher transaction costs. Advantages include the potential to attract customers, investors, and employees who may be drawn to the company's social purpose. Choosing a BC or PBC form may lend greater credibility to the company's claims of doing business differently in a way that is ultimately better for everyone. These hybrid forms may also enable founders to avoid hostile takeovers with the sweet pill. Perhaps most important, social entrepreneurs may like the idea of a legal entity type that reflects their profoundly held ideals.

The new forms may also offer some advantages over a nonprofit. Although BCs and PBCs offer no tax advantages, they are simpler to set up and maintain than nonprofit corporations, especially those hoping to qualify for § 501(c)(3) status. And they should offer better and more predictable governance. Most important, BCs and PBCs offer the possibility of financial rewards when the businesses are successful and can seek capital from investors.

In the next chapter, we explore how these investors might think about hybrid business forms.

## SEVEN

## SHOULD INVESTORS SUPPORT HYBRID FORMS?

### Investors' Importance to Entrepreneurs

Paul Tsongas's father was a Greek immigrant who ran a dry cleaners. Raised in Lowell, Massachusetts, Tsongas secured degrees from Dartmouth, Yale, and Harvard despite his humble beginnings. He served on Lowell's city council, as a US representative, and as a US senator. Near the end of his first term in the Senate, Tsongas's political career was derailed when he was diagnosed with non-Hodgkin's lymphoma. Undeterred, he beat back the cancer and then entered the race for US president in 1991. Tsongas positioned himself as a probusiness liberal, which at the time seemed a potentially winning platform. But his campaign ran out of steam when it ran out of money.[1] As Tsongas explained in his concession speech, "The problem is that we were starved, and if money is the mother's milk of politics, our mothers didn't show up until late January."[2]

If money is important to a political campaign, it is critical to founding a new business. Lack of capital is a major reason that new companies fail, perhaps the *most* important reason.[3] It takes time and usually considerable resources to nurture a new business until it becomes self-sustaining. For

148

example, Tesla did not declare an annual profit until 2020, eighteen years after its founding in 2003.[4] Until that time, it had to keep raising new capital from investors to fund its operating and development costs. Had Tesla's investors—its "mothers"—not shown up during that period, the company would have failed.

While some company founders are fortunate enough to have the resources to self-fund their new enterprises with personal or family resources, most require outside capital from early-stage investors such as angels—the earliest-stage professional investors—and venture capitalists. These investors will expect hefty profits to compensate them for the considerable risk of investing in a new, unproven enterprise.

Typically these early-stage investors realize a return either by selling the company as a whole or by going public in an initial public offering (IPO) or through a merger with a special-purpose acquisition company (SPAC). Angels and venture capital funds' willingness to invest therefore turns on their perception of the eventual interest of either public investors (in the case of an IPO or SPAC) or a financial or strategic investor (in the case of a sale of the entire company). Will investors—whether at early or late stages of the company's development—be interested in risking their money with companies that are legally required to pursue interests that may result in lower profits?

## Types of Investors

Before we dive into this question, we need to introduce a little bit of nuance about the different types of investors. Investors not only invest in different stages of companies' development, they also have different investment strategies and even different goals that may help determine their interest in BCs and PBCs.

We can usefully divide investors into two groups: those who invest solely to maximize their returns (profit-only investors) and those who may be willing to sacrifice some return in order to produce other social benefits (profit-plus investors). Note that both groups very much want to earn a profit on their capital; they are investors, not donors. Some entrepreneurs considering a BC or PBC legal form may also be considering forming their company as a nonprofit corporation, in part because a nonprofit may be able to attract donations. We discussed the relative merits of nonprofit corporations and BCs and PBCs in Chapter 6. In this chapter, our concern is with the ability of BCs and PBCs to interest investors, whom I distinguish from donors precisely in that investors are interested in earning a financial return on capital while donors are not.

Even within this group of profit seekers, some are willing to forgo a degree of profit in order to help the world in some meaningful way. For example, Triodos Investment Management, an impact investment fund based in the Netherlands, is a profit-plus investor. The company states that it "invests to generate social and environmental impact alongside a healthy financial return."[5] Its goal is to generate a good return for its investors while simultaneously "us[ing] money as a driving force towards a society that is humane, ecologically balanced and works for the benefit of all."[6]

Triodos measures its success not only on its financial performance but also by the progress it has made toward solving social problems. For example, its 2020 report highlights that it avoided emissions of 288,000 tons of carbon dioxide, provided 267,000 households with clean electricity, and generated 779,000 megawatts of electricity.[7] In a recent vision paper, Triodos Bank, the parent company of Triodos Investment Management, explained its philosophy: "Triodos Bank envisions a new economic model—built on generating benefits instead of financial value alone. An economic model based on fair social foundations and limited by ecological ceilings. Aimed at financing an economy that is distributive and regenerative by design."[8]

Profit-plus investors like Triodos (including both the bank and its subsidiary, the investment company) are not just interested in making money; they are willing to *sacrifice* money—at least sometimes—in the cause of doing good. Triodos's customers and investors know when they put their money in a Triodos account or buy Triodos equity that they may earn a lower interest rate or see less capital appreciation because of the company's commitment to improving society and the environment.

In fact, Triodos's equity holders also give up all control over the bank. The parent company's voting stock is owned by a foundation. To secure capital, the foundation sells depository receipts that entitle the holders to the economic rights associated with stock (such as dividends) but no voting rights.[9] The parent company set up this structure to protect the company's social mission from shareholder pressure to sacrifice mission for profits.

Profit-only investors are much more familiar to us than profit-plus investors like Triodos. Profit-only investors put their capital at risk for the sole purpose of attaining the highest possible returns for a given risk profile. They encompass investors at all stages (and risk levels) of a business's life cycle, from the earliest stages, when angels and then venture capitalists fund an enterprise, to shareholders in mature public entities. These investors may have different risk tolerances, time horizons, and industry-specific expertise, but they have in common their solitary goal of profit maximization.

One such company that has been particularly successful is the venture capital firm Andreessen Horowitz. The firm was an early investor in many now-famous companies such as Box, Coinbase, Facebook, GitHub, Instagram, Lyft, Oculus VR, Roblox, Slack, and Skype. Andreessen Horowitz's two cofounders, Marc Andreessen and Ben Horowitz, made their fortunes by selling Opsware, a company they had founded together with two others, to Hewlett Packard for a reported $1.65 billion in cash. After spending a number of years investing in start-ups as angel investors, they decided to form a venture capital firm together. Andreessen Horowitz has been laser focused on generating profits, with legendary results.

Two subcategories of profit-only investors merit our special attention. The first of these are what I call "purpose-for-profit" investors. These are investors who have adopted an investment thesis—supported by a significant number of academic studies—that companies that are more socially responsible are also more profitable.[10] For example, Sherbrooke Capital is a venture capital fund that invests in companies that are self-consciously prosocial because Sherbrooke believes those companies will inspire greater customer loyalty and therefore generate higher profits. As Sherbrooke explains:

> For consumers, a product's worth is no longer simply measured by how well it performs. Today's increasingly informed and engaged consumers are looking for something more from their products and the companies that provide them—authenticity, purity, innovation, value, and goodness. Consumers not only want to be satisfied by their products, but also believe in the brands behind the products. We at Sherbrooke seek to partner with companies that can deliver on these attributes and provide consumers the products and services that support healthy, active and sustainable living.[11]

There are several different versions of this thesis. Investors who adopt a minimalist view of this good = profits perspective filter out companies that seem like particularly bad actors. Depending on the particular strategy adopted, the companies that fall prey to this sort of negative screening might include oil companies, gun companies, mining companies, tobacco companies, energy utilities that rely on coal-generated power plants, or any other type of company that one might argue causes significant social harm.

Other investment funds take a somewhat more intensive approach by seeking out investment targets that have high ESG scores. There are quite a few different measures of ESG, but they all attempt to measure companies' performance across the three dimensions of environment, social, and governance. The environmental component of this score is fairly self-explanatory: How good is this company for the planet? The social aspect of an ESG score asks how the company treats its employees, suppliers, customers, and the communities in which it functions. The social aspect also incorporates diversity, equity, and inclusion concerns. Finally, the governance piece of an ESG score attempts to measure how effectively the company governs itself. How independent are the company's directors? How knowledgeable are the directors and officers about the business? How carefully is the company monitored and audited? Investment funds each have their own reasons for choosing a particular ESG measure (or sometimes a set of different measures). Regardless of which ESG measure they choose, though, the goal is to find a measure that will pick out the companies whose good corporate behavior will generate higher returns with lower risk.

The investors who are most serious about investing in prosocial companies take a triple-bottom-line approach, which refers to people, planet, and profits. The idea of this approach is to find companies whose business model includes a mission to excel at all three dimensions. These triple-bottom-line investment funds look for companies that will generate tremendous customer and employee loyalty through their outstanding reputations.

Whether an investment fund employs negative screening, ESG searches, or the triple bottom line, it is adopting an investment strategy, not a moral philosophy. The goal is still to maximize profits for a given level of risk. These funds may also do some good along the way with their investments, but that is a bonus, not the purpose of their strategy. If the investors have to choose between profit and purpose, they will choose profit. They might argue that such forced choices will be rare, because purpose produces profit most of the time. But in a situation where one option would demonstrably result in greater profits at the expense of purpose, they would presumably choose profits. These are still profit-only investors; they just happen to believe that the best path to profit lies through credibly adopting a social purpose.

The other subgroup of profit-only investors that merits special attention is the "universal owner." Universal owners are the result of orthodox finance theory's recommendation that investors diversify their portfolios by buying a wide spectrum of asset classes and of assets within each class. The goal of this strategy is to reduce risk while still achieving high returns. A diversified investor will not achieve the extraordinary returns of someone who guesses right about the future by, say, buying Tesla stock at its IPO and holding it through November 2021 (and maybe beyond). (I was not perspicacious enough to do that, to my everlasting regret.) But a diversified investor can earn the returns of the market as a whole while dampening the vicissitudes in value that any individual stock or other asset may suffer.

My point here is not to advocate for diversification as an investment strategy but just to acknowledge that investment advisers have been advocating this strategy for decades. Most professional investors—including institutional investors who manage trillions of dollars of other people's money—employ some version of a diversification strategy. The more diversified an investor is, the closer that investor becomes to a universal owner, someone who owns the entire market.

This is actually simple for even a small investor to accomplish. Anyone who wants to buy all the major companies in the US stock market can do so by buying an index mutual fund or exchange traded fund (ETF). The major investment companies all offer such funds, usually for an annual fee that is very close to zero. For example, Vanguard's S&P 500 ETF currently charges .03 percent per year, which would amount to a fee of $3 per year for a $10,000 investment. Vanguard also allows its customers to trade this ETF without any commission.[12] (I am not pushing Vanguard here; the other major investment companies offer similar terms.) Diversification is not limited to buying stocks. Investors can employ similar strategies to purchase broad investments in real property and even in artwork.[13]

Investors who diversify their portfolios approach universal ownership. Universal owners possess a portion of every company (and perhaps a large swath of other asset classes). A true universal owner should think differently about how corporate boards should run their companies. Someone who owns only Tesla stock might want Tesla to destroy its competing car manufacturers. But for someone who owns a roughly equal stake in all the car companies, the money Tesla earns by dominating the competition will be offset by the money its competitors lose.

A universal owner has to care about the fate of *all* companies. They cannot improve their investment returns by helping one company outcompete others; they benefit only when the economic system as a whole flourishes. As a result, the economic infrastructure's health matters much more to a universal owner than the relative success of any particular company. As Rick Alexander, founder of The Shareholder Commons and a prominent advocate for BCs and PBCs, has argued, "Continued healthy markets will depend on responsible investors recognizing their own universal ownership and working to improve the beta of their portfolios (not to mention the health of their society and the planet), rather than only viewing responsible investing as a means by which to increase individual company performance."[14]

Universal owners have a strong financial incentive to prevent companies from imposing negative externalities on the system as a whole—such as by polluting the planet or by paying their workers too little to live on—because the universal owners ultimately bear the cost of those externalities. An individual company can profit by externalizing costs to the rest of the economic system, but universal owners *are* the rest of the economic system. There is no free lunch for a universal owner.

## Investors' Theoretical Interest in BCs and PBCs

Now that we have a sense of the different categories of investor, we can think more deeply about how each of these categories might feel about investing in a BC or a PBC.

### Profit-Plus Investors

Profit-plus investors seek to make investments in companies that earn a reasonable return but also contribute toward solving social problems. They are willing to accept somewhat lower earnings in exchange for these nonfinancial rewards to society as whole. As we discussed in Chapter 6, depending on how this group is defined, these investors could represent a significant amount of capital. Unfortunately, the studies that attempt to measure social impact capital tend to conflate what we are calling profit-plus investors and purpose-for-profit investors. These two groups might well react differently to BCs and PBCs, and we do not have good data on their relative economic importance. Even looking at the more restrictive definitions and commensurately smaller estimates, though, profit-plus investors seem to command a significant amount of capital. Will BCs and PBCs appeal to this type of investor?

BCs and PBCs should have special appeal to profit-plus investors if the legal governance rules for these forms assure investors that BCs and PBCs are more likely than traditional entities to create social benefits beyond those that any successful enterprise would generate (such as jobs and a good or service that people value). At first glance, this seems likely to be true. Both BCs and PBCs are required by statute to create a public benefit, so profit-plus investors should feel fairly confident that a company that has chosen one of these forms will provide greater social benefits than traditional companies do.

Two issues. however, may undermine profit-plus investors' faith in BCs and PBCs. The first issue involves the statutory definition of "public benefit." Both the BC and the PBC statutes define the term very broadly, which raises the possibility that a company could operate in a way that is indistinguishable from a traditional company and still fulfill all the legal obligations of being organized as a BC or PBC. A company could define its public benefit as, for example, providing new technology to consumers who like the company's products. All successful technology companies do this, so there is nothing in what such a company is doing that would give a profit-plus investor any comfort that this is the type of company such investors should favor. For this reason, the mere fact that a company has chosen to organize as a BC or PBC may not suffice to attract a profit-plus investor's interest.

The second area for concern lies in the enforcement mechanisms the BC and PBC statutes contain. We discussed these in depth in Chapter 5 when we examined the risk that BCs and PBCs might be used for purpose washing, claiming to pursue a social purpose without actually behaving much differently from purely profit-seeking companies. As we saw in that chapter, the legal mechanisms designed to ensure that BCs and PBCs fulfill their social missions are considerably weaker than we might expect.

Both concerns are rooted in purpose washing. Profit-plus investors should be interested in investing in BCs and PBCs to the extent that the adoption of one of these legal forms helps ensure that the businesses will be run in a way that is meaningfully better for society. But these investors could prove skeptical about this proposition because of the broad definition of social purpose in the statutes and because of the weakness of the legal devices designed to ensure that BCs and PBCs pursue their social missions. We will see a bit later in this chapter what the empirical data show us about how profit-plus investors are reacting to BCs and PBCs.

### Profit-Only Investors

Even the most generous estimates of the amount of investment capital in the profit-plus category would have to concede that the lion's share of investment resources falls into the profit-only group.[15] It might be possible for profit-plus investors alone to sustain a limited number of BCs and PBCs, but ultimately the movement's success will turn on the willingness of profit-only investors to take a chance on these new forms of business organization. Profit-only investors' attitude toward BCs and PBCs is therefore critical. Will these investors refuse to risk their capital, or will they treat BCs and PBCs as acceptable legal forms?

#### GENERALLY

Although an increasing number of profit-only investors are either adopting one of the purpose-for-profit strategies or acknowledging the strategic implications of their status as universal owners, the bulk of investment capital still falls outside these categories.[16] These investors are not interested in companies with a social purpose as a strategy to earning more profits, nor are they concerned with the negative externalities companies generate that damage other investments in their portfolio. Instead, they consider each potential investment based on its potential to grow its profits without regard to any social benefits or harms it may create. This is the traditional approach to investing and still seems the most common. Can BCs and PBCs compete for such investors' capital?

We can easily see reasons why they might fail. BCs and PBCs are required to pursue a social mission. They are also required to balance their pursuit of profits against that social mission when making corporate decisions. They must take into account the impact of business decisions on other corporate constituencies. Often these requirements will not hinder the company's quest to increase its earnings; in fact, they may help guide the company toward highly profitable strategies. A strong social mission can provide an effective brand for a company that helps it attract customers and loyal employees, leading to an improved bottom line. Paying attention to the needs of employees, customers, and communities can also improve profitability, both directly and again through advantageous branding.

We must assume that these legal requirements will hurt a company's profitability at least some of the time, though. Paying employees a living wage may increase productivity enough to offset the greater labor expense, but it seems unlikely that this would always be true. Similarly, pursuing a social mission may yield tremendous benefits from increased brand authenticity that translates into greater sales and lower employee turnover. But the social mission could also easily cost more than it produces in reputational benefits, especially in industries that are inherently difficult to square with a positive social mission. No matter how hard ExxonMobil tries to rebrand itself as green, it seems unlikely to succeed.[17] Resources spent trying to persuade the public that an oil company is fighting to combat climate change are likely to be wasted.

Investors in this category who take the social mission and balancing requirements of BCs and PBCs seriously, then, could easily and reasonably conclude that they are not worthy investment targets. Yet these investors might at least sometimes believe that the company's business model, leadership team, and/or market position warrants an investment despite a less-than-ideal legal structure. The company's legal form might impose some costs, but in an environment with a lot of investment capital seeking relatively few high-quality opportunities, investors might prove willing to compensate for the inferior legal structure by negotiating for more advantageous deal terms, such as a lower price per share. Alternatively, they might reason that the broad definition of social purpose, combined with the very limited legal enforcement of the balancing requirement, means that BCs and PBCs do not really have to be managed any differently from traditional corporations. If so, then as long as the leadership team can be trusted to behave "reasonably" (from the investors' perspective), there is no meaningful difference between investing in a BC or PBC and investing in a traditional corporation.

These are not happy stories for those who hope the new legal forms will transform American capitalism. The largest group of investors may abstain from investing in BCs and PBCs, or they may invest only under the condition that they maximize profits and ignore any of the new requirements that impose net costs. Neither alternative bodes well for the movement to reform how companies do business. Only the "investment scarcity" hypothesis suggests that profit-only investors will invest in BCs and PBCs without requiring that they abandon their social mission whenever it conflicts with profit maximization. Even that theory suggests that profit-only investors will be somewhat reluctant to invest in BCs and PBCs. They will invest only because they cannot find equivalently promising companies with traditional legal structures, and they may reduce the risk they perceive comes with the new legal forms by investing less money or by insisting on cheaper pricing for the companies' equity, or both. This reasoning suggests that BCs and PBCs will likely have some trouble securing capital from the largest group of investors. Still, two subsets of this group may offer greater promise for BCs and PBCs: purpose-for-profit investors and universal owners.

### PURPOSE-FOR-PROFIT INVESTORS

Purpose-for-profit investors have no intrinsic interest in their investment targets improving society. They are aware, though, of the extensive academic literature that often shows that companies with a social mission are more profitable than their less idealistic competitors.[18] They see in this insight a chance to seize a competitive advantage. By investing in companies with a strong social mission, they hope to achieve a higher return, a lower risk profile, or both, giving them a significant advantage over investors who ignore social mission when evaluating a potential investment. Companies like Sherbrooke Capital prefer socially minded investment targets, then, not because they intrinsically believe that companies have a social obligation to improve their communities or the environment but because the social mission itself reduces risk or improves financial performance. or both.

Investors like Sherbrooke might see a company's choice to incorporate as a BC or PBC as a credible commitment to behave better than most traditional corporations. Given the academic findings on companies with social missions having better financial performance, these investors might believe that BCs and PBCs will tend to outperform on the metric that matters to them: profitability. This thesis turns, though, on the question of whether it is reasonable to think that a company will behave differently—better— because it is a BC or a PBC.

Here again, we find ourselves having to examine whether a company's BC or PBC status alone will ensure that the company will act more responsibly than traditional corporations do. As discussed in Chapter 5, some mechanisms in the BC and PBC statutes are designed to foster better behavior. BCs and PBCs are required to take into account the impact of their choices on constituencies other than shareholders, such as the company's employees, customers, and communities, as well as the environment. They must also attempt to produce either a general public benefit or a specific public benefit, depending on the statute, and balance this public benefit against the pursuit of profits as well as their impact on other corporate constituencies. This balancing requirement can be enforced by sufficiently large shareholders through litigation in a benefit enforcement proceeding or a derivative suit, depending on the statute. In addition, BCs and PBCs must disclose at least to their shareholders (and sometimes to broader groups) how well they are performing at producing the required general or specific public benefit.

These requirements, however, may not suffice to guarantee that BCs and PBCs behave materially differently than traditional corporations do. The broad definition of *public benefit* under both BC and PBCs statutes discussed in Chapter 4 should add to this concern.

We saw these same concerns just above when we considered the likelihood that profit-plus investors would find BCs and PBCs particularly appealing. The concerns may be somewhat attenuated for purpose-for-profit investors, though, since they do not care about companies producing social benefits per se. Instead, they are interested only in the financial benefits that may be associated with companies that espouse a social mission. To the extent these benefits materialize for BCs and PBCs even without significantly different corporate behavior, these investors should remain interested in providing capital to BCs and PBCs.

Is this possible? If BCs and PBCs are no more likely to create social benefits than traditional corporations, why would they demonstrate the investment benefits (higher returns at a lower risk) that many academic studies associate with companies that have a social mission? The answer turns on the underlying cause of the better financial performance. If the improved returns and lower risk are truly the product of a company's production of social benefits, then the fact that a company chooses a BC or PBC form alone does not guarantee an impact on its financial performance. But if the financial results stem at least in part from a public *perception* that the companies are better for the world, then the adoption of a BC or PBC form might well suffice to capture some of the associated benefits.

In other words, if the public believes—evenly incorrectly—that BCs and PBCs behave better, these companies may benefit from improved customer and employee loyalty, for example, even without actually spending resources on social benefits. This is a serious concern for those who hope that BCs and PBCs will change the way our economy works. But it could result in more investment by purpose-for-profit investors in BCs and PBCs, even without any meaningful assurance that these companies will act differently than traditional corporations do.

More optimistically, there are reasons to believe that BCs and PBCs will end up producing social benefits despite the weaknesses in the statutes' enforcement mechanisms. We discussed these reasons for hope in Chapter 5. To the extent that BCs and PBCs really are better for the world, they should produce better financial returns at lower risk and attract purpose-for-profit investors.

## UNIVERSAL OWNERS

Universal owners hold richly diversified portfolios. They recognize that since they effectively own the market, they cannot benefit by one company imposing externalities on the system in order to secure a profit for itself. Those externalities will harm the returns of the other companies in the universal owner's portfolio. Universal owners should most benefit when all companies minimize their externalities, when they behave as responsible corporate citizens. We would expect rational universal owners then to prefer companies that improve the entire system by minimizing their externalities, thereby improving the owners' financial return.

Universal owners, like profit-plus investors, should prefer to invest in BCs and PBCs to the extent these legal forms either signal or induce better corporate behavior. Unlike with purpose-for-profit investors, BCs and PBCs that claim to behave more responsibly but instead engage in purpose washing will not fulfill universal owners' goals. They need companies to behave better, in fact; the mere appearance of producing social value will not suffice.

A company that persuades its employees that it is environmentally friendly while actually dumping toxic waste into the local water system may benefit from greater customer loyalty, at least until the employees discover the truth. But such a company is imposing significant externalities on the economy as a whole. The logging company downstream will suffer reduced profits when its trees sicken and die from the pollution. A universal owner who owns stock in both the polluting company and the logging company will benefit from the decreased costs the polluting company enjoys by dumping its waste instead of disposing of it safely, but that owner will also lose money from its investment in the logging company. The investor may also lose money on any investment in a fishing company that sources its fish from the polluted water, a tourism company that takes customers rafting down the polluted rivers, and a real estate company that built housing near the polluted river and dying forest. The universal owner may eventually suffer increased taxes due to the government's need to clean the water supply. In all, the universal owner is likely to lose money on net, not gain, from the first company's pollution, even if that particular company sees some increase in profits from both its purpose washing (greater customer loyalty) and pollution (reduced disposal costs). The first company's purpose washing may boost its profits, but it ultimately harms the universal owner.

Just like profit-plus investors, universal owners need meaningful change to make the economy as a whole function better and produce more efficiently; purpose washing will do them little good overall. They should prefer BCs and PBCs, then, if and only if BCs and PBCs behave better—from the perspective of the economy as a whole—than traditional companies do. As we have discussed both here and in Chapter 5, there are reasons for both optimism and pessimism on this question.

So far, we have tried to predict whether different types of investors might be willing—or even eager—to invest in BCs and PBCs. Our theoretical analysis was inconclusive; we could see reasons why each category of investor might prove interested in BCs and PBCs, but we could also imagine some rationales for each group to avoid them. What we need to help us answer this question is some good old-fashioned data. Fortunately, my colleagues and I gathered some in a study I describe in the next section.

### An Empirical Study on Venture Capitalists' Willingness to Invest in BCs and PBCs

Steven Davidoff Solomon is about as close to a celebrity as a corporate law professor can be. Although a tenured professor at the University of California, Berkeley and a highly prolific and influential scholar, Solomon's greatest acclaim likely comes from the fact that for many years, he wrote a weekly *New York Times* column on developments in corporate law under the title, "The Deal Professor." James Hicks was Solomon's graduate student at Berkeley and is a rising star in his own right.

I was very fortunate that, like me, both Solomon and Hicks were interested in this new phenomenon of BCs and PBCs. They agreed that the most critical question surrounding the new legal business forms was whether they could attract early-stage investment in sufficient volume. Together, we mapped out a research strategy to secure and analyze data that would help us answer this question.

We decided to focus on Delaware PBCs for two reasons. First, as we have discussed before, Delaware is by far the most important state for corporate law in the United States. The majority of publicly traded corporations are registered in Delaware, which means that Delaware law governs any issues regarding these companies' internal affairs (disputes among or between a company's officers, directors, and/or shareholders). Companies that hope one day to go public tend to register in Delaware from the outset to avoid any complications arising later from having to shift their registration to Delaware before staging their initial public offering (or merging with a special-purpose acquisition company—SPAC). Sophisticated early-stage investors and their lawyers are deeply familiar with Delaware law, and they tend to expect companies in which they invest to be registered in Delaware. For all these reasons, we suspected that the companies that were most serious about pursuing outside investment would choose Delaware as their state of incorporation. We therefore hypothesized that if we looked at Delaware PBCs, we would capture the bulk of the venture capital investment that was going to BCs and PBCs.[19]

The second reason we focused on Delaware PBCs was more practical. Although the majority of state legislatures in the United States have passed legislation enabling either BCs or PBCs in their states, they have generally not provided any funding to administer the new forms. As a result, most secretary of state offices are treating their BCs and PBCs as though they were no different from traditional corporations in their databases. We were told by many different state offices that they had no way to identify which companies were BCs or PBCs and which were traditional corporations.

Delaware was the notable exception. Delaware's database allows anyone to look up any company registered in Delaware and see, for free, some of the company's relevant legal characteristics. Most important for our purposes, Delaware's system lists what form the entity is, whether an LLC, a traditional corporation, or a PBC. Even better, the Delaware Secretary of State's Office generously provided us with a comprehensive list of every PBC registered in the state. At the time (in late 2019), the list consisted of just under two thousand companies. By comparing the PBCs on Delaware's list to a commercial database of venture capital (VC) investments, we were able to determine which Delaware PBCs had secured such investments. We were also able to compare the characteristics of the funded PBCs to those of traditional Delaware corporations that VCs also funded.

The results were astonishing. Out of fewer than two thousand Delaware PBCs, 295, or over 10 percent, had secured funding. Many of these PBCs were small enterprises with no ambitions to grow quickly and so had no need for venture capital. The success rate of the PBCs that did seek venture capital money was likely quite high. From 2014 to 2019, Delaware PBCs secured over $2.5 billion in equity funding, without even counting the company that raised the most money, Laureate Education. (We excluded Laureate Education from our study since it had gone public by the time of our analysis and so was in a category different from the other companies in our data sample.)[20]

When we remember that there were significant theoretical reasons to doubt that investors would be willing to risk their capital with PBCs, the large number of PBCs that were awarded funding and the significant total amount of funding are both optimistic signs for the movement. On the other hand, when we parsed the data more closely, we did see two causes for concern.

The first potential issue involved the type of companies that received funding. We found that companies that sold their goods or services to the public rather than to other companies tended to receive more funding. Although there were roughly twice as many companies in the funded group that did not serve consumers directly, the two groups received approximately equal amounts of total funding. In other words, PBCs that sold directly to the public on average received twice as much funding as those that did not. While this could just be an artifact of the data, with a few large consumer-facing companies accounting for a disproportionate amount of funding, it could also be a signal that investors are interested in purpose washing. They might fund PBCs that sell directly to consumers more richly because they believe that consumers will—perhaps falsely—credit PBCs' claims of providing social good and buy these PBCs' goods and services ahead of those offered by traditional companies. Or perhaps the investors believe that this same consumer advantage stems from the real social good these PBCs are doing. There is no way for us to distinguish these possible causes from our data.[21]

The other cause for concern came from the amount of money PBCs raised at each stage of their development. We were not able to identify each investor, but for the many investors we could identify, we compared the amount they invested at each round of investment in PBCs to the amount they invested in the same round at non-PBC companies. (Early-stage companies go through different stages, or rounds, of investment as they develop, usually raising larger and larger amounts as they progress.)

We found that at each round, PBCs raised less money than their traditional counterparts (measured by the median amount raised in each round). This difference was not very large at the earliest fundraising stages, but in later rounds, those that typically involve more sophisticated and better-funded VCs, the difference grew dramatically. In late-stage VC rounds, for example, the median amount PBCs raised from VCs was $5 million, while the median amount raised by traditional companies was a whopping $21 million, over four times as much. This large difference in amounts of funding might mean that investors consider PBCs riskier bets than traditional companies and that they are hedging their risk by investing less, especially at later stages when the stakes are much higher. Even if that is the correct explanation of this result, though, it may be an effect that attenuates over time as VCs become more familiar with BCs and PBCs and the lingering legal questions gradually become settled.

Despite these two concerns, overall, the study's results seem promising for PBCs. A surprisingly large percentage of the existing Delaware PBCs succeeded in raising money, and the total amount of money they raised was considerable. The source of the funds was also noteworthy. While we might have expected profit-plus investors to shop for PBC investments, the vast majority of both the amount and number of investments came from traditional venture capital funds in the profit-only category. This last result might raise some concerns about purpose washing, but it should also mean that BCs and PBCs (or at least Delaware PBCs) have a reasonable chance of securing early-stage financing, comparable (and perhaps even superior) to the odds of success for traditional corporations and LLCs.[22]

## Publicly Traded BCs and PBCs

VCs' continued willingness to invest in BCs and PBCs will likely turn on their ability to sell the companies for a large profit to either another investor or the public through an initial public offering or a merger with a SPAC. Why is this so? After all, if the BC or PBC is profitable, the investors can earn their return over time through dividends without ever selling the company. Many wealthy families have done precisely this, to the profit of multiple generations of owners.

VCs, though, have a different incentive structure than long-term owners like families do. They have investors of their own, usually large institutions and very wealthy individuals. The VC firms promise these investors that they will keep the investors' capital for a limited period, typically about ten years. At the end of this period, the VCs pledge to return their investors' money, along with whatever returns they have earned. For this reason, the VCs' investment time horizon is limited. They cannot simply buy and hold on to a company forever, collecting dividends. Instead, they must liquidate their investments to return their investors' capital within their contractual time limit. They have little choice but to find a buyer for their portfolio companies within that period, whether that buyer is a strategic purchaser in the same industry, another institutional investor such as a hedge fund or private equity fund, or the investing public in an IPO or SPAC.

The public markets are a particularly important source of liquidity for VCs. Not only are they a ready source of capital, but they also provide both publicity and legitimacy. IPOs and SPACs get a lot of coverage in the media, so when BCs and PBCs go public, they provide highly visible evidence that BCs and PBCs are salable, that VCs will not get stuck with an investment they cannot liquidate.

For much of the new forms' short history, there was little evidence that the public markets had much appetite for BCs and PBCs. The first PBC to go public was Laureate Education, in 2017. Laureate's IPO took place just seven years after the first state legislature (Maryland's) authorized BCs and just four years after Delaware's legislature passed its PBC statute. Laureate seemed a promising and quick start at first, but it remained alone for quite some time. Other companies that seemed likely to follow turned aside. For example, Etsy, the craft e-commerce company, was a certified B Corp for several years and remained one after its IPO. To remain certified as a B Corp, Etsy was required to convert to a BC or PBC or make equivalent changes to its corporate charter. As the deadline for changing its corporate status approached, it experienced a decline in its business. Ultimately, it decided to drop its B Corp certification rather than convert its legal status to a BC or PBC.[23] It explained its decision by complaining that conversion was "a complicated and untested process for existing public companies."[24]

In 2020, though, the tide turned. Lemonade and Vital Farms, both already PBCs, staged successful IPOs.[25] Kronos Technologies, already publicly traded in the over-the-counter market, converted to a PBC.[26] These success stories encouraged other companies to move forward. As of this writing in mid-2022, in addition to the four already mentioned, Allbirds,[27] Amalgamated Bank,[28] AppHarvest,[29] Broadway Financial Corporation,[30] Coursera,[31] Planet,[32] United Therapeutics,[33] Veeva Systems,[34] Warby Parker,[35] Zevia,[36] and Zymergen[37] have gone public as PBCs or converted to a PBC form when already public.

PBCs remain a small minority of publicly traded companies to date, but the fifteen companies that have made the leap have at least proven the concept. Public investors do not reject PBCs categorically. In fact, some of the

PBCs have been lauded as "hot IPOs,"[38] and AppHarvest's stock price shot up 44 percent on its first trading day.[39] It remains to be seen how these public PBCs will do over time from a purely profit-oriented perspective. They are too new and too few in number to make possible an empirical comparison to traditional public companies. If they perform tolerably well financially, it seems reasonable to believe that the trend will continue, and perhaps even accelerate, justifying the faith many VCs have already placed in this new form. The more publicly traded BCs and PBCs there are, the more normal they will seem. In time, I hope that investors will see them as perfectly sound, and perhaps even preferable to traditional corporations and LLCs.

———

In this chapter, we discussed the different types of investors and analyzed the advantages and disadvantages of BCs and PBCs for each category. We learned that the most important type of early-stage investor, the profit-only VC, has invested substantially in companies organized as PBCs, though perhaps with some hesitation. The recent trend toward increasing numbers of publicly traded PBCs should bolster VCs' faith in the new form and encourage even larger capital investments going forward.

In the next chapter, we take up the requirement that BC and PBC boards balance profit against other social goals. We also explore a few techniques boards might use to fulfill this requirement in a transparent manner.

# EIGHT

## HOW SHOULD BENEFIT CORPORATIONS BALANCE PROFIT AND PUBLIC GOOD?

### The Balancing Requirement

Some of the best conversations of my life took place while sitting around a college dorm room, eating late-night pizza with my roommates. We discussed philosophy, politics, religion, relationships, and how we planned to transform the world. Although these conversations had an enormous impact on my developing worldview, none of them led to the formation of a billion-dollar company.

A conversation that did give birth to a major corporation took place in 2010 at a Wharton computer lab. Neil Blumenthal, Andrew Hunt, David Gilboa, and Jeffrey Raider, the four cofounders of Warby Parker, met at Wharton while studying for their MBAs. Gilboa had lost his glasses on a recent trip and was complaining about the high cost of replacing them. Before starting business school, Blumenthal had worked for VisionSpring, a nonprofit that provided glasses to people in developing countries who could not afford them. Blumenthal therefore had some insight into the glasses market.[1]

The group determined to sell eyeglasses online to cut costs and make buying glasses more convenient and less expensive. They founded Warby

Parker while still in business school, shaking off an admired professor's skepticism about their business model.[2] Warby Parker's glasses start at $95 a pair, much cheaper than most fashion brands offer. In 2021, the company went public in a direct listing that valued the company at over $6 billion.[3] The once skeptical professor—who had turned down a chance to invest at the very beginning—now deeply regrets the missed opportunity.[4]

One might think that a company whose core strategy was to sell its product at a steep discount to the competition's prices would be laser-focused on cutting costs. Giving away a free pair of glasses to those who cannot afford to pay for them for every pair of glasses sold would seem like a terrible idea for such a company; the donations would necessarily increase the cost of each pair and cut into a profit margin that was already much slimmer than the competition's. But that "buy one, give one" concept is exactly the strategy Warby Parker adopted.

By the time it went public, Warby Parker had given away in excess of *8 million* pairs of glasses in over fifty countries.[5] Those glasses must have come at a significant cost, though Warby Parker's prospectus does not reveal what that cost was.[6] But the fact that the company was still not profitable at the time it sold shares to the public may be attributable at least in part to its buy one, give one program.[7]

Warby Parker converted into a Delaware public benefit corporation shortly before going public.[8] As we discussed in Chapter 3, PBC boards have a fiduciary duty to balance "the stockholders' pecuniary interests, the best interests of those materially affected by the corporation's conduct, and the public benefit or public benefits identified in its certificate of incorporation."[9] Warby Parker has adopted the specific public benefit of "provid[ing] access to products and services that promote vision and eye health and . . . work[ing] towards positively impacting the communities in which we operate."[10] Warby Parker's board must therefore balance the company's quest for profits against *both* the provision of these two specific public benefits— promoting vision and eye health and positively benefiting Warby Parker's communities—*and* against the best interests of all those "materially affected" by the company's activities, whether or not they are within the scope of the company's specific public benefits.

For most of its existence, Warby Parker gave away free glasses despite being organized as a purely profit-maximizing entity. During that period, it presumably justified the donations as part of its marketing, arguing that its buy one, give one policy distinguished it from its competitors, built its brand, and helped it take market share. Customers might have bought Warby Parker's glasses because they liked the frames or the company's lower prices, but competitors quickly sprang up to offer low-priced designer frames once Warby Parker began to have some success. Warby Parker's buy one, give one strategy gave customers another reason to buy from Warby Parker and not a competitor's similar product; they knew that in buying glasses from Warby Parker, they were also giving the gift of vision to someone who otherwise could not afford it. In other words, it paid for Warby Parker to be generous.

As a traditional corporation, Warby Parker's management team could make a fairly straightforward calculation to decide whether its buy one, give one policy was worth the expense of giving away all those glasses. The team could use focus groups, customer surveys, and trial and error to test how they could boost sales the most while giving away as little as possible. (I am not suggesting that this was how Warby Parker's management approached this question, only that the law permitted and encouraged this type of thinking while Warby Parker was organized as a traditional corporation.)

Now that Warby Parker is a PBC, it is *obligated* to weigh its provision of these benefits—and its impact on all those affected by its conduct—against the pursuit of profits. That obligation means that even if the board became convinced that giving away free glasses was unprofitable despite the positive marketing—that the giveaway program cost more than it gained the company in increased sales—it might still decide to continue the program in order to pursue the company's specific public benefits and help those materially affected by the company's activities. Shareholders who objected to the board's decision to give up some profits in order to pursue other social goals would have no legal leg to stand on in litigation. The Delaware PBC statute clearly authorizes boards to make precisely such trade-offs.

On the other hand, Warby Parker's board would also be within its legal powers if it chose to cut back on its donations by giving away one pair of glasses for every two pairs sold for example or if it decided to eliminate the donation program entirely. The statutory obligation is for the board to balance these different considerations, not to achieve some particular result. The statute does not give any guidance to boards at all as to how much to weigh profits versus the company's specific public benefit(s) versus the company's impact on affected parties.

Both Delaware's PBC statute and the Model Act rest the ultimate decision-making power in the board. Boards of directors must consider these separate interests, but the final choice is up to the directors. Presumably a board that always chose profit over purpose would end up with little credibility with relevant groups—customers, employees, communities—when it claimed its company was better for the world than a traditional corporation. Conversely, a board that always pursued purpose regardless of the cost could quickly drive the company to bankruptcy. Between these two extremes lies a broad range of possible actions. How should boards of BCs and PBCs use the enormous discretion the law gives them?

## Some Concerns about Balancing

Warby Parker's public disclosures provide few clues to how the company balances profit with purpose. The company's prospectus explains that Delaware law requires its board to balance, then cautions investors that this may sometimes mean that the board will make decisions that will result in earning lower profits. The prospectus states:

> In the event of a conflict between the interests of our stockholders and the interests of our specific public benefit or our other stakeholders, our directors must only make informed and disinterested decisions that are not such that no person of ordinary, sound judgment would approve; thus, there is no guarantee such a conflict would be resolved in favor of our stockholders, which could have a material adverse effect on our business, financial condition, and results of operations, which in turn could cause our stock price to decline.[11]

However, the prospectus is silent about *how* the board will make decisions about these trade-offs. Is the buy one, give one policy written in stone, so that the board will continue to give away free glasses even if the company continues to lose money? Or is there some point at which the policy might be modified, or even abandoned, in an effort to earn a profit? Conversely, if the company becomes profitable, might the board consider giving away more glasses? Are there other social policies the board might enact? If so, what are they, and under what circumstances might the board implement them? The prospectus leaves investors entirely in the dark as to all of these important questions. The prospectus discloses that the board has the right to sacrifice profit for purpose but gives no hints on its decision-making process.

Warby Parker is not unique in its reticence to commit publicly to a particular balancing methodology. I have examined the securities filings of a number of publicly traded PBCs, and not one of these companies provided meaningful details about how its board intended to balance the company's public purpose against its profitability.[12] For example, Allbirds, the eco-conscious shoe manufacturer, gave a few examples of decisions the company might make that would prioritize its environmental values over the company's profitability.[13] But nowhere in its securities filings did the company explain its criteria for making these decisions.

United Therapeutics Corporation provided one of the deeper discussions of the balancing requirement I found in public securities filings, but even it said very little about the board's balancing methodology. United Therapeutics was already publicly traded when it converted to PBC status. In seeking shareholder approval for the conversion, United Therapeutics explained to its shareholders the costs and benefits of its proposed new legal form of organization. As part of that explanation, the company provided its view of the board's balancing duties. In essence, the company argued that over the long term, the interests of shareholders would not conflict with those of other stakeholders, so shareholders should not be concerned about the new balancing requirement. The company concluded its discussion with the caution, "That said, we may at times find it appropriate to pursue initiatives that are consistent with our goals of treating patients and employees well and seeking sustainable results that do not have immediate or short-term financial benefits to our shareholders."[14] Since the company believed that—at least over the long run—profit and purpose could not conflict, it presumably saw no need to explain how it would decide when to sacrifice one for the other.

Many knowledgeable commentators would likely be unsurprised by companies' reticence to commit publicly to a particular balancing methodology. Critics have argued that the balancing process is completely unworkable. Since no coherent decision-making process is possible, boards have reasonably avoided trying to articulate one. These critics contend that balancing profits against a social mission is too complex a task to perform with any consistency. It is impossible, they say, to satisfy all the corporate constituents; any decision that favors one group will necessarily displease another. To take a simple example, paying workers more will please the employees, but the increased labor costs will likely reduce profits and so upset shareholders and creditors. Faced with the impossibility of pleasing everyone, directors could be excused if they avoided the issue altogether to protect themselves from the emotional burden of making a decision that is bound to fail to satisfy some important corporate constituency.[15]

Rather than worry about everyone, directors might choose simply to please themselves. This is the concern of some critics who worry that the balancing requirement will raise "agency costs,"[16] which are inefficiencies that stem from a person acting as an imperfect agent, often resulting from agents' conflicts of interest. Agency costs also include the costs employers bear to prevent agents' opportunistic behavior.[17] For example, when a manager hires a relative to work for a company despite the fact that other, nonrelated candidates are superior, the company suffers an agency cost consisting of the inferior work produced by the hired relative. If the company imposes an anti-nepotism policy to prevent this sort of behavior, the expense of drafting, implementing, and enforcing the policy would also count as an agency cost, as would the loss of the contributions of relatives who might have been superior employees if not banned by the anti-nepotism policy.

Shareholders face agency costs when trying to supervise corporations' boards of directors. Directors may pay themselves high salaries, enter into contracts between the corporation and friends and relatives, or simply slack off. When the corporation's goal is only to earn profits, shareholders can measure the corporation's output—its profitability—as an indirect way to determine whether the directors are acting in the shareholders' interests. If the company's net earnings grow quickly, chances are that the directors are doing their jobs. Less robust financial results signal to shareholders that perhaps they should supervise the directors more closely or replace them entirely.

Supervising directors may become more difficult and expensive if the corporation's goal is not just to make money but also to produce some social good or advance some cause. Shareholders then need to look at the balance the board is striking between producing too much social good—at the expense of the company's earnings—and producing too little. Shareholders may be divided among themselves about the right level of social good to produce, so they cannot cooperate or rely on larger shareholders to supervise the board with the same degree of confidence they would have if the company's sole goal was to increase profits.[18]

In the end, critics complain, directors may yield to shareholders' interests and focus primarily on increasing the company's profits. In both BCs and PBCs, shareholders elect the directors.[19] Shareholders are also the only group that can bring a suit to enforce the company's obligation to balance profits against the provision of some form of social good.[20] Directors might naturally then cater to the shareholders' interests. Shareholders might disagree about the optimal level of social good the company should produce, but they all should be happy to collect more profits. Faced with complex balancing decisions, directors might choose the actions they are most certain will please the most shareholders: maximizing profits.[21]

## Three Goals for Balancing Strategies

These concerns about the balancing requirement in BCs and PBCs seem overblown. Some of these critiques implicitly—and likely incorrectly—assume that shareholders care only about profit. As we discussed in Chapter 7, shareholders are quite likely to care about corporations' social purposes, especially if shareholders are diversified. These universal investors calculate that they cannot benefit from the success of one corporation at outcompeting its rivals if that success comes at the expense of imposing costs on the system as a whole. If the winning corporation's advantage comes from polluting the environment or depriving workers of a living wage, for example, the costs of its activities will ultimately be borne by other members of society. A universal investor recognizes that costs imposed by one corporation are ultimately paid by other corporations and their shareholders, either directly or through the taxation system. In addition, some investors prefer to invest in companies that pursue some social good as part of their business model or alongside it. These investors willingly sacrifice some degree of financial return in exchange for companies' contributions to improving society.

Investors who genuinely care about corporations' conduct should push directors to steer their companies toward better behavior. Shareholders may have different views about the amount of social good a company should produce, and correspondingly, how much profit the company should sacrifice. These differences, however, are analogous to the different time horizons and risk profiles that shareholders have. Directors regularly handle these differences, even though a twenty-five-year-old shareholder saving for retirement will generally have markedly different preferences from a seventy-five-year-old living on investment income.

The law deals with these issues by granting the board discretion to make whatever investment decisions it wants, so long as the board makes those decisions in good faith after gathering a reasonable amount of information.[22] As long as boards are transparent about their strategies and as long as they articulate those strategies in a way that can be measured and verified, investors can make their investment decisions based on the boards' declared intentions. A young investor with high risk tolerance and a desire for long-term growth may invest in companies that embrace a high-risk, high-reward strategy, while a more senior investor reliant on current investment income for daily needs might invest in more cautious companies. In purely for-profit companies, boards' articulation of transparent, credible, and measurable goals allows the system to work well for traditional corporations.

Those same requirements should empower BCs and PBCs to deal with investors' different preferences for the trade-offs between profit and purpose when those trade-offs are necessary. They should also help investors cope with the agency costs potentially associated with granting boards broader latitude to forgo profits, as the law does for boards of BCs and PBCs.

Transparency is the first requirement for the BC/PBC balancing system to work properly. Investors who care about companies' values cannot choose among different possibilities without knowing the strategies that each company will pursue to blend the pursuit of profits with a dedication to a social mission. Similarly, other constituencies that might favor the corporation because of the social benefits it provides, such as employees and customers, need to know about those benefits before they can, for example, accept a position at a lower salary because of the company's devotion to a mission that is important to them. A company that anonymously donates 10 percent of its profits to provide veterans with job training may produce a lot of good, but the company will not get credit from its constituents without telling the public about its contributions.

It is not enough for a company to proclaim publicly that it uses electricity only from renewable sources or pays its workers to spend three days a year volunteering for a charity of their choice. Many companies claim to embrace environmental values or to treat their employees like family members, but those claims must be credible if corporate constituencies are to treat these companies differently. Credibility is therefore the second requirement for the BC/PBC balancing system to function well. For a statement to be credible, people must have reason to believe it is truthful.

Chevron's landing page on the day of this writing proudly announced, "Chevron sets net zero aspiration and new GHG [greenhouse gases] intensity target" while displaying a photo of a cell phone or tablet with the slogan "climate change resilience—advancing a lower carbon future."[23] These are remarkable statements coming from an oil extraction company, a business whose profits come directly from taking carbon out of the ground and putting it into the air. And Chevron is trumpeting its environmental claims at the very top of its website, not burying them under some subsidiary page where only environmentalists might find them. Should people who worry about global warming (but still drive cars that run on gas) now seek out Chevron stations for their refueling needs, even if Chevron's gas is more expensive or its station is less convenient than others in the neighborhood?

Most readers of Chevron's claims will likely be skeptical that Chevron is serious about achieving carbon neutrality. The company's business model requires it to add more carbon to the atmosphere; there is no apparent way for the company to make money from its huge oil reserves without digging that oil up and selling it to people who will burn it for fuel. Chevron might try to offset the carbon output from its operations by planting trees or building a network of carbon capture devices. But given the company's enormous scale, it is hard to imagine that it could truly pull anywhere near as much carbon out of the air as it is busily putting into it.

Clicking on the link to see the company's press release reveals that the details of Chevron's plans might validate this skepticism. The bulk of Chevron's carbon reductions—including its net zero pledge by 2050—refer only to its "Scope 1" and "Scope 2" emissions. These are emissions that stem from direct emissions from Chevron's operations and indirect emissions from imported electricity and steam. The net zero pledge specifically excludes "Scope 3" emissions that Chevron produces through consumers' use of its products, that is, burning gasoline. [24]

The implicit message of Chevron's headline claims is that Chevron is a green company that plans to reduce its net carbon emissions to zero. That message is transparent—it appears very prominently on the company's website—but it is not credible. Chevron's shareholders, employees, and customers are unlikely to take it very seriously or to privilege Chevron over other oil extraction companies when making investment, employment, or purchasing decisions. Credibility is key to shaping constituents' behavior.

Credibility may come in a variety of ways—from the company's reputation, from trusted sources vouching for the company's claim, from legal penalties tied to misrepresentations, from the claim's inherent plausibility—but simply believing a company is truthful is not sufficient. It is important for people to believe a claim is true *and* meaningful. To be meaningful, a claim must include some relevant measure. A company can claim to be environmentally conscious, but if that is the sum total of the company's claim, then the claim is essentially empty of content, even if true and credible. But if a company states that it now receives 80 percent of its power from renewable sources, that statement is meaningful. Measurability is therefore the third requirement that must be met if BCs and PBCs are to differentiate themselves from traditional companies.

Measurability may also be the toughest standard to meet. While some claims are very concrete and easily measurable, others are far more challenging. Warby Parker says it donates one pair of glasses for every pair of glasses it sells. That is a straightforward claim to measure; we only need to know the number of pairs Warby Parker has sold and the number it has donated. Not surprisingly, Warby Parker is happy to publicize this number, and the public has an easy time understanding it. [25] Other claims, though, are much harder to measure. Environmental claims may be particularly tough. Is an electric car better for the environment than a comparable sedan powered by an internal combustion engine? Intuitively, we might feel strongly that the answer is yes. After all, the whole point of trying to electrify the world's automotive fleet is to reduce the world's carbon emissions. And internal combustion cars clearly produce a lot of carbon by burning gas, while electric cars emit nothing at all.

As it turns out, the calculation is far more complex than it first appears. Electric cars rely on lithium-ion batteries for power, and these batteries contain some elements, such as lithium and cobalt, that are environmentally problematic to mine. The lithium mining process used in Argentina and Chile—the source of about one-third of the lithium in the world—requires an enormous amount of water, some 500,000 gallons for every ton of lithium, in an area where farmers already struggle to find sufficient water to grow crops.[26] The process also frequently results in toxic chemicals leaking into the local water supply, killing fish and sometimes even larger animals such as cows and yaks. These toxic chemicals have been documented to impact wildlife over long distances, as far as 150 miles, from the lithium mine.[27]

Even ignoring the broader environmental impact and focusing only on emissions of gases that contribute to global warming, the comparison between electric and internal combustion engines is far from simple. The *Wall Street Journal* performed an in-depth analysis of the contributions toward global warming made by electric cars versus the emissions produced by internal combustion cars over the course of their respective useful lives. The *Journal* concluded that building an electric car generates 65 percent more global warming gases than building an equivalent car powered by an internal combustion engine. However, the electricity that powers electric cars generally comes from much cleaner sources than the gasoline that powers internal combustion engines. Electric cars generate about one-third of the emissions as internal combustion engines do per mile based on the average emissions from US electrical generation, and much less if the electricity is generated using a clean, renewable source such as wind or solar. As a result, the farther electric cars drive, the more the overall global warming impact shifts in their favor. Taking the average emissions for electricity generation in the United States, the break-even point occurs when the cars have been driven 20,600 miles. After that, every mile driven increases the advantage of electric cars over internal combustion engines. By 200,000 miles, the electric car has generated less than half the emissions of the internal combustion model.[28]

Note that even this fairly sophisticated calculation looks only at greenhouse gas emissions. How do we factor in the other environmental harm caused by mining lithium? And what about nonenvironmental factors? For example, cobalt is often mined in Africa by children under dangerous working conditions.[29] How do we weigh the harm to these children against the environmental benefits of electric cars? As this example demonstrates, it may not always be possible to measure a company's contribution to social goals in a straightforward, uncontroversial way. But the better is companies' measurement of their progress toward their stated and credible goals, the easier it will be for those companies to persuade corporate constituents such as employees and customers to take the companies' social stances into account when making employment and purchasing decisions.

Two leading corporate law scholars, Jill Fisch and Steven Davidoff Solomon, have pointed out that the specific public benefits that large PBCs have adopted are quite vague.[30] For example, they point out that the insurance company Lemonade, a Delaware PBC, has adopted as its specific public benefit the desire to "'harness technology and social impact to be the world's most loved insurance company.'"[31] I suppose Lemonade could conduct surveys to measure its popularity relative to other insurance companies, but Fish and Solomon are correct that Lemonade's specific public benefit has few details that would give confidence to shareholders or other corporate constituents that the company is somehow better for the world than its competitors.

This lack of specificity in companies' corporate charters might not trouble us very much. Corporate charters are analogous to the corporations' constitutions; they can and usually do contain only broad, fundamental rules for how the company will operate. In most cases, they do not even state what type of business the company will run, leaving the board with the power and authority to adopt different business models over time.

Similarly, perhaps BCs and PBCs should leave the details of their social goals to board bylaws. Fisch and Solomon argue for more detailed and measurable public benefit purposes, a proposal with which I wholeheartedly agree. These specifics, though, can and maybe in many cases should be the subject of board bylaws, not charter provisions, so that the board can adapt the company's goals as needed to meet changing conditions. With that one quibble, I join with Fisch and Solomon in calling for measurable social benefit goals.

By pursuing goals that are transparent, credible, and measurable, BCs and PBCs can bring agency costs down to a level that may prove comparable to those shareholders face normally in purely for-profit companies. The concerns that agency costs will be unworkably high in BCs and PBCs stem primarily from the perception that by ordering directors to consider other goals besides profits, the BC and PBC statutes will both give directors too much freedom to act in their own interests and make the task of monitoring directors more difficult for shareholders, even shareholders who want companies to pursue social goals alongside profits. If a BC or PBC board publicizes credible, measurable goals for the company's social purpose(s), those goals will constrain the board's freedom of action. The more specific and detailed the goals and the more accurate and verifiable the measures, the greater will be the constraint on the directors' ability to pursue their own interest instead of the corporation's. Transparent, credible, and measurable goals will also make it easier for shareholders to monitor the directors to ensure they are fulfilling their pledge to balance profits against purpose in a particular way.

The BC and PBC statutes have provisions that will help boards ensure that their balancing techniques meet at least two of these three requirements. The Model Act requires BCs to prepare an annual benefit report. This benefit report must describe the extent to which the BC successfully contributed to the general public benefit and any specific public benefit the BC has committed to produce. The report must also assess the company's overall social and environmental performance, measured using a standard created by a third party.[32] The Model Act requires BCs to post their benefit reports on their websites, if they have websites, and otherwise to make the reports available to anyone who asks for them.[33]

Similarly, the Delaware PBC statute requires PBCs to issue a statement at least every other year reporting on the company's promotion of the specific public benefits adopted by the PBC. The statement must also report on the company's success in fostering the well-being of those materially affected by the company's activities. Delaware requires PBCs to measure these social factors against some standard, though unlike the Model Act, this standard does not have to be the creation of a third party. Delaware requires PBCs to provide the statement to shareholders but does not adopt the Model Act's policy of mandating that PBCs post the statement on the company's website or make it available to anyone who asks for it.[34]

Both the Model Act and the Delaware PBC statute therefore demand transparency regarding companies' fulfillment of their social missions, at a minimum to shareholders and in the Model Act's case to anyone who is interested. Both also require companies to use some standard to measure their progress in creating a public benefit and balancing the needs of other corporate constituents against the quest for profits.

The one factor the statutes do not facilitate directly is credibility. Credibility stems from boards' sincerity and the social mission's compatibility with the company's core business and past practice. It is hard to imagine how a statute could legislate either.

Although the statutes require transparency and a degree of measurability, they do not provide for rigorous enforcement of either. Nevertheless, the statutory requirements should encourage directors who are earnest in their desire to provide social benefits to try to measure those benefits and let at least the company's shareholders know how the company is doing.

## Balancing Strategies

Boards will still face the challenge of finding a method of balancing profit and purpose that fulfills these requirements. Just as there is no single business strategy that fits all companies, so there is no single balancing method that will be appropriate for every BC and PBC. The fact that setting up a balancing system can be complicated does not mean that the challenge is insurmountable, as some critics have argued. On the contrary, there is a range of different types of strategies a company could pursue; some are relatively simple to understand and implement and others are more complex.

The strategies I describe are all capable of fulfilling the goals of transparency, credibility, and measurability. That does not mean that adopting one of these strategies automatically guarantees that a company will fulfill these goals. Boards continually need to monitor the company's implementation of its strategy to ensure that the company's execution of the strategy is fulfilling the strategy's purpose.

At the same time, the three strategies I discuss are not the only balancing methods that companies could employ that would meet these three requirements. My purpose here is not to create an exclusive list of strategies but to illustrate that transparent, credible, and measurable strategies are possible in more than one way. I hope that this discussion will inspire boards to think creatively about other ways to balance as well.

### Minimum Thresholds

One way to balance social purpose against profit is for the board to set a minimum threshold for each. This strategy requires companies to have some measure of the social good they are producing or at least of the core aspect of their social mission. It also requires companies to adopt a particular measure of profitability, whether that be gross revenue, net earnings, profit margins, or some other metric. Once the board has chosen how it will measure both its profitability and its social mission, it can set a minimum level for each. If the company is failing to meet its goal for either profit or social good production, it must adjust its strategy to sacrifice the more successful dimension until both aspects are above the floors the board has set.

Suppose, for example, a marketing firm was a BC or PBC, and that the firm's board chose to focus on improving its employees' well-being as its primary social goal. (Remember that BCs must promote the general social good, and that PBCs must consider their impact on all affected by their activities, so that neither can pursue only one aspect of social good to the exclusion of all other aspects. Still, it is reasonable for a BC or PBC to choose one or two aspects of social good for special attention.) The firm has decided to promote its employees' well-being in three ways: paying above-market salaries, allowing employees to devote some paid work time to volunteering for a charity of their own choice, and scheduling meetings between the CEO and a small group of randomly selected employees to provide an opportunity for employees to give the CEO feedback and suggestions for improving the company. The firm's board of directors decided that at a minimum, the company must pay 10 percent over market wages, grant employees one day per month of volunteer time, and schedule one CEO-employee meeting per month. The board also chose to set a minimum net earnings target of $1 million per month.

The marketing firm exceeded all the board's profit goals for several years. As long as the firm was exceeding the board's profit goals, the board allocated all profits over the minimum $1 million per month evenly between the shareholders and the employees. The board spent half the excess profits on paying dividends to shareholders and spent the other half on bolstering its employee well-being programs. This allocation was in accordance with its stated plan. A month ago, however, the owner of the building the firm leases for its offices gave notice that she was raising the firm's rent by 20 percent, in line with the increase in commercial rents throughout the city. The board investigated moving to a different building but found that there was no appropriate space available at a lower rate than what the current landlord proposed to charge. With the increase in rent, the firm's profits would fall below the floor of $1 million per month, though it would remain profitable.

Under these conditions, the minimum thresholds strategy would suggest that the board should cut back on its employee well-being programs. The most obvious way to do so would be to shrink employees' pay. The pay program is almost certainly the most expensive component of the program, and even after the cuts, the employees would still enjoy above-market wages, making it unlikely that they would quit to work for another company. Cutting pay would certainly hurt morale. However, if the board was transparent about its balancing methodology from the outset, employees would know that this was a possibility, reducing the harm to morale somewhat. Alternatively, the board could also reduce the number of volunteer days. The extra days of work might improve revenue, which could also increase profitability. Moreover, the reduction in volunteer days is likely to have less of a negative impact on employee morale than a pay cut would. Reducing the number of CEO meetings with employees is probably the least effective technique to improve profitability, so the board should likely look elsewhere for cuts to its employee well-being program. The board would face a challenging decision under these circumstances, but the minimum thresholds strategy does provide substantial guidance.

What if the scenario is even more challenging? Suppose that the company could only return to exceeding its profitability floor by cutting pay below the board's minimum threshold of 10 percent over market? In other words, what if it is impossible at some point for the company to meet either its profitability or its social purpose goals?

As unpleasant as the prospect might be of failing to meet either dimension of its minimum goals, the board should plan for this possibility as well when designing its balancing plan. It should decide in advance what to prioritize when the business is failing to meet either goal. One natural response would be to prioritize profitability until the company is at least breaking even. The rationale for this choice is straightforward: without continuing infusions of cash from outside investors or lenders, a business that is losing money will eventually cease to exist. Prioritizing profitability until the business is financially sustainable is therefore a sensible strategy in most situations. Once the company is profitable, the board might choose to devote resources evenly to both social and profitability goals until either the profitability floor or the social floor is met. At that point, the board might focus on the lagging floor until the business is exceeding both floors.

Although focusing on profitability when the business is in real trouble will often make sense, it may not always be possible. Some social goals are so enmeshed in the company's business model that they cannot be sacrificed, even when the company might need to do so in order to stem losses. For these "rigid floor" companies, there is no escape hatch. The company must meet its floor social goal even if that means losing money or going out of business entirely.

Allbirds provides an excellent example of a rigid floor company. Allbirds manufactures and sells shoes made from sustainable materials—primarily wool and tree fiber.[35] The company markets its shoes to customers who care about the environment and want their clothing to be made in an environmentally friendly way. If Allbirds were failing to meet its profitability goals or even losing money, it would likely find it impossible to cut back on its environmental commitments in order to improve its finances. The heart of the brand's cachet lies in the shoes' sustainable manufacturing; Allbirds' customers would likely ditch the brand if the company abandoned its environmentally friendly manufacturing methods and materials.

As of this writing, Allbirds is in fact losing tens of millions of dollars per year yet shows no signs of changing its strategy.[36] It remains in business because outside investors continue to infuse it with new capital in the hope that it will eventually become profitable. If that willingness flags before Allbirds achieves profitability, the company will likely fail. Allbirds' environmental mission *is* its brand. Changing to traditional shoe materials such as leather is not a feasible strategy, even if the alternative is bankruptcy. Rigid floor companies have the potential to build very strong brands due to the credibility their business strategies bring to their social mission, but that credibility comes at the expense of their flexibility to pivot if their business strategies prove unprofitable.

*Trade-Off Ratios*

An alternative balancing strategy to minimum thresholds is for the board to set a fixed ratio between profit and social purpose. Like minimum thresholds, trade-off ratios need boards to adopt a measure of the company's social mission. Unlike minimum thresholds, these ratios require a formula that can translate a unit of social good to a unit of profit. Boards that use this strategy must choose measurements for profit and social good and declare the relative importance of each.

Imagine a BC or PBC that built apartment buildings and whose primary social mission was to provide low-income housing. The company's board could decide up front what percentage of each building's units would be allocated for low-income tenants and what percentage would be rented at the full market price. In this example, the ratio is straightforward because both the profit measure (the number of market-rent apartments) and the social good measure (the number of apartments reserved for low-income tenants) are measured by the same units: apartments. Investors could use the ratio to calculate their expected return based on the profitability of each market rate unit versus the lower profit or net loss allocated to each low-income unit. Similarly, employees and tenants could easily understand how important a priority providing affordable housing was to the company; a low ratio of affordable units to market-rate units would show that the company was mostly concerned with earning a high return, while a high ratio would demonstrate the company's strong commitment to providing housing to those who could not afford to pay market rents.

Setting a trade-off ratio is more challenging when the measures of profit and social good are unrelated. For example, a car parts manufacturer might send its employees to a local public school to tutor students one afternoon a week and pay its employees for this time as if they were working at the factory. The company's profit measure would likely be net earnings or something similar, measured in dollars. The measure of social good the company produced— aside from the usual incidents of any profitable business such as jobs, products, and taxes—would be the number of hours of free tutoring provided or perhaps the improved grade point average of the students who received tutoring.

Setting a trade-off ratio for this manufacturing company would involve using different measurement units. The board might decide that each hour of tutoring per month was equivalent to the company earning $100. If so, then the board could balance its social mission against profit by donating tutoring time up to the point that the next hour of tutoring would cost the company more than $100 in profits. Setting the trade-off ratio allows the board to maximize "profits" by counting the donated time as a profit center.

An advantage of trade-off ratios is that those who participate in the enterprise can know what percentage of the company's resources will be allocated to profits and what percentage to fulfilling its social mission. Trade-off ratios also permit the board to set its priorities with some precision.

A disadvantage is that it is less flexible than minimum thresholds, since the ratio is fixed regardless of the company's circumstances. Of course, a board could remedy this problem by employing a mix of minimum thresholds and trade ratios, setting a trade ratio that applies only after the minimum thresholds are satisfied. Remember that with minimum thresholds, we suggested that once the company was exceeding its minimum thresholds for both profit and social purpose, it would allocate its resources evenly in producing more of each thereafter. A company could just as easily choose some other allocation method at that point, though, including a trade ratio.

### Maximizing Subject to Constraints

This balancing strategy involves a bit of mathematics. For some readers, the techniques involved will be familiar and comfortable. For others, they may raise the specter of high school math classes they would prefer to forget. Since the first group will not need much explanation of the details of these techniques and the second group would likely skip over any detailed discussion even if I provided one, I will stick to a conceptual overview that I hope will satisfy both. I also provide some resources in the endnotes for those who would like more detailed information.

Mathematicians long ago worked out techniques to maximize a function subject to a constraint. That sounds very technical, and it can be, but the basic concept is straightforward. We can often describe a company's goal with an equation, which mathematicians sometimes call a function. We can keep the equation simple, which will help with analysis but sacrifice some accuracy, or we can try to capture most of the important variables, which will make the equation harder to work with but more accurate. For most companies, no equation can perfectly capture all the variables that are important to its business, so we need to be humble about how precisely the math will provide the right result. But we can often model real life reasonably well with math, or at least well enough to provide useful insights.

Imagine a company that sells cakes and wants an equation that will describe its profits. The major variables are the cost of the cake's ingredients, the cost of the labor to make a cake, the costs associated with marketing and sales for each cake, the price at which it sells each cake, and the number of cakes it sells. Note that even for this simple business, I am omitting some important factors. I have not included rent or the cost of the baking equipment, and there may be other costs I am skipping over such as back-office functions. I am also lumping some variables in together that might usefully be separated, such as the cost of the ingredients. We could separate out the costs of the eggs, flour, sugar, chocolate, salt, and whatever else we plan to put into the cake, and for some purposes, we might want to do that. To illustrate the concept, none of that is necessary.

The profits from the business will be the total amount it takes in from sales (the number of cakes sold times the price for each cake) minus the total cost of each cake (the sum of the materials, labor, and marketing and sales expenses on a per cake basis). We could express all this with the following equation:

$$\text{Profits} = [\text{Number sold}] \times [(\text{price}) - (\text{materials}) - (\text{labor}) - (\text{marketing and sales})].$$

Once an equation incorporates the function, we can then maximize that function subject to a constraint. The cake business might have a number of constraints. Labor costs, for example, might go up the more cakes the business bakes. If it is only a few cakes, it can employ a single baker to work in the kitchen. But if it wants to bake a lot of cakes, it might have to squeeze quite a few bakers into the kitchen, making each baker less efficient so that each baker can bake fewer cakes per day. At some point, the kitchen might not be large enough to fit an additional baker, and perhaps there are no other kitchens available in the short term, so there will be a cap on its total manufacturing capacity. We might describe the labor constraint with an equation such as this:

$$\text{Cakes per baker per day} = 10 - (\text{number of bakers}).$$

This equation indicates that for each additional baker, the productivity of every baker goes down by 1 cake per day. When there is 1 baker, that baker can produce 9 cakes. When 2 bakers are working, each can bake 8 cakes, a total of 16. When there are 10 bakers, the kitchen is so crowded no one can get any work done at all. The business should stop hiring well short of that cap because once it has 5 bakers working, adding a baker will actually reduce the total number of cakes they can bake. With 5 bakers, each baker can make 5 cakes per day, for a total of 25 cakes. With 6, each can bake only 4 cakes per day, for a total of 24 cakes. There is no point in paying for an additional baker if the result is fewer cakes!

We can now use this productivity function together with our profit function to calculate the ideal number of bakers to maximize profits. We first need some data points, though, including the daily cost of hiring each baker, the price at which the cakes are sold, the cost of the ingredients, and the sales and marketing costs. Let us say that each baker receives $200 a day in pay, the cakes sell for $50 each, the ingredients cost $5 per cake, and the sales and marketing costs are $10 per cake. How many cakes should it bake?

Because this example is so simple, we can use the brute force method: trying each number of bakers and then calculating profits. We know that there is no point in hiring more than five bakers, so we only need to try five possibilities. When we do this, we find the following results:

| Number of Bakers | Total Profit |
|:---:|:---:|
| 1 | $115 |
| 2 | $160 |
| 3 | $135 |
| 4 | $40 |
| 5 | ($125) |

The bakery can maximize profits by hiring just two bakers. Hiring a third baker would result in lower profits because the increase in labor costs of the additional baker more than offsets the additional cakes produced with 3 bakers rather than two (21 cakes instead of 16).

Although I used simple math to solve this maximization under a constraint problem, there are much more sophisticated techniques for solving more complex problems. Two of those techniques are the Lagrange multiplier method and linear programming. The Lagrange method works only for equations; linear programming works even when there are inequalities as constraints, such as a constraint that said we can have at most five bakers. The details of these methods are beyond the scope of this book, but the endnote contains some resources for those who would like to learn more, and many additional resources are available with a simple Google search.[37]

In the cake example, our task was to maximize profits subject to a labor productivity constraint. We could easily imagine applying similar techniques to maximizing profits subject to a social good production constraint or maximizing social good production subject to a profit constraint. Using these mathematical techniques, we could have quite sophisticated and complex interactions between a company's pursuit of social good and its quest for profits. Greater complexity would allow for more precision and would permit companies to balance more variables, such as providing low-income housing, above-market wages for the company's workers, and profits.

This technique also comes with some disadvantages. Larger and more complex companies will have difficulty reducing the variables that affect their business to equations or inequalities. Just as important, the more complex the balancing model, the more difficult the model will be to explain to corporate constituents such as investors, customers, and employees. A complex model then, while more sophisticated and nuanced, might be less transparent. Still, for some companies, especially those with particularly sophisticated employees, investors, and customers, the reduced transparency might be a worthwhile price to pay in exchange for enhanced nuance and precision in the balancing methodology.

———

In this chapter, we discussed the balancing requirement boards of BCs and PBCs face. We examined the nature of the statutory mandate and analyzed the critiques of that mandate on both feasibility and desirability grounds. We then considered that the balancing requirement might be both feasible and desirable so long as boards adopted policies that met three goals: transparency, credibility, and measurability. The three balancing methods we examined at the end of the chapter all have the potential to meet these three requirements if they are properly structured. They are not the only balancing methods that could do so, however, and I hope they will serve as a spur to boards' creativity to come up with others.

In the next chapter, we examine the impact that going public may have on the risk of BCs and PBCs engaging in purpose washing.

## NINE

# THE PUBLICLY TRADED
# PUBLIC BENEFIT CORPORATION

In the beginning, there was Laureate Education. Laureate owns and runs a network of for-profit educational institutions that offer both undergraduate and graduate degrees.[1] It operated as a traditional corporation for much of its life, then converted to a PBC in 2015 while still privately held.[2] When Laureate then went public in 2017, it became the first publicly traded PBC in the world.[3]

For several years, Laureate remained the only publicly traded PBC. In 2020 and 1921, though, the number of publicly traded PBCs mushroomed, with companies like Lemonade Insurance and Allbirds going public, and public companies like Amalgamated Bank and United Therapeutics converting to PBC status.[4] As of this writing, there are at least fifteen publicly traded PBCs.[5] In addition, there are several large PBC or BC subsidiaries of publicly traded corporations where the parent is organized as a traditional corporation, including the largest PBC in the world, Danone North America.[6] Others include household names such as the Gap's Athleta, Campbell Soup's Plum Organics, and Unilever's Ben & Jerry's Homemade.

The recent influx of publicly traded PBCs provides a huge boost to the credibility of this still relatively new and untested legal form. Investment banks' willingness to underwrite these companies' offerings and institutional investors' willingness to purchase their stock demonstrate that PBCs' obligation to pursue social purpose alongside profits does not disqualify them in the eyes of sophisticated market participants. The successful public offerings of a critical mass of PBCs also signals to venture capital firms that their initial faith in these companies was justified;[7] if a PBC is successful in building a profitable business, the public markets will provide an exit opportunity for early-stage investors in the form of an initial public offering.

The public nature of these firms not only enhances the utility of the PBC form, it also may reduce PBCs' ability to purpose-wash. To understand how going public may impede purpose washing, we need to take a short detour to explore the federal securities laws that are most likely to have an impact on PBCs. We will keep the detour to a brief overview to provide just the background necessary to understand how going public might bear on some of the special features of PBCs. (The securities laws will have a similar impact on BCs, but to date, there are no publicly traded BCs. As we discussed in Chapter 2, Delaware, which has authorized only PBCs, not BCs, dominates registrations of publicly traded corporations, so this outcome should not be surprising.)

## Securities Regulation Overview

A central purpose of the federal securities laws is to provide investors with the information they need.[8] The securities laws and related exchange listing rules also impose some substantive governance rules, such as the requirement that publicly traded corporations have a majority of independent directors (in essence, directors without direct or indirect financial ties to the company other than stock ownership and their compensation as directors) and that their boards include certain committees.[9] But a core function of the federal securities statutes is to provide accurate disclosure to investors.

The most important federal securities statute for our purposes is the 1934 Securities and Exchange Act (the '34 Act), which governs the ongoing disclosure obligations of publicly traded companies. It also established the Securities and Exchange Commission (SEC), the government agency empowered to create regulations to implement the securities statutes and enforce the securities laws.

Stocks of US companies are generally traded on one of the two major national securities exchanges, the New York Stock Exchange (NYSE) or the Nasdaq. Both exchanges impose their own rules that apply to their listed companies. These rules must be approved by the SEC and so are often quite similar to one another. Many of the rules that control companies' governance come in the form of these exchange rules. For example, the rule requiring independent directors comes from the exchange rules rather than the '34 Act or an SEC regulation.[10]

The disclosure obligations form the bulk of the securities regulations, and they are also the rules that are most likely to have a special impact on PBCs' ability to purpose-wash. The '34 Act requires public companies to engage in disclosure every quarter, every year, whenever asking its shareholders to vote, and upon the occurrence of certain special events.[11] There are other occasions companies are required to disclose information, but these are less likely to have an impact on purpose washing.[12]

Whenever the securities laws require disclosure, they specify the information that the corporation must supply to the public. For example, every year when a corporation files its annual report on Form 10-K, it must respond to the items required by the form, including certain specified information required by Regulation S-K and Regulation S-X. The forms contain a long list of matters the corporation must discuss, but it is a defined list, not a general requirement to disclose all information in the corporation's possession that a shareholder conceivably might want to know.[13] That said, if a company's response to a disclosure category would be misleading without additional material information, then the company must disclose that additional information even though it is not specifically called for by the relevant form.[14] To that extent at least, there is something of a general disclosure obligation.

The disclosure requirements are often further limited by the materiality of the information. The point of the securities laws is not to drown investors in irrelevant information; it is to provide them with the information they need to make informed investment decisions. For this reason, the securities laws usually do not require companies to disclose information that a reasonable investor would not want to know. These laws generally define the term *material* this way, as the information a reasonable person would want to know in making whatever decision is at issue given the total mix of information, whether that be a decision to buy or sell stock or a decision to vote.[15] While the SEC does require disclosure of some information that might not be considered material, the instructions to Regulation S-K are riddled with the materiality modifier. In fact, the word *material* appears in the instructions nearly 600 times.[16]

To ensure that companies tell the truth when they disclose information to the public, the securities laws prohibit fraud in a number of different contexts. For example, section 18 of the '34 Act says that anyone who knowingly makes a false or misleading statement in a document filed with the SEC will be subject to civil liability.[17] Under this statute, if a company knowingly exaggerated its profits when filing its annual report with the SEC, for example, the company could be liable to those who relied on that misstatement. Even more powerfully, Rule 10b-5 imposes both civil and potentially criminal liability on anyone who commits fraud or employs a manipulative or deceptive device in connection with the purchase or sale of a security.[18] If an officer of a publicly traded company knowingly or even recklessly makes a material and false statement to the public, the officer could be liable to anyone who traded on the basis of that statement for any resulting losses the traders might suffer.

Similarly, Rule 14a-9 prohibits false or misleading statements made in connection with a solicitation of a shareholder's vote by proxy. Most shareholders of public companies do not appear at shareholder meetings in person. Instead, they vote their shares by mailing in a proxy form that instructs a neutral agent, or "proxy," how to vote their shares. Companies solicit these proxies before each annual meeting to ensure enough shares are "present" for the meeting to count. As part of that solicitation process, they also provide an annual report with a great deal of information. Candidates running for director seats therefore are susceptible to liability if they knowingly misrepresent information while asking for shareholders' votes. Imagine if political elections ran under such stringent rules!

## Impact on PBCs

There are four ways that going public might have an impact on a PBC's ability to engage in purpose washing: enhanced disclosure requirements, enhanced internal control requirements, greater enforcement options, and a higher public profile. We discuss each in turn.

### Enhanced Disclosure Obligations

Becoming a publicly traded company may have two effects on the scope of a PBC's disclosure obligations. The first involves the impact of the securities laws on a PBC's state law obligation to produce and distribute a benefit report. The second stems from the disclosure obligations imposed directly by the federal securities laws.

In Chapter 5, we learned that the disclosure obligations the Delaware PBC statute imposes are fairly limited and that they are not being enforced vigorously. The Model Act imposes somewhat more rigorous disclosure obligations on BCs, but most states are not enforcing those rules either.[19] Companies that have been producing and distributing benefit reports are often using them more as marketing tools than as serious disclosure vehicles.

Public companies may not retain the luxury of producing lax benefit reports that private companies have. When a publicly traded company makes a statement to the public, that statement is subject to Rule 10b-5, one of the federal antifraud provisions. Rule 10b-5 bars fraud in connection with the purchase or sale of a security. If an issuer makes a material statement knowing it is false, an investor who purchases or sells the security on the basis of that statement can sue under Rule 10b-5 to recover the investor's resulting losses.[20] When a publicly traded PBC sends its benefit report to its shareholders or posts it on its website, it therefore risks liability under Rule 10b-5 for any material, false statements in the report. As a result, publicly traded PBCs may take greater care to ensure that anything they say in their benefit reports is accurate. They still may choose not to produce a benefit report at all, as we discussed in Chapter 5, or to say very little in any report they do produce, but at least a publicly traded PBC has a strong incentive to be truthful in any benefit report it disseminates.

Also, once a company becomes public, the federal securities laws impose much more extensive disclosure obligations. Publicly traded PBCs may find that this disclosure requires them to say quite a bit about their social mission.

Perhaps the item most likely to provoke this type of disclosure is Regulation S-K's Item 101, the description of the business.[21] Recall that companies must disclose information responsive to the long list of prompts in Regulation S-K whenever they file their annual report, or Form 10-K. One of those items, Item 101, commands issuers to "describe the general development of the registrant, its subsidiaries, and any predecessor(s)."[22] (The securities rules tend to refer to companies that issue securities as either "registrants," because they have registered with the SEC under the securities laws, or "issuers," because they have issued stock to investors.) Under this item, there is a long list of specific categories of information that companies must disclose. For example, issuers must describe "the business done and intended to be done," "revenue-generating activities, products and/or services," "status of development efforts for new or enhanced products, trends in market demand and competitive conditions," "resources material to a registrant's business," and "the registrant's human capital resources, including the number of persons employed by the registrant, and any human capital measures or objectives that the registrant focuses on in managing the business."[23]

Although none of the matters listed under Item 101 specifically ask for disclosure about a PBC's social mission, most publicly traded PBCs will likely find that some discussion of their social mission is necessary in responding to a number of the matters that are asked. It would be difficult for a PBC to describe its development without explaining why it made the choice to file as a PBC rather than as a traditional corporation. A PBC would also likely need to explain its social mission as part of any description of the business it has done, its revenue-generating activities, and its development of new products and services. For many PBCs, the social mission will be integral to its business model, so it would be impossible to discuss its strategy for making money without also talking about its social goals. Even for PBCs whose social mission is less organically intertwined with their businesses, the devotion of resources to their social mission will require some explanation. Capital spent pursuing a social mission is unavailable for reinvestment or for distribution to shareholders, and a publicly traded PBC should explain this. Moreover, since PBCs must take the impact of their activities on their employees into account, they should also discuss how they take care of their workers as part of discussing their human capital resources.

Another area of Regulation S-K that would likely elicit a discussion of a PBC's mission is Item 105, which asks about risk factors.[24] This item asks issuers to provide "the material factors that make an investment in the registrant or offering speculative or risky."[25] One factor that could make an investment in a PBC riskier is that the board is required to balance the interests of all stakeholders, even when doing so results in their sacrificing profit for other goals. There are reasons to think that managing a business with an eye toward the benefit of all stakeholders and pursuing a social purpose may result in higher profits. There may also be times when a PBC board chooses to sacrifice profits for these other interests. Those decisions may prove beneficial for society as a whole but may sometimes come at shareholders' expense. As a result, Item 105 would generally require disclosure of this possibility.

Item 105 might also require disclosure of any particular instances where this express trade-off occurred. That sort of disclosure to shareholders would risk raising the ire of shareholders who care only about profits. Boards could likely avoid this issue, though, by arguing that any short-term costs incurred to favor the interests of other stakeholders will ultimately redound to the shareholders' benefit in the form of higher long-term profits. I expect most PBCs will craft boilerplate disclosures of the possibility of sacrificing profits but will not delve into any particular decisions the board made.

We can gain a sense of how PBCs will interpret these rules by examining some of the filings by the PBCs that are already publicly traded. These demonstrate that, as predicted, publicly traded PBCs do discuss their social purpose. They also demonstrate, though, that this discussion may not cover all the topics in the sort of detail that investors who care deeply about the company's social purpose (or beneficiaries of the company's social purpose) might wish. The current SEC rules were not designed with social purpose disclosure in mind, which leaves a great deal to each company's discretion when it comes to the discussion of social purpose.

The shoe company Allbirds furnishes an illustrative example. Its Form 10-K filed on February 28, 2022, was its most recent annual report as of this writing. The 10-K demonstrates how truly extensive disclosure on social issues can be for a publicly traded company. It also demonstrates the limitations on those disclosures, though, in the absence of SEC rules that specify what social disclosures are required. On environmental issues and, to a lesser extent, labor issues, Allbirds' disclosures are immensely impressive. Even on these topics, though, it focuses on the positive without a deep discussion of the trade-offs it faces in pursuing these admirable goals.

Allbirds explains that environmentalism is core to its culture and business strategy. The "Who We Are" section declares that Allbirds holds three "fundamental beliefs" about young consumers: (1) they believe climate change is an existential threat, (2) they want their products to have a lower impact on the environment, and (3) they do not want to sacrifice product appearance or quality while purchasing sustainable products.[26] In other words, Allbirds explains why its commitment to sustainability is also a pathway to profits, based on the preferences of its customer base. The remainder of that section goes into considerable detail about how Allbirds fulfills its environmental commitments, including information about the steps the company takes to ensure that its suppliers employ sustainable practices throughout the supply chain.[27] Allbirds has published elsewhere its methodology for measuring the carbon emissions created across the life cycle of each of its products, and it labels each of its products with its carbon footprint to encourage consumers to consider emissions when they make their purchasing decisions.[28]

Most impressive, Allbirds provides its responses to the Sustainability Accounting Standards Board's (SASB) industry standards relevant to the company's business. These include a long list of environmental and labor issues. Allbirds also provides responses to the Financial Stability Board's Task Force on Climate-Related Financial Disclosures. These are entirely focused on environmental issues. By including all of these disclosures in its Form 10-K, Allbirds has subjected its responses to the antifraud provisions of the securities laws. In other words, Allbirds has committed to the truthfulness of these disclosures in a highly credible manner.

When it comes to the conflict between purpose and profit, though, Allbirds' disclosures are less comprehensive. It trumpets its commitment to the environment and to nonshareholder stakeholders, especially its employees, but says nothing about how those commitments will be actualized when they conflict with maximizing profits. In fact, Allbirds does not even mention the possibility of such a conflict in its primary discussion of these issues. Beyond the many statements promoting the profit potential in All-birds' environmental purpose, there is very little of substance in the Form 10-K about the costs involved in its commitment to sustainable manufac-turing or pledge to pay attention to the interests of nonshareholder stake-holders. It does list these issues under the section that discusses risks to its business, but these read as lawyerly caution rather than an integrated part of the company's philosophy.[29] To the contrary, Allbirds' view seems to be that its social mission will help drive profits. As Form 10-K states, "Our core strengths work in unison to allow us to make better things in a better way, tread lighter, and help our consumers to live life in better balance. Our core strengths also create a competitive moat that sets us apart from competi-tors."[30] Allbirds also states that its status as a PBC and a certified B Corp adds to the brand's authenticity.[31]

Allbirds apparently saw no reason to discuss a tension between profits and purpose because the company's philosophy asserts that purpose drives profits; therefore, there is no conflict between the two. Allbirds makes a convincing case that its environmental values will ultimately reduce costs and boost sales. But its discussion of how it considers its customers' inter-ests is fairly sparse, saying only that the company offers great, sustainable products and provides information about the products' carbon footprint.[32]

It is also somewhat disappointing that Allbirds did not incorporate its benefit report into its Form 10-K. It did publish its benefit report on its website, something it is not required to do under Delaware law. But incor-porating the report into its Form 10-K, as it did with its SASB disclosures, would have made a strong statement about how seriously it takes its obli-gation to produce an accurate benefit report. That said, much of the Form 10-K's discussion of Allbirds' environmental and labor policies appears very similar to the parallel discussions in its 2020 benefit report.[33] Incorporating the report by reference therefore might not have added much material in-formation. Still, incorporating the benefit report into the Form 10-K would have sent a beneficial message about the benefit report's seriousness.

Allbirds does better in describing its commitment to the community, listing a number of worthy charitable endeavors it has pursued, most no-tably donating more than 267,000 pairs of gently worn shoes to a charity that distributes them to those in need in developing countries.[34] Also as expected, Allbirds did mention its PBC status as a risk factor for shareholders, cautioning that its PBC status could have a negative impact on its financial performance and that the company could be subject to derivative suits by shareholders alleging the company's board failed to balance stockholders' interests with the company's social goals.[35]

Overall, then, Allbirds' disclosure of its social goals and the degree to which it is meeting them is impressive. The information it provides goes far beyond what most private companies have provided in their benefit reports. There are some gaps in their disclosures, particularly in terms of how they weigh the competing interests of shareholders, employees, customers, and the community, but I have no trouble counting Allbirds as a positive example of the enormously beneficial impact going public can have on a PBC's disclosure of its social impact.

Not all publicly traded PBC choose to be as admirably forthcoming as Allbirds. Eyeglass manufacturer Warby Parker, for example, provides very little information about its environmental impact in its 2021 Form 10-K.[36] It does publish an annual impact report that measures its performance using both the Global Reporting Initiative standards and SASB's. The impressively detailed information in that report, though, was not incorporated into Warby Parker's Form 10-K, either by reference or (as Allbirds essentially did) by repeating the information there.[37]

The sharp contrast between how these two prominent PBCs saw their disclosure obligations highlights both the potential of the securities laws to enhance disclosure greatly and the significant problems with using the current rules to cover disclosure of companies' social impact. The SEC could ameliorate this discrepancy by imposing a uniform disclosure requirement for PBCs. If the SEC imposed a rule on publicly traded PBCs that regulated their disclosure of their efforts to fulfill their social goals, then all publicly traded PBCs would be subject to the same requirement. My hope is that any such rule would require reasonably comprehensive disclosure of material information. This type of rule would impose some additional cost on PBCs, but the SEC could avoid a PBC penalty by imposing the same rule on all publicly traded companies. In other words, the SEC could require standardized disclosure of every publicly traded company's performance along a number of social metrics such as their environmental performance, their treatment of their employees, and their contributions to other social goals. Some scholars have advocated that the SEC impose uniform social disclosure requirements, at least for PBCs and BCs.[38]

The SEC is already taking an important step along the path of requiring all companies to engage in social disclosure with its proposed rule governing public companies' environmental impact. On March 22, 2022, it proposed a new rule that would require disclosure of an issuer's climate-related risks, greenhouse gas emissions, and certain climate-related financial metrics.[39] The proposal is quite extensive and represents an ambitious and sweeping change from prior law.

The SEC justified the rule by pointing to the impact of climate risk on companies' financial performance, not because climate change is important in its own right.[40] Nevertheless, the proposed rule has drawn considerable criticism from congressional Republicans, the US Chamber of Commerce, and a group of prominent law professors, among others.[41] The SEC may choose to retract or amend the rule because it has attracted so much criticism. If it nevertheless finalizes the rule, there will no doubt be litigation over whether it exceeded its authority in passing the rule. But if the rule survives these formidable challenges, it will represent a major step toward a broad requirement that publicly traded corporations disclose their impact on society.

Requiring a much smaller group of companies—publicly traded PBCs—to disclose a considerably broader range of information does not seem out of the question, especially considering the existing state law requirement that they do so. Such a rule could again be justified by investor interest, just as the SEC justified its new environmental disclosure rules, since investors in PBCs are presumably interested in the companies' social impact. Some investors are likely interested only as an indirect method of securing greater profits, while others may be interested for the benefit of society as a whole. Either way, investor interest could support the adoption of a new disclosure rule on social impact for publicly traded PBCs.

Any such proposal seems unlikely to come soon, however. The SEC is likely to want to see how its environmental disclosure rule fares before plunging deeper into the social impact pool. Also, even with the recent mushrooming number of publicly traded PBCs, they still represent a very small percentage of the total number of publicly traded companies. The

SEC seems unlikely to devote resources to regulating such a small group unless and until the number grows considerably. Still, the environmental disclosure rule is an important precedent, and its fate may reveal a great deal about the potential for more comprehensive disclosure rules concerning social impact in the future.

### Enhanced Internal Controls Requirements

Disclosure can be helpful in preventing purpose washing only to the extent that the information companies release is accurate.[42] While the general disclosure laws have rules that prohibit lying, companies might lack rigorous internal control systems that would ensure corporate officers have the most accurate information in their possession. Corporate officers can disclose only what they know, and without a strong internal control system, they may lack information that investors would find highly material. Two federal statutes impose obligations on public companies to maintain effective internal controls, helping to ensure that companies have accurate information about their financial results: the Foreign Corrupt Practices Act (FCPA) and the Sarbanes-Oxley Act.

The FCPA requires public companies to "keep books, records, and accounts, which, in reasonable detail, accurately and fairly reflect the transactions and dispositions of the assets of the issuer."[43] It also requires public companies to "devise and maintain a system of internal accounting controls sufficient to provide reasonable assurances" that (1) the company's management has authorized the company's transactions, (2) the company records transactions in order to permit it to prepare accurate financial statements, (3) its assets can be accessed only with management's approval, and (4) it regularly compares its asset records against existing assets.[44]

Sarbanes-Oxley requires the CEO and CFO of publicly traded companies to certify the accuracy of every annual and quarterly financial report the company files with the SEC. In particular, these corporate officers must certify that they have reviewed the report in question, that based on their knowledge, the report does not contain any untrue material statement or omission that would make the report misleading, and that based on the officer's knowledge, the financial sections of the report fairly present the company's financial condition and results of operations.[45] Sarbanes-Oxley also imposes an obligation on the signing officers to establish and maintain the company's internal controls in such a way that ensures they are in possession of the material information they need to make these certifications.[46] The company's auditors must "attest to, and report on" the assessment made by the officers of the effectiveness of their internal control system.[47]

These safeguards focus on public companies' disclosure of their financial results, not on the companies' provision of nonfinancial social benefits. There is nothing specific in either the FCPA or Sarbanes-Oxley that requires companies to maintain accurate records regarding any social purpose a company has adopted. To the extent a company's financial reporting also implicates social issues, though, these statutes may assist in preventing purpose washing. Such instances may not prove to be very common.

Even so, the system of internal controls that companies put in place to ensure accurate reporting of financial results often may be adaptable to police the companies' success at pursuing their social goals.[48] How feasible this adaptation is will depend on the nature of the company's existing internal control system and on the type of social mission the company pursues. In all likelihood, adapting an existing system of internal controls to meet the needs of tracking a social mission will be considerably easier than implementing an internal control system in a company that has never had one. Public companies, which are required to have an internal control system for financial matters, may therefore have an easier time tracking their success in meeting their social goals than private companies.

To the extent a company chooses to do this and publicize the results, it will enhance the credibility of its social claims and gain a greater share of the benefits from customers, employees, and investors that we discussed in Chapter 6. Public companies that choose not to take this step will, by implication, seem much more likely to be engaging in purpose washing. Publicly traded BCs and PBCs, then, would seem to have a significant incentive to extend their systems of internal controls—which the law already requires them to implement for financial matters—to their social missions in order to bolster their social claims and avoid the implication that they are engaging in purpose washing.

### The Potential for Better Enforcement by Shareholders

So far, we have seen that going public may require PBCs to disclose more information about their social purposes and to take greater care to ensure that any public disclosure they make is accurate, including the benefit report. We have also seen, though, that the amount of disclosure PBCs make about their social purposes will still largely remain within their discretion in the absence of a new SEC rule or more aggressive enforcement by states of the benefit report requirement.

Another impact that going public will have on PBCs is that there may be more vigorous enforcement of both the accuracy of the PBC's disclosures (including the benefit report) and of the board's balancing duty. The '34 Act includes a number of provisions intended to ensure that publicly traded companies' disclosures do not include any fraudulent misstatements or omissions. As we will see, though, the securities laws may prove helpful to shareholders complaining about a PBC that invested too much in its social missions but not very helpful to those who argue a PBC did too little to pursue its social mission. Therefore, the federal securities fraud laws may not end up being very helpful as mission enforcement tools.

The most common provision likely to be useful in this context is Rule 10b-5, which bars fraud in connection with the purchase or sale of a security. The US Supreme Court has articulated the "elements" or requirements for a Rule 10b-5 suit as " (1) a material misrepresentation or omission by the defendant; (2) scienter [an intent requirement]; (3) a connection between the misrepresentation or omission and the purchase or sale of a security; (4) reliance upon the misrepresentation or omission; (5) economic loss; and (6) loss causation."[49]

There is a host of subtleties involved in applying Rule 10b-5, but the one that concerns us most in our context is the economic loss requirement, as law professor Joan Heminway has pointed out.[50] To explain the issue, let us consider a hypothetical. Suppose that an imaginary PBC we can call Hats, PBC adopted the social purpose of providing a free hat to the underprivileged for every hat it sold. In its securities filings, Hats made a representation about the cost and quality of the hats it donated to the underprivileged. We should consider two possible scenarios. In the first scenario, which we can call "Cheap Hats," Hats stated that the hats it distributed to the underprivileged were much cheaper to manufacture (and of lower quality) than the hats it sold to its customers. In the second scenario, which we can call "Expensive Hats," Hats stated that the hats it donated were of the same quality and cost the same to manufacture as the hats it sold to its customers.

Suppose that under both scenarios, Hats's statement in its securities filings about the quality and manufacturing cost of its hats was a lie. That is, under the Cheap Hats scenario, the hats it gave to the underprivileged actually cost the same to manufacture as the hats it sold, and under the Expensive Hats scenario, the hats it donated were actually much cheaper to manufacture (and of poorer quality) than the hats it sold.

Who will be upset in each scenario? In the Cheap Hats scenario, where Hats claimed the donated hats were cheap but they were actually expensive, shareholders who care most about earning a profit are likely to be upset. They bought stock in Hats thinking that while the company did have a nice social mission, that mission would not eat into the company's profits unduly because the hats it donated were cheap to make. Conversely, in the Expensive Hats scenario, where Hats claimed the donated hats were expensive (and of high quality) but they were actually cheap (and of poor quality), the shareholders who care most about the company's social mission are likely to be upset. They bought stock in Hats thinking they were supporting a serious social mission, but the truth is that Hats was providing much less charity than they believed.

Which of these groups is more likely to be successful in a Rule 10b-5 suit against Hats? Remember that in both scenarios, Hats has lied to its shareholders and the public at large in its securities filings. Let us also assume that in both cases, the lie was important, or "material," to a reasonable investor. Note, though, that in the Expensive Hats scenario, that will require more of a stretch from traditional profit-centered norms than the courts are accustomed to and so is still an open question. In both scenarios, Hats knew it was misrepresenting the facts when it made its filing, so in both cases the element of scienter, or intent, was met. Only a shareholder who either bought or sold stock in Hats after Hats lied to the public will have a right to sue (that is, standing). For those shareholders, there will be a connection between the misrepresentation and the purchase or sale of Hats's stock since its stock price probably changed in response to the release of this material information. Reliance is usually met in these cases through a complicated legal doctrine known as the "fraud on the market theory."[51] For our purposes, we'll assume that the reliance requirement is met here as well. Transaction causation is really just another term for reliance.[52] So far, then, in both scenarios, the irate shareholders would have a Rule 10b-5 claim.

The problem arises with the economic loss requirement (again assuming that the materiality element is met, though it may not be in the Expensive Hats scenario). Notice that the loss must be economic in nature. The courts have never recognized a Rule 10b-5 cause of action based on psychological or emotional harm. To earn a favorable verdict, the complaining shareholders must prove that they lost money because of the defendant's fraudulent statement or omission.

The shareholder plaintiffs in the two scenarios therefore have very different chances of success, at least under the traditional understanding of the securities laws. In the Cheap Hats scenario, the shareholders are complaining that the lie resulted in lower profits for the company. Hats said it was spending relatively little on the donated hats, when in fact it was spending quite a bit, reducing the company's profits and therefore its share price (at least once the truth came out). These shareholders have a clear claim under Rule 10b-5 because they have suffered an economic loss. In the Expensive Hats scenario, in contrast, the shareholders are *better* off economically because of the lie. They bought stock in Hats when the market believed— falsely—that Hats was spending a great deal of money on the donated hats. The market would have reduced the price of Hats's stock because of the impact these expensive donations would have had on the company's profits. After the truth emerged, the stock price likely rose considerably as the market increased its projection for the company's future profits. The injury these shareholders are claiming is not strictly economic, at least not in the first instance. They have suffered an *emotional* loss because the good they thought they were doing for the world turned out to be considerably less than they expected when they bought the stock, but they have if anything gained a *financial* windfall. Under the traditional understanding of the securities laws, these shareholders would lack a valid claim under Rule 10b-5.

The securities laws will continue to help shareholders for whom profit is the primary goal, but they will not, at least under the view the courts have adopted thus far, assist the shareholders who want to enforce the company's social mission. Courts might adopt a different view, though, at least for PBCs. They might reason that "universal shareholders," who invest in all the publicly traded companies in the market, care a great deal about the health of the economic system as a whole. That health affects all of their investments. To the extent a company's social mission improves the health of the economy by, for example, ensuring that everyone has sufficient clothing and is therefore warm enough to stay healthy and work, that social mission can have a significant economic impact on universal shareholders' total financial return. In recent years, the percentage of the market owned by such universal investors has grown markedly, especially with the increased popularity of index funds.[53] This is the reasoning advanced by Rick Alexander in regard to disclosure obligations more generally.[54] Whether courts will adopt this reasoning when evaluating securities fraud claims against PBCs remains to be seen.

While the availability of the securities laws may turn out to be the most important enforcement-related change PBCs experience when they go public, another shift may also have an important impact: the change in the identity of the company's shareholders. This shift is not about a change in the laws that govern these companies when they go public but rather how their capital structure alters. This shift is important because of its impact on the likelihood of the board's being sued for failing to pursue its social mission adequately or failing to balance the interests of the company's other constituencies against those of the shareholders.

While a company is privately held, it has a small group of shareholders that usually consists of the founders and the early outside investors such as venture capital firms. The shareholders are either actively involved in managing the company—in the case of the founders—or at least frequently in touch with the managers and in agreement with the managers' strategies. It would be unusual for someone from this group to launch a lawsuit against the company, both because the early shareholders' views about how the company should be run tend to be reasonably aligned and because when there are disagreements, these shareholders have other means of exercising power to effect the changes they want. Venture capital investors generally demand a fair degree of power over governance as a condition of investment, so they rarely need to launch a formal lawsuit against the company to change its management strategy.

Once the company goes public, though, many new shareholders enter the mix. Some of these will be retail shareholders—people who buy the stock for their personal portfolios based on their own research or the recommendation of an investment adviser. Most, however, will typically be institutional investors—large companies such as mutual funds and pension funds that invest money on behalf of other people. Although institutional investors often are not the beneficial owners of the shares they purchase on others' behalf—they do not profit directly from any increase in the shares' value or suffer any direct loss when prices decline—they still are the legal owners of the shares. Legal ownership grants standing to sue.

As noted in Chapter 3, most states grant standing to launch benefit enforcement proceedings only to shareholders who own a great deal of the company's stock. Both Delaware and the Model Act require shareholders to own 2 percent of the company's stock to bring these suits.[55] Delaware's statute also offers standing to shareholders whose stake in the company is worth at least $2 million, when that represents a lower threshold than the 2 percent requirement.[56] (It is worth noting that California's statute grants standing to any shareholder, even someone who owns only a single share, but this permissive approach is rare among the states.[57])

It would require a very wealthy retail investor to qualify for standing with either option under Delaware law, but institutional shareholders—who have billions or even trillions of dollars to invest—often will. Institutional investors are quite different from the controlling group in a closely held enterprise. They are far more removed from the company and its founders than venture capitalists. Unlike the founders or VCs, the institutional investors were not involved at the early stages of the company, did not fight shoulder to shoulder in the trenches while struggling to make the company a success, and did not have a major voice in shaping the company's business strategy. They therefore are likely to have fewer compunctions about suing the company's board if the directors diverge from what the investors consider optimal behavior. In addition, some institutional shareholders might care about enforcing a PBC's social mission either because the social mission aligns with the investor's strategy to maximize returns or because the investor cares about the mission for its own sake. In sum, while shareholder suits to enforce a PBC's social mission seem likely to be rare among privately held PBCs, they might become more common after a PBC goes public. Once a PBC's stock is traded on a national securities exchange, it might very well have some shareholders with the necessary stake to qualify for standing and perhaps the willingness to sue to enforce the board's duty to balance purpose and profits.

Some scholars have expressed skepticism about institutional investors' willingness to pursue these suits. For example, Steven Solomon and Jill Fisch have argued that institutional investors "face a variety of structural and reputational constraints that make their leadership in policing PBCs unlikely."[58] This skepticism may be warranted based on institutional investors' track record of rather limited involvement in shareholder litigation in other contexts, even when it would appear in their financial interest to participate actively.[59]

Nevertheless, with the increasing interest in investing in socially active companies, institutional investors may find it advantageous to position themselves as guardians over companies' claims of social consciousness. In addition, activist organizations may sometimes decide that the impact such a suit can have would be worth investing $2 million in a PBC for the sole purpose of gaining standing to sue. Few activist organizations would have the requisite resources to pursue this strategy, but even a handful of these suits might produce a strong deterrent effect against purpose washing.

## Public Pressure

The final change PBCs may experience when they enter the public equity markets is that they are likely to obtain a substantially higher public profile. [60] The popular press often pays more attention to publicly traded companies, as do websites and bloggers that target investors as their primary audience. The press may be particularly attracted to stories about publicly traded PBCs for a number of reasons. First, they are still relatively rare, and therefore interesting. Second, there has been a great deal of coverage of the current trend favoring social investing and companies focusing on environmental, social, and governance factors, and a publicly traded PBC fits nicely into that theme. Finally, to the extent a publicly traded PBC fails to live up to its promises to focus on its social mission, the press is likely to take great joy in highlighting the company's perceived hypocrisy.

The higher profile of a publicly traded PBC may provide an additional tool to reinforce the company's social mission. One advantage the PBC form may confer on companies is that the legal form may lend greater credibility to a company's claims to care about a social mission that is broader than just earning profits by selling a valuable good or service. Companies with a reputation for caring about society may garner greater loyalty from a customer base that increasingly says it cares about companies' social profile when making purchasing decisions.[61] Companies can quickly lose this advantage, though, if stories begin circulating that accuse it of purpose washing. The implicit pressure of losing market share, then, may act as a significant deterrent against PBCs' abandoning their social missions. That pressure may be considerably greater once a company goes public and its actions increasingly play out in public view.

Customers are likely to be the primary source of this pressure, but employees can also demonstrate considerable persuasive power. Employees may work harder, stay longer, and accept lower pay when they believe their company is dedicated to important goals.[62] PBCs risk losing that benefit as well if they pay only lip service to their social missions. Again, the attention that comes with going public makes it much harder for a PBC to hide any flaws in its execution of its social mission and so puts it at greater risk of losing its employees' loyalty.

———

In this chapter, we discussed the federal securities laws that are most likely to have an impact on PBCs and their ability to engage in purpose washing after they go public. These laws include both significant disclosure obligations and antifraud provisions that apply to companies' public statements. The disclosure requirements may result in PBCs providing significant information that the public can use to determine whether the companies are providing the social benefits they purport to be serving. In the absence of new regulations by the SEC, though, PBCs retain considerable discretion in determining how much disclosure to provide about their social missions. The antifraud provisions may encourage publicly traded PBCs to take greater care to ensure that anything they say publicly about their pursuit of a social mission is materially accurate. Here too, though, we saw that the technicalities of these antifraud rules may prevent them from becoming as useful as they might be. We also discussed how the weaker connections of institutional shareholders to a given PBC may make it more probable that they would sue a PBC for failing to balance its profit-making and social goals appropriately. Finally, we discussed the likelihood that going public would result in companies attracting greater attention from the popular press and others who follow companies' actions closely. That greater attention may help deter publicly traded PBCs from shirking their social missions.

Overall, going public is unlikely to serve as a panacea for the flaws in the BC and PBC statutes. But there are important ways in which publicly traded PBCs may be more deterred from purpose washing than PBCs that remain privately held.

# CONCLUSION

As a reader of this book, you should now have a deep and nuanced understanding of a number of important questions concerning BCs and PBCs. You know the history of the corporate purpose debate in the United States. You have a grasp on the fundamental principles of American corporate law. You have a detailed knowledge of how the BC and PBC statutes change those principles for these new forms of business organization. You explored what types of social purposes these companies are pursuing and debated whether the statutes that permit such a broad range of social purposes should be narrowed. You learned why entrepreneurs and investors might be interested in choosing these new forms for the companies they build. You analyzed different methods boards might use to balance profit and purpose that are transparent, credible, and measurable. You surveyed the risk that BCs and PBCs will engage in purpose washing and examined how going public might reduce that risk.

At this point, you have the knowledge base to step back and examine the two bottom-line questions:

1. Are BCs and PBCs a reasonable legal form for entrepreneurs and investors?

2. Will these new legal forms produce companies that do a better job of internalizing their negative externalities and producing positive externalities, resulting in an economy that works better for people and the planet?

The answer to the first question is, in my view, an enthusiastic yes. There is little downside to adopting the BC or PBC form, even for publicly traded companies. The risk of additional liability for directors is very small, especially in states that have specifically insulated directors from personal liability by statute. There are additional disclosure obligations, and companies that take these seriously could incur costs. I would argue, though, that the resulting information about the company's impact on its employees, its customers, the environment, and others materially affected by its activities is something all companies—not just BCs and PBCs—should consider when making business decisions. At a minimum, this information may help profit-focused entities discover hidden costs and opportunities to improve their relationships with customers that may boost their profitability. For companies that care about their impact as a value separate and apart from earnings, the legal requirement to gather this information can act as a spur to self-reflection that aligns with their values. At least for companies with compatible cultures and business models, the BC and PBC forms offer potentially significant benefits at a modest cost.

The second question is more challenging. As I argued earlier in the book, BCs and PBCs offer impressive reinforcement tools but inadequate enforcement mechanisms. The lack of powerful enforcement devices is a significant weakness for those who look to the new forms to force companies into different behavior patterns. Nevertheless, both the balancing and disclosure requirements can support companies' existing desire to take their impact—both positive and negative—into account in shaping business strategy. The new forms are not a panacea, by any means. But they may help companies shift their perspective and reshape their corporate cultures by not only permitting but requiring boards to think about more than maximizing profits. That is a radically different message than directors and officers have been hearing from the shareholder-centric profit-maximization school. I hope it is one that shareholders and managers of all companies are ready, willing, and able to hear and heed.

# NOTES

**Acknowledgments**

1. Michael B. Dorff, James Hicks, and Steven Davidoff Solomon, "The Future or Fancy? An Empirical Study of Public Benefit Corporations," *Harvard Business Law Review* 11 (2021).

**Introduction**

1. The original And1 mixtape is available on YouTube: https://www.youtube .com/watch?v=TA04S4yOA_0 (last viewed Nov. 15, 2019).

2. Richard Feloni, "More Than 2,600 Companies, Like Danone and Patagonia, Are on Board with an Entrepreneur Who Says the Way We Do Business Runs Counter to Human Nature and There's Only One Way Forward," *Business Insider*, Dec. 8, 2018, https://www.businessinsider.com/b-corporation-b-lab-movement-and-1-cofounder-2018-11 (last viewed Nov. 15, 2019).

3. Ryan Honeyman, *The B Corp Handbook: How to Use Business as a Force for Good* 10 (Berrett-Koehler 2014).

4. Fair Trade Certified, "Why Fair Trade," https://www.fairtradecertified.org/why-fair-trade/our-global-model (last viewed Nov. 15, 2019).

5. Michael B. Dorff, "Assessing the Assessment: B Lab's Effort to Measure Companies' Benevolence," 40 *Seattle University Law Review* 515, 523 (2017).

6. Email from Susan Mac Cormac, March 24, 2023 (on file with the author).

7. *Id.* The social purpose corporation contains features that are very similar to the public benefit corporation that Delaware ultimately passed.

8. Delaware State Bar Association, "About the Section of Corporation Law,"https://www.dsba.org/sections-committees/sections-of-the-bar/corporation -law/ (last viewed Nov. 19, 2019).

9. Frederick H. Alexander, *Benefit Corporation Law and Governance: Pursuing Profit with Purpose* 3 (San Francisco: Berrett-Koehler 2017).

10. *Id.*

11. You can read more about The Shareholder Commons at https://frederickalex ander.net/the-shareholder-commons/.

## Chapter 1: What Is a Corporation's Purpose?

1. Jack Ewing, "Volkswagen C.E.O. Martin Winterkorn Resigns Amid Emissions Scandal," *New York Times*, Sept. 23, 2015, https://www.nytimes.com/2015/09/ 24/business/international/volkswagen-chief-martin-winterkorn-resigns-amid -emissions-scandal.html (last viewed Aug. 9, 2022).

2. Kevin Granville, "Facebook and Cambridge Analytica: What You Need to Know as Fallout Widens," *New York Times*, Mar. 19, 2018, https://www.nytimes.com /2018/03/19/technology/facebook-cambridge-analytica-explained.html (last viewed Aug. 9, 2022).

3. James Walsh, "Boston Scientific to Pay $30 Million in Defective Devices Case," *Star Tribune*, Oct. 17, 2013, https://www.startribune.com/boston-scientific-to -pay-30-million-in-defective-devices-case/228211891/ (last viewed Aug. 9, 2022).

4. Robin Marantz Henig, "The Dalkon Shield Disaster," *Washington Post*, Nov. 17, 1985, https://www.washingtonpost.com/archive/entertainment/books/1985/11/ 17/the-dalkon-shield-disaster/6c58f354-fa50-46e5-877a-10d96e1de610/ (last viewed Aug. 9, 2022).

5. Ariane DeVogue, Dennis Powell, & the Associated Press, "Documents: Firestone Knew of Tire Defects in '97," *ABC News*, Sept. 6, 2000, https://abcnews.go. com/US/story?id=95866&page=1 (last viewed Aug. 8, 2022).

6. Ben Wojdyla, "The Top Automotive Engineering Failures: The Ford Pinto Fuel Tanks," *Popular Mechanics*, May 20, 2011) https://www.popularmechanics.com/ cars/a6700/top-automotive-engineering-failures-ford-pinto-fuel-tanks/ (last viewed Aug. 9, 2022).

7. Sarah Kaplan, "By 2050, There Will Be More Plastic Than Fish in the World's Oceans, Study Says," *Washington Post*, Jan. 20, 2016, https://www.washing tonpost.com/news/morning-mix/wp/2016/01/20/by-2050-there-will-be-more -plastic-than-fish-in-the-worlds-oceans-study-says/ (last viewed Aug. 9, 2022).

8. Thomas Pikkety, *Capital in the Twenty-First Century* (Harvard University Press 2013).

9. Solomon E. Asch, *Social Psychology* 450–59 (Oxford University Press 1952).

10. https://www.latimes.com/business/story/2019-09-04/hiltzik-medical-bank ruptcy-american-scandal

11. Moddassir Ahmed, Muhammad Rauf, Zahid Mukhtar, & Nasir Ahmad Saeed, "Excessive Use of Nitrogenous Fertilizers: An Unawareness Causing Serious Threats

to Environment and Human Health," 24 *Environmental Science and Pollution Research* 26893 (Dec. 2017); Artemis Dona & Ioannis S. Arvanitoyannis, "Health Risks of Genetically Modified Foods," 49 *Critical Reviews in Food Science and Nutrition* 164, Feb. 2009.

12. Darby Saxbe, "The Social Media Disconnect," *Psychology Today*, Feb. 26, 2018, https://www.psychologytoday.com/us/blog/home-base/201802/the-social-media -disconnect (last viewed Aug. 9, 2022).

13. World Bank, "GDP," last consulted Mar. 31, 2023.

14. https://www.cia.gov/library/publications/the-world-factbook/fields/224 .html

15. https://www.epi.org/publication/charting-wage-stagnation/

16. *Id.*

17. *Id.*

18. For a discussion of the phenomenon of cohesive groups known as group-think, see Irving L. Janis, *Groupthink: Psychological Studies of Policy Decisions and Fiascoes* (2d ed. Houghton Mifflin 1982), and Michael B. Dorff, "The Group Dynamics Theory of Executive Compensation," 28 *Cardozo Law Review* 2025 (2007).

19. Frank H. Easterbrook & Daniel R. Fischel, *The Economic Structure of Corporate Law* 36–39 (Harvard University Press 1991). *also* Ian B. Lee, "Efficiency and Ethics in the Debate about Shareholder Primacy," 31 *Delaware Corporate Law Journal* 533, 537–38 (2006) (explaining this theory); Lynn A. Stout, "Bad and No-So-Bad Arguments for Shareholder Primacy," 75 *Southern California Law Review* 1189, 1192–93 (2002) (same).

20. Hannah Zhang, "Dick's Sporting Goods Will Stop Selling Guns at 440 More Stores," *CNN*, Mar. 10, 2020, https://www.cnn.com/2020/03/10/business/dicks -sporting-goods-remove-guns-from-440-stores/index.html (last viewed Sept. 7, 2022).

21. See, *e.g.*, Lucian Ayre Bebchuk, "Federalism and the Corporation: The Desirable Limits on State Competition in Corporate Law," 105 *Harvard Law Review* 1435, 1492 (1992); David L. Engel, "An Approach to Corporate Social Responsibility," 32 *Stanford Law Review* 1 (1979); Walter Werner, "Corporation Law in Search of Its Future," 81 *Columbia Law Review* 1611, 1651 (1981) (describing the pragmatist position).

22. *Citizens United v. Federal Election Commission*, 558 U.S. 310 (2010).

23. *Edgar v. MITE Corp.*, 457 U.S. 624, 645 (1982).

24. John C. Carney, *Fiscal Year 2021 Governor's Recommended Budget*, last consulted Mar. 31, 2023. https://budget.delaware.gov/budget/fy2021/documents/operating/ introduction.pdf.

25. See, *e.g.*, William L. Cary, "Federalism and Corporate Law: Reflections upon Delaware," 83 *Yale Law Journal* 663 (1974).

26. Ralph K. Winter, "State Law, Shareholder Protection, and the Theory of the Corporation," 6 *Journal of Legal Studies* 251 (1977).

27. Jill E. Fisch, "Institutional Competition to Regulate Corporations: A Comment on Macey," 55 *Case Western Reserve Law Review* 617, 619 (2005).

28. Delaware Division of Corporations, "Annual Report Statistics" (2021), https://corp.delaware.gov/stats/ (last viewed Aug. 10, 2022).

29. *Dodge v. Ford Motor Company*, 204 Mich. 459, 170 N.W. 668 (Mich. 1919).

30. *Id.* at 671.

31. *Id.* at 684.

32. *Id.*

33. *Id.*

34. Jeffrey N. Gordon, "The Rise of Independent Directors in the United States, 1950–2005: Of Shareholder Value and Stock Market Prices," 59 *Stanford Law Review* 1465, 1511–14 (2007).

35. Peter F. Drucker, *The Concept of the Corporation* (Transaction 1946); Peter F. Drucker, "They're Not Employees, They're People," *Harvard Business Review* (Feb. 2002), https://hbr.org/2002/02/theyre-not-employees-theyre-people (last viewed Aug. 10, 2022).

36. Milton Friedman, "The Social Responsibility of Business Is to Increase Its Profits," *New York Times Magazine*, Sept. 13, 1970.

37. *Id.*

38. Michael B. Dorff, *Indispensable and Other Myths: Why the CEO Pay Experiment Failed and How to Fix It* 18 (University of California Press 2014).

39. *Id.*

40. *Unocal Corp. v. Mesa Petroleum Co.*, 493 A.2d 946, 955 (Del. 1985). In *Unocal*, the Delaware Supreme Court held that in considering whether a corporate takeover defense was reasonable in response to the threat posed by a hostile bid (and therefore permitted under Delaware law), the board could consider the threat not only to the company's shareholders but also to other corporate constituencies. The court defined these other constituencies broadly, as including "creditors, customers, employees, and perhaps even the community generally."

41. *Revlon, Inc. v. MacAndrews & Forbes Holdings, Inc.*, 506 A.2d 173, 176 (1986).

42. *eBay Domestic Holdings, Inc. v. Newmark*, 16 A.3d 1 (2010).

43. *eBay*, 16 A.3d at 34 (internal citation omitted).

44. Even if Professor Stout were correct and shareholder primacy were not the law in Delaware, BCs and PBCs would retain much of their usefulness. Because there is little legal enforcement of shareholder primacy (or, for that matter, of the balancing requirement imposed by BCs and PBCs, as we discuss later in the book), the primary benefits of the BC and PBC forms are (1) cultural, by setting different expectations for managers and investors and (2) reinforcement of the founder's social values through mechanisms such as periodic reporting on the company's progress in advancing its social goals and the mandate that the board balances profit against other social goals. These tools would be useful even if Delaware law did not require traditional corporations to focus only on pursuing profits through legal means.

45. Lynn A. Stout, *The Shareholder Value Myth* 31 (Berrett-Koehler 2012).

46. *Id.* at 28. Stout makes this point as an argument in favor of latitude, pointing out that few if any charters mandate shareholder primacy. But there she mistakes the default rule, which is shareholder primacy. Companies that do not opt out of shareholder primacy are bound by it under Delaware law.

47. Leo E. Strine Jr., "The Dangers of Denial: The Need for a Clear-Eyed Understanding of the Power and Accountability Structure Established by the Delaware General Corporation Law," 50 *Wake Forest Law Review* 761, 768 (2015).

48. Jonathan D. Springer, "Corporate Constituency Statutes: Hollow Hopes and False Fears," 1999 *Annual Survey of American Law* 85 (1999); Julian Velasco, "The Fundamental Rights of the Shareholder," 40 *U.C. Davis Law Review* 407 (2006).

49. See, *e.g.*, *AP Smith Mfg. Co. v. Barlow*, 98 A.2d 581 (New Jersey 1953) (approving a company's charitable donations to Rutgers and Princeton).

50. Larry Fink, "A Sense of Purpose" (2017), https://www.blackrock.com/corporate/investor-relations/2018-larry-fink-ceo-letter.

51. Marc Benioff, "We Need a New Capitalism," *New York Times*, Oct. 14, 2019, https://www.nytimes.com/2019/10/14/opinion/benioff-salesforce-capitalism.html.

52. Business Roundtable, "Statement on the Purpose of a Corporation" (2019), https://opportunity.businessroundtable.org/wp-content/uploads/2019/09/BRT-Statement-on-the-Purpose-of-a-Corporation-with-Signatures-1.pdf.

53. Accountable Capitalism Act, S. 3348, 115th Cong. (2018), https://www.warren.senate.gov/imo/media/doc/Accountable%20Capitalism%20Act.pdf

54. Office of Senator Elizabeth Warren, "Warren Introduces Accountable Capitalism Act" (Aug. 15, 2018), https://www.warren.senate.gov/newsroom/press-releases/warren-introduces-accountable-capitalism-act.

55. See, *e.g.*, Lucian A. Bebchuk & Roberto Tallarita, "The Illusory Promise of Stakeholder Governance," 106 *Cornell Law Review* 91, 101–102 (2020); J. S. Liptrap, "The Dark Side of Colombia's Benefit Corporation," *Oxford Business Law Blog* (June 8, 2022), https://www.law.ox.ac.uk/business-law-blog/blog/2022/06/dark-side-colombias-benefit-corporation (last viewed August 10, 2022).

## Chapter 2: Corporate Law Basics

1. 8 Del. Gen. Corp. L. § 141(a).

2. Kelli A. Alces, "Beyond the Board of Directors," 48 *Wake Forest Law Review* 783 (2011).

3. Dorothy S. Lund, "Nonvoting Shares and Efficient Corporate Governance," 71 *Stanford Law Review* 687, 712–13 (2019).

4. Generally, Jill Fisch & Steven Davidoff Solomon, "The Problem of Sunsets," 99 *Boston University Law Review* 1057 (2019).

5. *Smith v. Van Gorkom*, 488 A.2d 858 (Del. 1985).

6. Delaware Courts, "Judicial Officers," https://courts.delaware.gov/chancery/judges.aspx (last viewed November 14, 2022).

7. Clark Neily, "There Are Way Too Many Prosecutors in the Federal Judiciary," *Slate,* Oct. 14, 2019, https://slate.com/news-and-politics/2019/10/too-many-prosecutors-federal-judiciary.html (last viewed Aug. 10, 2022).

8. You can see the commercial here: https://www.countryliving.com/life/entertainment/a37477/coca-cola-super-bowl-ad-reunion/ (last viewed Nov. 22, 2019).

9. Many of these ads can be seen here: https://www.youtube.com/watch?v=guMrgRKKENI (last viewed May 19, 2022).

10. Sound like a familiar story? It is loosely based on Kendall Jenner's Pepsi ad. You can see the ad and a brief explanation of the controversy it provoked here: https://www.youtube.com/watch?v=bTivpgMkGKA.

11. *Steiner v. Meyerson*, 1995 WL 441999, at *5 (Del. Ch. 1995) (Allen) ("But rarest of all-and indeed, like Nessie, possibly non-existent-would be the case of disinterested business people making non-fraudulent deals (non-negligently) that meet the legal standard of waste!"). But see *Sanders v. Wang*, 1999 WL 1044880 (Del. Ch. 1999) (denying a motion to dismiss a waste claim in an executive compensation case).

12. The most famous case to do so is *Smith, supra* note 5.

13. See, *e.g., Benihana of Tokyo, Inc. v. Benihana, Inc.*, 891 A.2d 150, 191–92 (Del. Ch. 2005) ("The duty of care includes a duty that directors inform themselves, before making a business decision, of all material information reasonably available to them. The duty also includes a requirement that directors reasonably inform themselves of alternatives. Director liability for breaching the duty of care 'is predicated upon concepts of gross negligence.'") (internal citations omitted, citing *Aronson v. Lewis*, 473 A.2d 805, 812 (Del. 1984)).

14. 8 Del. Gen. Corp. L. § 102(b)(7) (permitting a corporation to include in its certificate of incorporation, "a provision eliminating or limiting the personal liability of a director to the corporation or its stockholders for monetary damages for breach of fiduciary duty as a director").

15. Harold J. Marsh, "Are Directors Trustees? Conflict of Interest and Corporate Morality," 22 *Business Lawyer* 35 (1966).

16. *In re Trados Inc. Shareholder Litigation*, 73 A.3d 17, 44 (Del. Ch. Ct. 2013).

17. 8 Del. Gen. Corp. L. § 144.

18. *Broz v. Cellular Information Systems, Inc.*, 673 A.2d 148 (Del. 1996).

19. *In re Walt Disney Co. Deriv. Litig.*, 906 A.2d 27, 67 (Del. 2006).

20. *Stone ex rel. AmSouth Bancorporation v. Ritter*, 911 A.2d 362, 370 (Del. 2006).

21. Generally, *Ryan v. Gifford*, 918 A.2d 341, 357–58 (Del. Ch. Ct. 2007) (ruling that backdating stock options constituted a breach of the duty of good faith).

22. *Unocal Corp. v. Mesa Petroleum Co.*, 493 A.2d 946 (Del. 1985).

23. For a description of the full test, you might read *Unitrin Inc. v. American General Corp.*, 651 A.2d 1361 (Del. 1995).

24. 506 A.2d 173 (Del. 1986).

25. Nearly identical transactions may have opposite results. A stock-for-stock merger with a publicly held buyer that has a controlling shareholder does trigger

*Revlon. Paramount Communications, Inc. v. QVC Network, Inc.*, 637 A.2d 34 (Del. 1994). But a stock-for-stock merger with a publicly held buyer that lacks a controlling shareholder does not trigger *Revlon. Paramount Communications, Inc. v. Time, Inc.*, 571 A.2d 1140 (Del. 1989). To a layperson, and even to many lawyers, this distinction may seem difficult to understand. (Some commentators have argued that when the directors are selling the company, they might feel less compelled to act in the shareholders' interests, and the buyer will often have a strong financial motive to try to bribe them to accept a lower price than they might otherwise demand. The buyer might be especially motivated to offer a bribe when the buyer is an individual or an entity that has a controlling shareholder. Such buyers benefit personally from the transaction in a way that mere managers of a buying company owned by others do not. , *e.g.*, Stephen Bainbridge, *Mergers and Acquisitions: Concepts and Insights* 314–15 (3rd ed. 2012).)

26. Although *Revlon* itself seemed to apply a relatively strict standard, the Delaware Supreme Court has since seemed to loosen up on its requirements, at least for corporations that have opted to protect their directors from liability for breaches of their duty of care. For such corporations, only a bad-faith failure to sell the corporation to the highest bidder can trigger *Revlon* liability. The Delaware Supreme Court has held that this means that directors will be liable under *Revlon* only if they "utterly failed to attempt to obtain the best sale price." *Lyondell Chemical Co. v. Ryan*, 970 A.2d 235, 243–44 (Del. 2009).

27. *Paramount Communications, Inc. v. QVC Network, Inc.*, 637 A.2d 34, 48 (Del. 1994) ("When a corporation undertakes a transaction which will cause: (a) a change in corporate control; *or* (b) a break-up of the corporate entity, the directors' obligation is to seek the best value reasonably available to the stockholders.").

28. *Americas Mining Corp. v. Theriault*, 51 A.3d 1213 (Del. 2012).

29. 8 Del. Gen. Corp. L. § 145.

30. *Parfi Holding AB v. Mirror Image Internet, Inc.*, 954 A.2d 911, 935 (Del. Ct. Ch. 2008).

31. *United Food and Commercial Workers Union and Participating Food Industry Employers Tri-State Pension Fund v. Zuckerberg*, 262 A.3d 1034, 1047 (Del. 2021).

32. *Aronson v. Lewis*, 473 A.2d 805, 817–18 (Del. 1984); *Brehm v. Eisner*, 746 A.2d 244, 256 at n. 33 (Del. 2000).

33. *Zuckerberg, supra* note 31, at 1058.

34. *Zapata Corp. v. Maldonado*, 430 A.2d 779, 788–89 (Del. 1981).

35. *Id.*

## Chapter 3: How Are BCs and PBCs Different?

1. B Lab, "Model Benefit Corporation Legislation with Explanatory Comments" (January 13, 2016) [hereafter Model Act], on file with the author. B Lab hosted a copy of the Model Act on its website until recently, but unfortunately no longer does. I have a copy on file and would be happy to share upon request.

2. *Id.* § 201(a).

3. *Id.* § 102.

4. *Id.*

5. *Id.*

6. *Id.* Note that although religion is not specifically enumerated, it should easily qualify within the catch-all provision of § 102(7).

7. *Id.* § 201(c) ("The creation of general public benefit and specific public benefit under subsections (a) and (b) is in the best interests of the benefit corporation.").

8. *Id.* § 301(a)(1).

9. *Id.* § 301(a)(2).

10. *Id.* § 301(a)(3).

11. Heather Boushey & Sarah Jane Glynn, "There Are Significant Business Costs to Replacing Employees," *Center for American Progress* (Nov. 16, 2012), https://www.americanprogress.org/article/there-are-significant-business-costs-to-repla cing-employees/ (last viewed July 13, 2022); Timothy R. Hinkin & J. Bruce Tracey, "Employee Turnover: When the Devil Is in the Details," 6 *Cornell Hospitality Report* 7 (Dec. 2006), https://ecommons.cornell.edu/bitstream/handle/1813/71149/Tra cey_202006_20The_20cost_20of_20employee_20turnover.pdf?sequence=1 &isAllowed=y (last viewed July 11, 2022).

12. Model Act. §305.

13. *Id.* at § 305(a) ("Except in a benefit enforcement proceeding, no person may bring an action or assert a claim with respect to: (1) failure of a benefit corporation to pursue or create general public benefit or a specific public benefit set forth in its articles of incorporation; or (2) violation of an obligation, duty, or standard of conduct under this [*chapter*].").

14. *Id.* at § 305(c)(2).

15. For example, the groups that are allowed to bring benefit enforcement proceedings are very limited and exclude the beneficiaries of the BC's general and specific public benefits. *Id.* § 305(c) ("A benefit enforcement proceeding may be commenced or maintained only: (1) directly by the benefit corporation; (2) derivatively . . . by: (i) a person or group of persons that owned beneficially or of record at least 2% of the total number of shares of a class or series outstanding at the time of the act or omission complained of; or (ii) a person or group of persons that owned beneficially or of record 5% or more of the outstanding equity interests in an entity of which the benefit corporation is a subsidiary at the time of the act or omission complained of.").

16. Louis D. Brandeis, *Other People's Money and How the Bankers Use It* 92 (Bedford/St. Martin's 1914).

17. Model Act § 401(a).

18. *Id.* § 102.

19. *Id.* § 401(a)(6).

20. *Id.* §401(a)(2).

21. You can also read a detailed analysis of the BIA at Michael B. Dorff, "Why Public Benefit Corporations?," 42 *Delaware Journal of Corporate Law* 77 (2017).

22. Model Act § 402.

23. *Id.* § 302.

24. See, *e.g.*, 8 Del. Gen. Corp. L. §102(b)(7).

25. *Id.* § 302(e).

26. Model Act §301(c).

27. *Id.* §§ 304 (authorizing the appointment of benefit officers), 302(b) ("A benefit director may serve as the benefit officer at the same time as serving as the benefit director.").

28. *Id.* § 302(e) ("[A] benefit director shall not be personally liable for an act or omission in the capacity of a benefit director.").

29. *Id.* § 103.

30. *Id.* §§ 104 (conversion rules), 102 (definition of "minimum status vote").

31. *Id.* § 104(b).

32. 8 Del. Gen. Corp. L. §362(a).

33. *Id.* § 362(b).

34. *Id.*, Model Act §102.

35. *Id.*, § 102.

36. 8 Del. Gen. Corp. L. § 362(a)(1).

37. *Id.* § 362(b).

38. Model Act §102; 8 Del. Gen. Corp. L. § 362(b).

39. 8 Del. Gen. Corp. L. § 362(a). *See also Id.* § 365(a) (using almost identical language to describe the directors' duties).

40. In the securities context, for example, the word *material* has been interpreted to mean information that a reasonable investor would consider important in making a decision such as how to vote or whether to buy or sell a security. *TSC Industries, Inc. v. Northway, Inc.*, 426 U.S. 438, 439 (1976).

41. *Id.* §102.

42. 8 Del. Gen. Corp. L. § 367.

43. *Id.* § 366.

44. For example, the board cannot delegate the authority to vote on any matter that requires a shareholder vote, such as a merger. *See id..* at §§ 141(c)(2) ("[N]o such committee shall have the power or authority in reference to . . . approving or adopting, or recommending to the stockholders, any action or matter (other than the election or removal of directors) expressly required by this chapter to be submitted to stockholders for approval."); § 251(c) (board must submit merger agreement to the shareholders for their approval).

45. *Id,* §102(b)(7).

46. *Id.* § 362(a).

47. *Id.* t § 362(c).

48. *Id.*

49. *Id.* §§ 242(b)(1), 251.

50. Delaware General Assembly, "Delaware House Bill 341," June 23, 2020, https://legis.delaware.gov/BillDetail?legislationId=48122 (last viewed June 30,

2020) (indicating that the bill making these changes had passed both houses of the Delaware legislature and was awaiting the governor's signature to become law).

## Chapter 4: What Public Purposes Can Benefit Corporations Serve?

1. Sramana Mitra, "A Late Bloomer on Building a Legitimate Unicorn: Veela Systems CEO Peter Gassner (Part I)", One Million by One Million Blog, https://www.sramanamitra.com/2016/06/27/a-late-bloomer-on-building-a-legitimate-unicorn-veeva-systems-ceo-peter-gassner-part-1/ (last viewed June 15, 2021).

2. *Id.*

3. *Id.*

4. Veeva Systems, "Veeva Systems Forms Board Committee to Explore Becoming a Public Benefit Corporation," https://www.veeva.com/resources/veeva-forms-board-committee-to-explore-becoming-a-public-benefit-corporation/ (last viewed June 15, 2021).

5. Jill E. Fisch & Steven Davidoff Solomon, "The 'Value' of a Public Benefit Corporation," in *Research Handbook on Corporate Purpose and Personhood* (Elizabeth Pollman & Robert B. Thompson, eds.) (Elgar 2021).

6. Del. Gen. Corp. L. § 362(a)(1).

7. *Id.* § 362(b).

8. B Lab, "Model Benefit Corporation Legislation" (Apr. 17, 2017), https://benefitcorp.net/sites/default/files/Model%20benefit%20corp%20legislation%20_4_17_17.pdf (last viewed June 21, 2021) [hereafter Model Act].

9. See, *e.g.*, William L. Cary, "Federalism and Corporate Law: Reflections upon Delaware," 83 *Yale Law Journal* 663 (1974).

10. "Model Act," 3 supra note 8, https://benefitcorp.net/sites/default/files/Model%20benefit%20corp%20legislation%20_4_17_17.pdf (last viewed June 21, 2021).

11. *Supra* Chapter 9.

12. Del. Gen. Corp. L. § 362(a).

13. *Id.*, at §365(a).

14. Model Act § 102.

15. Del. Gen. Corp. L. § 362(a).

16. Model Act § 301(a)(1).

17. *Supra*, Chapter 2.

18. Cary Funk & Brian Kennedy, "How Americans See Climate Change and the Environment in 7 Charts," *Pew Research Center* (Apr. 21, 2020), https://www.pewresearch.org/fact-tank/2020/04/21/how-americans-see-climate-change-and-the-environment-in-7-charts/ (last viewed June 24, 2021).

19. Aldatu Biosciences, "Our Goal," https://www.aldatubio.com/our-story/ (last viewed June 24, 2021).

20. Drip Drop Hydration, "Our Mission" https://www.dripdrop.com/mission/our-mission (last viewed June 24, 2021).

21. Chiesi U.S.A., "Mission and Values," https://www.chiesiusa.com/about-us/mission-values/ (last viewed June 24, 2021).

22. 42 Strategies, PBC, "Our Mission," https://42strategies.com/about/ (last viewed June 25, 2021).

23. Charity Charge, PBC, "How Does It Work for Individuals?" https://www.charitycharge.com/about-us/ (last viewed June 25, 2021).

24. Acid Zebra, PBC, "Gamify Your Event," https://www.acidzebra.com/ (last viewed June 25, 2021).

25. Agents and Corporations, "Certified B Corp.," https://www.incnow.com/about-us/ (last viewed June 25, 2021).

26. See, e.g., Megafood, a vitamin supplement producer committed to organic agriculture, https://www.megafood.com/who-we-are.html (last viewed July 9, 2021).

27. See, e.g., Aggressively Organic, a company that manufactures and sells Micro Dendritic Pods, that it says can grow as much lettuce in a 10 × 10 room as a traditional farm could grow on a half-acre of land, https://aggressivelyorganic.com (last viewed July 9, 2021).

28. See, e.g., Blazin' Babes, a professional networking organization for women, https://blazinbabes.org (last viewed July 9, 2021).

29. See, e.g., Chronically Capable, a company that helps the disabled and the chronically ill find flexible and remote work opportunities, https://www.wearecapable.org/about (last viewed July 9, 2021).

30. See, e.g., Enlight, a company that trains Ugandans to become solar power installers, https://www.enlightinstitute.org/solartrainings (last viewed July 9, 2021).

31. See, e.g., Shadow, a free app that helps reunite lost pets with their families, https://shadowapp.com/ (last viewed July 9, 2021).

32. 26 U.S.C. § 501(c)(3).

33. *Bob Jones University v. U.S.*, 461 U.S. 574 (1983).

34. Rev. Ruling 78–305, 1978–2 C.B. 172 (1978).

35. ExxonMobil, "Sustainability: Environmental Protection," https://corporate.exxonmobil.com/Sustainability/Environmental-protection (last viewed July 8, 2021).

## Chapter 5: Purpose Enforcement Mechanisms

1. https://www.youtube.com/watch?v=j9x15lR9VIg (last viewed Apr, 7, 2022).

2. Daniel Victor, "Pepsi Pulls Ad Accused of Trivializing Black Lives Matter," *New York Times*, Apr. 5, 2017, https://www.nytimes.com/2017/04/05/business/kendall-jenner-pepsi-ad.html (last viewed Apr. 7, 2022).

3. , *Id.*; Alexander Smith, "Pepsi Pulls Controversial Kendall Jenner Ad after Outcry," *NBC News*, Apr. 5, 2017, https://www.nbcnews.com/news/nbcblk/pepsi-ad-kendall-jenner-echoes-black-lives-matter-sparks-anger-n742811 (last viewed Apr. 7, 2022).

4. *Id.*, Smith.

5. Porter Novelli, "Purpose Perception: Implicit Association Study" (2021), at 17, https://www.porternovelli.com/wp-content/uploads/2021/02/Porter-Novelli -Purpose-Perception-Implicit-Association-Study.pdf (last viewed Apr. 11, 2022).

6. *Id.* at 11.

7. Edelman, *Edelman Trust Barometer 2022* 13–16, https://www.edelman.com/sites/g /files/aatuss191/files/2022-08/2022%20Edelman%20Trust%20Barometer%20Spe cial%20Report%20Trust%20in%20the%20Workplace%20FINAL.pdf (last viewed Nov. 12, 2022).

8. Rachel Barton, Kevin Quiring, & Bill Theofilou, "From Me to We: The Rise of the Purpose-Led Brand" (Dec. 5, 2018), https://www.accenture.com/us-en/in sights/strategy/brand-purpose?c=strat_competitiveagilnovalue_10437227&n= mrl_1118 (last viewed Apr. 11, 2022).

9. *Id.*

10. Biljana Cvetanovski, Orsi Jojart, Brian Gregg, Eric Hazan, & Jesko Perrey, "The Growth Triple Play: Creativity, Analytics, and Purpose" (June 21, 2021), https://www.mckinsey.com/business-functions/marketing-and-sales/our-insights/ the-growth-triple-play-creativity-analytics-and-purpose (last viewed Apr. 11, 2022).

11. Vittorio Cerulli & Annabel Beales, "How Can We Save Purpose from Purpose-Wash?" (Sept. 13, 2019), https://businessfightspoverty.org/how-can-we -save-purpose-from-purpose-wash-2/ (last viewed Apr. 11, 2022) (citing a report by Business in the Community).

12. Michael B. Dorff, *Indispensable and Other Myths: Why the CEO Pay Experiment Failed and How to Fix It* (University of California Press 2014).

13. David I. Walker, "The Economic (In) Significance of Executive Pay ESG Incentives," (Feb. 14, 2022), https://ssrn.com/abstract=4034877 (last viewed Apr. 11, 2022).

14. *Id.* at 23.

15. Tom Gosling & Phillippa O'Connor, "Executive Pay and ESG Performance," *Harvard Law School Forum on Corporate Governance* (Apr. 12, 2021), https://corpgov.law. harvard.edu/2021/04/12/executive-pay-and-esg-performance/ (last viewed Apr.11, 2022).

16. B Lab, "Model Benefit Corporation Legislation" (Apr. 17, 2017), https:// benefitcorp.net/sites/default/files/Model%20benefit%20corp%20legislation%20_ 4_17_17.pdf (last viewed June 21, 2021) [hereafter Model Act]. Model Act § 305.

17. *Id.*

18. See, *e.g.,* Cal. Corp. Code § 14623; New Mexico Statutes Ann. § 53-12-7(G)(2).

19. Del. Gen. Corp. L. § 367.

20. *Id.* § 364.

21. *Supra,* Chapter 3.

22. *United Food and Commercial Workers v. Zuckerberg,* 262 A.3d 1034 (Del. 2021).

23. For example, see *Shields v. Singleton,* 15 Cal. App. 4th 1611 (1993) (laws of Cal-

ifornia and Delaware in regard to evaluating demand futility in a derivative suit are identical).

24. Yahoo Finance, https://finance.yahoo.com/quote/WRBY/ (last viewed May 3, 2022).

25. New Mexico Statutes Ann. §53-12-7(G)(1) (2021).

26. Cal. Corp. Code § 14623. New York does not provide for benefit enforcement proceedings at all, but presumably the balancing requirement could still be enforced by a traditional derivative suit. Derivative suits in New York State may be brought by any shareholder who was a shareholder from the time of the action that is the subject of the suit through the end of the litigation. New York B.C.L. § 626(b).

27. Model Act § 301(d); Del. Gen. Corp. L. § 365(b). *also, e.g.*, New York B.C.L. § 1707 (c).

28. Model Act § 301(c).

29. For a discussion of attorneys' fees in derivative suits, *see Americas Mining Corp. v. Theriault*, 51 A.3d 1213 (Del. 2012).

30. See, *e.g.*, Cal. Corp. Code § 14623(c) (benefit corporation not liable in damages but no express liability protection for directors); New Mexico Statutes Ann. § 53-12-7 (no express liability protection); New York B.C.L. § 1707 (no express liability protection).

31. Del. Gen. Corp. L. § 102(b)(7).

32. Model Act § 301(e); Del. Gen. Corp. L. § 365(b).

33. *Smith v. Van Gorkom*, 488 A.2d 858 (Del. 1985).

34. Model Act § 401.

35. Del. Gen. Corp. L. § 366.

36. Louis D. Brandeis, "What Publicity Can Do," 58 *Harper's Weekly* 10 (Dec. 20, 1913).

37. *Supra* Chapters 6 & 7.

38. 17 C.F.R. §229.

39. Model Act §§ 102, 401(a).

40. Del. Gen. Corp. L. § 366(b).

41. J. Haskell Murray, "An Early Report on Benefit Reports," 118 *West Virginia Law Review* 25 (2015); Maxime Verheyden, "Public Reporting by Benefit Corporations: Importance, Compliance, and Recommendations," 14 *Hastings Business Law Journal* 37 (2018). Three states do impose penalties on companies that fail to file their benefit reports: Minnesota, New Hampshire, and New Jersey. Brent J. Horton, "Rising to Their Full Potential: How a Uniform Disclosure Regime Will Empower Benefit Corporations," 9 *Harvard Business Law Review* 101, 127–28 (2019).

42. Murray, *supra* note 41; Verhevden, *supra* note 41.

43. Minnesota Statutes Annotated §304A.301(5).

44. Verhevden, *supra* note 41.

45. B Lab has at least one competitor, Responsible 100, but B Lab has roughly ten times as many customers as Responsible 100 as of this writing. Responsible

100, "Frequently Asked Questions," https://responsible100.com/FAQs.html (last viewed May 5, 2022) (claiming to work with over 600 businesses); B Lab, "Make Business a Force for Good," https://www.bcorporation.net/en-us/?_ga=2.202562 129.1959003398.1651796475-1065746884.1651620296 (last viewed May 5, 2022) (claiming to have certified over 5,000 companies). There are other entities that are at least adjacent to what B Lab does, but no others attempt a comprehensive measure of a company's policies across all five dimensions. Horton, *supra* note 41, at 129 (describing other measures such as the Global Reporting Initiative—which allows users to focus on only one of three dimensions (environmental, economic, or social)—and Green America—which focuses only on environmental concerns). The Sustainability Accounting Standards Board perhaps comes closest to what B Lab and Responsible 100 do, but SASB's metrics are focused on factors that have an impact on profits; environmental and social concerns are not valued in their own right. Sustainability Accounting Standards Board, "SASB Conceptual Framework," at 9 (2017), https://www.sasb.org/wp-content/uploads/2020/02/SASB_ Conceptual-Framework_WATERMARK.pdf (last viewed May 6, 2022) ("SASB standards address the sustainability topics that are reasonably likely to have material impacts on the financial condition or operating performance of companies in an industry.") The Conceptual Framework is under review, but this core concept is not being questioned. Sustainability Accounting Standards Board, "Proposed Changes to the SASB Conceptual Framework & Rules of Procedure," at 4 (2020) https://www.sasb.org/wp-content/uploads/2021/07/PCP-package_vF.pdf (last viewed May 6, 2022) ("[I]t is not the intent of the Standards Board to fundamentally change its approach to sustainability accounting or the processes it uses to conduct standard setting.").

46. B Lab, "About B Corp Certification," https://www.bcorporation.net/en-us/ certification (last viewed May 5, 2022).

47. *Id.*

48. B Lab, "B Impact Assessment," https://www.bcorporation.net/en-us/ programs-and-tools/b-impact-assessment (last viewed May 5, 2022).

49. *Id.*

50. B Lab, "The Legal Requirement for Certified B Corporations," https://www .bcorporation.net/en-us/about-b-corps/legal-requirements (last viewed May 6, 2022).

51. B Lab, "About B Corp Certification," https://www.bcorporation.net/en-us/ certification (last viewed May 6, 2022); *compare* B Lab, "Pending B Corps," https:// www.bcorporation.net/en-us/programs-and-tools/pending-b-corps (last viewed May 6, 2022) *with* B Lab, "B Corp Certification Guide for Large Enterprises," https://assets.ctfassets.net/l575jm7617lt/2Q8x6Q7QoOWnoVDgVUuu2R/cbdd 1d3be195247819121862d296ce8e/Certification_Guide_-_Large_Enterprise_12 _Jan_2022.pdff (last viewed May 6, 2022).

52. B Lab, "About B Lab," https://www.bcorporation.net/en-us/movement/ about-b-lab (last viewed May 6, 2022).

53. B Lab, "Standards Advisory Council," https://www.bcorporation.net/en-us/standards/advisory-council (last viewed May 6, 2022).

54. B Lab, "About B Corp Certification," *supra* note 51.

55. B Lab, "Preparing for the Assessment Review: Documentation Tips," https://kb.bimpactassessment.net/support/solutions/articles/43000501783-preparing-for-the-assessment-review-documentation-tips (last viewed May 6, 2022); Michael B. Dorff, "Assessing the Assessment: B Lab's Effort to Measure Companies' Benevolence," 40 *Seattle Law Review* 515, 540 (2017).

56. Dorff, *supra* note 55, at 527.

57. *Id.* at 534.

58. *Id.* at 527.

59. *Id.* at 532–34.

60. *Id.* at 535–37.

61. B Lab, "B Impact Assessment," https://www.bcorporation.net/en-us/programs-and-tools/b-impact-assessment (last viewed May 5, 2022).

62. Dorff, *supra* note 55, at 537–39.

63. Cal. Corp. Code §§ 5110, 5111.

64. Anup Malani & Eric Posner, "The Case for For-Profit Charities," 93 *Virginia Law Review* 2017, 2018 (2007).

65. Emilie Aguirre, "Beyond Profit," 54 *U.C. Davis Law Review* 2077 (2021).

66. Aguirre's plan also requires the BCs and PBCs subject to her proposal to tie a meaningful component of their executive compensation to the companies' progress in achieving their social missions. *Id.* I think this proposal is unlikely to achieve what she hopes for a variety of reasons. Most important, traditional corporations have attempted to achieve greater financial success by tying executive pay to various financial metrics, especially stock price, for over forty years, yet there is no persuasive evidence that tying executive pay to corporate performance results in better corporate performance. Dorff, *supra* note 12. There seems little reason to believe that BCs and PBCs would have any greater luck tying executive pay to companies' social performance.

67. David Gelles, "Billionaire No More: Patagonia Founder Gives Away the Company," *New York Times*, Sept. 14, 2022, nytimes.com/2022/09/14/climate/patagonia-climate-philanthropy-chouinard.html#:~:text=Rather%20than%20selling%20the%20company,trust%20and%20a%20nonprofit%20organization (last viewed Nov. 13, 2022).

68. *Id.*

69. *Id.*

70. Another wealthy person who made a similar decision though to pursue the opposite values was Barre Seid, who gave away 100 percent of his electronics company to a nonprofit organization devoted to conservative causes, including efforts to *prevent* action on climate change. *Id.* Seid donated his company to a § 501(c)(3) organization and so did garner a very substantial tax deduction, unlike the Chouinards. *Id.*

71. Impact Makers, "About Impact Makers," https://www.impactmakers.com/aboutus/ (last viewed May 9, 2022).

72. *Pirron v. Impact Makers,* No. CL19003073–00, Complaint (May 8, 2019), https://michaelpirron.com/wp-content/uploads/2019/05/Pirron-v-Impact-Makers_Stamped-w-Exhibits.pdf [hereinafter "Complaint"].

73. *Id.* at 8–9.

74. *Id.* at 9–12.

75. *Id.* at 11–12, 16–19.

76. Brent J. Horton, "Terra Incognita: Applying the Entire Fairness Standard of Review to Benefit Corporations," 22 *University of Pennsylvania Journal of Business Law* 842, 897 (2020).

77. 26 U.S.C. § 4958.

78. Dana Brakman Reiser & Steven A. Dean, *Social Enterprise Law: Trust, Public Benefit, and Capital Markets* (Oxford University Press 2017).

79. *Id.*, Reiser and Dean also proposed a purely private ordering method of reinforcing companies' social mission through their financing method. They created the notion of flexible, low-yield debt, or "FLY paper." FLY paper would have many of the aspects of traditional debt instruments, but the lenders would have the power to convert their debt to equity—perhaps even a controlling stake—should the borrowing BC or PBC fail to live up to its social mission. FLY paper lenders would also have the right to veto any change of control transaction. Their idea is that "impact-first investors" (what I call concessionary investors) would lend money to BCs and PBCs this way. As Reiser and Dean recognize, there are many problems with this approach, foremost of which is that it requires investors willing to accept a lower than market return for a long period of time while still investing resources in monitoring and policing companies' pursuit of a social mission. Their proposal seems unlikely to me either to provide a source of ample funding to BCs or PBCs or to enforce their social missions.

80. Emily Winston, "Benefit Corporations and the Separation of Benefit and Control," 39 *Cardozo Law Review* 1783 (2018).

81. Sarah Dadush has also argued persuasively for involving beneficiaries when establishing governance standards for BCs and PBCs. Sarah Dadush, "A New Blueprint for Regulating Social Enterprises," in *Cambridge Handbook of Social Enterprise Law* (Benjamin Means & Joseph Yockey, eds.) (Cambridge University Press 2018).

82. *Infra*, Chapter 8.

83. Winston, *supra* note 80.

84. Model Act §302(a).

85. *Id.* § 302(c).

86. *Id.* § 304.

87. *Id.* § 304(b).

88. See, *e.g.,* R. J. Iannotti, "Effect of Role-Taking Experiences on Role Taking, Empathy, Altruism, and Aggression," 14(2) *Developmental Psychology* 119 (1978); Wei

Peng, Mira Lee, & Carrie Heeter, "The Effects of a Serious Game on Role-Taking and Willingness to Help," 60 *Journal of Communication* 723 (Dec. 2010).

89. Frederick H. Alexander, *Benefit Corporation Law and Governance: Pursuing Profit with Purpose* 135–38 (Berrett-Koehler 2017).

90. *Id.* at 142–46.

91. *Id.* at 149–52.

92. *Id.* at 152.

93. *Id.* at 153  55. Note that recently a few states, including Delaware, have passed legislation enabling a new form of business organization, the benefit limited liability company, that is analogous to a BC or PBC for a corporation but takes the form of a limited liability company. It remains to be seen how successful this experiment will be. *Id.* at 155.

94. GA Code §§ 14-2-1801 to 14-2-1807 (2021); Ala. Code §§ 10A-2A-17.01 to 10A-2A-17.06 (2021).

95. I do not mean to argue that the combination is impossible to overcome. Etsy's story is certainly a cautionary tale. But the fact that this combination is not invincible does not undercut the point that it is incredibly powerful.

## Chapter 6: Should Entrepreneurs Choose a Hybrid Form?

1. Nick Paumgarten, "Patagonia's Philosopher-King," *New Yorker*, Sept. 12, 2016, https://www.newyorker.com/magazine/2016/09/19/patagonias-philosopher-king (last viewed Aug. 11, 2022).

2. Patagonia, Inc., "What We're Doing about Our Plastic Problem," https://www.patagonia.com/stories/what-were-doing-about-our-plastic-problem/story-72799.html (last viewed Aug. 11, 2022).

3. Paumgarten, *supra* note 1.

4. Lemonade, Inc., "Executive Management," https://investor.lemonade.com/governance/executive-management/default.aspx (last viewed Aug. 11, 2022).

5. Lemonade, Inc., "The Lemonade Giveback," https://www.lemonade.com/giveback (last viewed Aug. 11, 2022).

6. Omar Faridi, "Insurtech Lemonade CEO Daniel Schreiber Shares Insights about Their Unique Business Model," *Crowdfund Insider*, July 27, 2021, https://www.crowdfundinsider.com/2021/07/178358-insurtech-lemonade-ceo-daniel-schreiber-shares-insights-about-their-unique-business-model/ (last viewed Aug. 11, 2022); Lemonade, Inc., "How Lemonade Works," https://www.lemonade.com/?f=1 (last viewed Aug, 11, 2022).

7. 8 Del. Gen. Corp. L. § 363 (requiring approval of an absolute majority of the outstanding shares to convert to a PBC); Model Act § 104 (requiring approval by a minimum status vote—two-thirds of the outstanding shares—for a traditional corporation to convert to a BC).

8. Delaware Secretary of State, "The Honest Company Entity Details," https://icis.corp.delaware.gov/Ecorp/EntitySearch/NameSearch.aspx (last viewed Aug. 8, 2022).

9. Derek Blasberg, "How Jessica Alba Built a Billion-Dollar Business Empire," *Vanity Fair*, Jan. 2016, https://www.vanityfair.com/style/2015/11/jessica-alba-honest-company-business-empire (last viewed June 23, 2020).

10. *Id.*

11. *Id.*

12. Serena Ng, "No Longer a Unicorn, Jessica Alba's Honest Co. Struggles to Grow," *Wall Street Journal*, Jan. 5, 2018, https://www.wsj.com/articles/no-longer-a-unicorn-jessica-albas-honest-co-faces-growth-challenges-1515157203 (last viewed June 24, 2020).

13. Blasberg, *supra* note 9.

14. The Honest Company, "The Honest Company: Proud to Be a B Corp," Dec. 31, 2012, https://www.honest.com/blog/lifestyle/purpose/the-honest-company-proud-to-be-a-b-corp/413.html (last viewed June 24, 2020).

15. Julia Horowitz, "Jessica Alba's The Honest Company Can't Catch a Break," *CNNMoney*, June 12, 2017, https://money.cnn.com/2017/06/12/news/companies/honest-company-problems/index.html (last viewed June 24, 2020).

16. Blasberg, *supra* note 9; Ng, *supra* note 12.

17. Horowitz, *supra* note 15.

18. Ng, *supra* note 12.

19. The Honest Company, *supra* note 14.

20. B the Change, "New Benefit Corp Sets the Bar for Being a Conscious Business in the CBD Business Boom," June 5, 2019, https://bthechange.com/new-benefit-corp-sets-the-bar-for-being-a-conscious-business-in-the-cbd-business-boom-28fabb6dd475 (last viewed June 25, 2020).

21. *Id.*

22. *Id.*

23. 26 U.S.C. Subchapter C.

24. The Honest Company, "Our Honest Purpose," https://www.honest.com/purpose (last viewed Aug. 8, 2022).

25. Chapter 1, *supra*.

26. *Id.*

27. 8 Del. Gen. Corp. L. § 367; Model Act § 305.

28. 8 Del. Gen. Corp. L. § 366 (b); Model Act § 401.

29. , *e.g.*, Rule 10b-5, 17 C.F.R. §240.10b-5 (unlawful to make any false or misleading material statement in connection with the purchase or sale of a security using interstate commerce or a national securities exchange or the mails).

30. Horowitz, *supra* note 15 (discussing suits alleging that The Honest Company misled consumers about the ingredients in its soap, laundry detergent, and baby formula, and that its sunscreen was not "natural" and failed to protect users from harmful solar radiation).

31. Delaware Division of Corporations, "DE PBC List 9.5.2019," on file with author.

32. Delaware Division of Corporations, "2019 Annual Report Statistics," on file with author.

33. In September 2017, the Delaware Division of Corporations was kind enough to furnish me with a list of all Delaware PBCs. At that time, there were not quite 1,000 PBCS. Two years later, the division provided an updated list with nearly 2,000 PBCs. Both lists are on file with me.

34. One case that might have raised some of these issues in Virginia was settled in 2019. John Reid Blackwell, "Richmond-Based Impact Makers and Its Founder Settle Lawsuit," *Richmond Times-Dispatch*, June 18, 2019, https://www.richmond.com /business/richmond-based-impact-makers-and-its-founder-settle-lawsuit/article_ f591f6b8-3925-5c9e-9f81-210480a31a34.html (last viewed June 30, 2020).

35. Model Act, §§ 102 (defining "Minimum status vote"), 104 (requiring a minimum status vote for conversion to a BC).

36. 8 Del. Gen. Corp. L. § 363 (2019). Originally, Delaware required shareholders to approve conversion by an astoundingly difficult to achieve 90 percent. Sandra B. Feldman, "Two Recent Changes Make It Easier to Convert to a Delaware Public Benefit Corporation," *Wolters Kluwer*, Oct. 8, 2015, https://ct.wolterskluwer.com/ resource-center/news/two-recent-changes-make-it-easier-convert-delaware -public-benefit-corporation (last viewed June 30, 2020).

37. Delaware General Assembly, "Delaware House Bill 341," June 23, 2020, https://legis.delaware.gov/BillDetail?legislationId=48122 (last viewed June 30, 2020) (indicating that the bill making these changes had passed both houses of the Delaware legislature and was awaiting the governor's signature to become law).

38. Warby Parker, Inc., "Buy a Pair, Give a Pair," https://www.warbyparker.com /buy-a-pair-give-a-pair (last viewed Aug. 8, 2022).

39. Yuliya Chernova, "Lemonade to Test IPO Waters as a Public Benefit Corporation," *Wall Street Journal*, June 12, 2020, https://www.wsj.com/articles/lemonade-to -test-ipo-waters-as-a-public-benefit-corporation-11591995018 (last viewed June 19, 2020).

40. Ryan Deffenbaugh, "Warby Parker Public Offering Brings Test for Companies Promising Societal Good," *Crain's New York Business* (Aug. 26, 2021), https:// www.crainsnewyork.com/technology/warby-parker-ipo-public-offering-brings -test-companies-promising-societal-good (last viewed Aug. 8, 2022).

41. Nielsen, "Global Consumers Are Willing to Put Their Money Where Their Heart Is When It Comes to Goods and Services from Companies Committed to Social Responsibility" (June 17, 2014), https://www.nielsen.com/us/en/insights/ reports/2015/the-sustainability-imperative.html (last viewed July 1, 2020); *see also* Mehdi Miremadi, Christopher Musso, & Ulrich Weihe, "How Much Will Consumers Pay to Go Green?," *McKinsey Quarterly* (Oct. 2012), https://www.mckinsey .com/business-functions/sustainability/our-insights/how-much-will-consumers -pay-to-go-green (last viewed July 1, 2020) (as many as 70 percent of consumers would pay 5% more for green products of similar quality).

42. Patagonia, "Family Business," https://www.patagonia.com/family-business/ ; Patagonia, "Activism," https://www.patagonia.com/activism/ (last viewed July 1, 2020).

43. State Bags, "Backpacks," https://statebags.com/collections/shop-backpacks (last viewed March 30, 2023) (the Lorimer Diaper Bag was listed as selling for $198 on March 30, 2023, with several types of backpack selling for $150 or more).

44. State Bags, "Give. Back. Pack.," https://www.statebags.com/pages/give-back -pack (last viewed July 1, 2020).

45. Michael B. Dorff, "Interview with Taylor Myers," Aug. 31, 2015, recording and transcript on file with the author.

46. Deloitte, "The 2016 Deloitte Millennial Survey," http://www2.deloitte.com /content/dam/Deloitte/global/Documents/About-Deloitte/gx-millenial-survey -2016-exec-summary.pdf. (last viewed July 2, 2020).

47. Edelman, "Edelman Trust Barometer 2022," pp. 13–16, https://www.edel man.com/sites/g/files/aatuss191/files/2022-08/2022%20Edelman%20Trust%20 Barometer%20Special%20Report%20Trust%20in%20the%20Workplace%20FI NAL.pdf (last viewed Nov. 12, 2022).

48. Charles Fishman, "The War for Talent," *Fast Company* (July 31, 1998), https: //www.fastcompany.com/34512/war-talent ("According to a yearlong study con-ducted by a team from McKinsey & Co.—a study involving 77 companies and almost 6,000 managers and executives—the most important corporate resource over the next 20 years will be talent: smart, sophisticated businesspeople who are technologically literate, globally astute, and operationally agile") (last viewed July 2, 2020); Susan Sorenson, "How Employee Engagement Drives Growth," *Gallup* (June 20, 2013), https://www.gallup.com/workplace/236927/employee-engagement -drivesgrowth.aspx ("Given the timing of the eighth iteration of this study, it also confirmed that employee engagement continues to be an important predictor of company performance even in a tough economy.") (last viewed July 2, 2020).

49. Theresa Agovino, "To Have and to Hold," *SHRM* (Feb. 23, 2019), https:// www.shrm.org/hr-today/news/all-things-work/pages/to-have-and-to-hold.aspx ("Each employee departure costs about one-third of that worker's annual earnings, including expenses such as recruiter fees, temporary replacement workers and lost productivity, according to the Work Institute.") (last viewed July 2, 2020).

50. Michael B. Dorff, "Interview with Michael Pirron," Nov. 25, 2015, recording and transcript on file with the author.

51. Abhilash Mudaliar & Hannah Dithrich, "Sizing the Impact Investment Market," (Apr. 2019), https://thegiin.org/assets/Sizing%20the%20Impact% 20Investing%20Market_webfile.pdf (finding that there were over 1,300 invest-ment organizations managing $502 billion in impact investment capital in 2018) (last viewed July 2,2020); US SIF The Forum for Sustainable and Responsible Investment, "Sustainable Investing Assets Reach $12 Trillion as Reported by the US SIF Foundation's Biennial Report on US Sustainable, Responsible and Impact Investing Trends" (Oct. 31, 2018), https://www.ussif.org/files/US%20SIF%20

Trends%20Report%202018%20Release.pdf (reporting that sustainable, responsible, and impact investing assets account for $12 trillion in assets under management in the U.S. alone) (last viewed July 2, 2020).

52. Michael B. Dorff, James Hicks, & Steven Davidoff Solomon, "The Future or Fancy? An Empirical Study of Public Benefit Corporations," 11 *Harvard Business Law Review* 113 (2020).

53. Constance L. Hays, "Ben & Jerry's to Unilever, with Attitude," *New York Times*, Apr. 13, 2000, https://www.nytimes.com/2000/04/13/business/ben-jerry-s-to-unilever-with-attitude.html (last viewed July 6, 2020).

54. Anthony Page & Robert A. Katz, "The Truth about Ben and Jerry's," *Stanford Social Innovation Review*, Fall 2012, https://ssir.org/articles/entry/the_truth_about_ben_and_jerrys#:~:text=If%20Ben%20%26%20Jerry's%20was%20a,this%20sale%20was%20its%20Altamont.&text='The%20board%20was%20legally%20required,public%20they%20had%20no%20choice.%E2%80%9D (last viewed July 6, 2020).

55. *Id.* (so arguing).

56. Michael B. Dorff, "Why Public Benefit Corporations?," 42 *Delaware Journal of Corporate Law* 77 (2017).

57. Crowdspending, "How It Works," www.crowdspending.com (last viewed July 6, 2020).

58. Michael B. Dorff, "Interview with Chris Norton," July 31, 2015, recording and transcript on file with the author.

59. 26 U.S.C. § 501(c)(3).

60. Michael B. Dorff, "Interview with Tayde Aburto," July 30, 2015, recording and transcript on file with the author.

## Chapter 7: Should Investors Support Hybrid Forms?

1. Nick DeCosta-Klipa, "A Look Back at Paul Tsongas's Unorthodox Bid for the White House, 25 Years Later," *Boston.com*, Mar. 19, 2017, https://www.boston.com/news/politics/2017/03/19/a-look-back-at-paul-tsongass-unorthodox-bid-for-the-white-house-25-years-later/ (last viewed July 26, 2021).

2. Paul Tsongas, "Archive," in *Tampa Bay Times*, Oct. 10, 2005), https://www.tampabay.com/archive/1992/03/20/text-of-tsongas-speech/ (last viewed July 26, 2021).

3. Robert N. Lussier, "Reasons Why Small Businesses Fail: And How to Avoid Failure," 1(2) *Entrepreneurial Executive* 10 (Fall 1996) (entrepreneurs whose businesses failed were most likely to cite lack of capital as a cause of the failure); Janet Rovenpor, "Explaining the E-Commerce Shakeout: Why Did So Many Internet-Based Businesses Fail?," 3(1) *e-Service Journal* 53 (Fall 2004) (start-ups that failed tended to run out of cash within about a year of founding).

4. Neal E. Boudette, "Tesla Has First Profitable Year, But Competition Is Growing," *New York Times*, Jan. 27, 2021, https://www.nytimes.com/2021/01/27/business/tesla-earnings.html (last viewed July 26, 2021).

5. Triodos Investment Management, "Strategies," https://www.triodos-im.com/about-us (last viewed July 26, 2021).

6. Triodos Investment Management, "Mission," https://www.triodos-im.com/about-us (last viewed July 26, 2021).

7. Triodos Investment Management, "Impact Highlights," https://www.triodos-im.com/impact-report/2020/energy-and-climate (last viewed July 26, 2021).

8. Triodos Bank, "Towards a Low Carbon Economy" at 29 (Sept. 2019), https://www.triodos.com/binaries/content/assets/tbho/position-papers/triodos-bank_ec-paper_towards-a-low-carbon-economy_sep-2019-3.pdf (last viewed July 26, 2021).

9. Triodos Bank, "Corporate Governance," https://www.triodos.com/governance#organisational-structure (last viewed July 27, 2021).

10. See, *e.g.*, Costanza Consolandi, Robert G. Eccles, & Giampaolo Gabbi, "How Material Is a Material Issue? Stock Returns and the Financial Relevance and Financial Intensity of ESG Materiality" (Apr. 12, 2020), https://ssrn.com/abstract=3574547 (last viewed Nov. 30, 2022); Gunnar Friede, Timo Busch, & Alexander Bassen, "ESG and Financial Performance: Aggregated Evidence from More Than 2000 Empirical Studies," 5 *Journal of Sustainable Finance & Investment* 210 (2015); Mozaffar Khan, George Serafeim, & Aaron Yoon, "Corporate Sustainability: First Evidence on Materiality," 91 *Accounting Review* 1697 (2016); Sakis Kotsantonis & Vittoria Bufalari, "Do Sustainable Banks Outperform? Driving Value Creation through ESG Practices," *Report of the Global Alliance for Banking on Values* (GABV) (2019), https://www2.deloitte.com/content/dam/Deloitte/lu/Documents/financial-services/Banking/lu-do-sustainable-banks-outperform-driving-value-creation-through-ESG-practices-report-digital.pdf (last viewed Nov. 30, 2022); Kelly van Heijningen, "The Impact of ESG Factor Materiality on Stock Performance of Firms," Erasmus Platform for Sustainable Value Creation working paper (2019), https://www.rsm.nl/fileadmin/Faculty-Research/Centres/EPSVC/The_impact_of_ESG_factor_materiality_on_stock_performance_of_firms_Heijningen.pdf (last viewed Nov. 30, 2022).

11. Sherbrooke Capital, "Our Strategy," https://www.sherbrookecapital.com/our-strategy/ (last viewed July 27, 2021).

12. Vanguard, "Vanguard S&P 500 ETF," https://investor.vanguard.com/etf/profile/fees/voo (last viewed July 28, 2021).

13. Investors can purchase a diversified portfolio of real property with a real estate investment trust. They can buy portions of artwork with companies like the Italian company Art Share. https://www.artsharesales.com/come-funziona/ (last viewed July 28, 2021).

14. Frederick H. Alexander, *Benefit Corporation Law and Governance: Pursing Profit with Purpose* 53–54 (Berrett-Koehler 2017).

15. A recent global survey by BNP Paribas found that a surprisingly large 22 percent of investors surveyed said that all or most of their portfolio incorporated ESG. Trevor Allen *et al.*, *The ESG Global Survey 2021* at 11, BNP Paribas (2021), https://www.theia.org/sites/default/files/2021-09/The%20ESG%20Global%20Survey%202021.pdf (last viewed Aug. 8, 2022). Even these ESG-focused investors, though, were motivated by financial considerations such as companies' brand and reputa-

tion and the improved long-term returns associated with ESG investing rather than an independent desire to promote social good. *Id.* at 7.

16. *Id.*

17. See, *e.g.*, Timothy Puko & Ted Mann, "Washington's Oil Lobby Pivoted on Climate Change—and Made No One Happy," *Wall Street Journal*, July 28, 2021, https://www.wsj.com/articles/api-oil-gas-lobby-reckoning-climate-change-116274 84072 (last viewed July 29, 2021).

18. *Supra,* note 10.

19. Michael B. Dorff, James Hicks, & Steven Davidoff Solomon, "The Future or Fancy? An Empirical Study of Public Benefit Corporations," 11 *Harvard Business Law Review* 113 (2021).

20. *Id.*

21. *Id.*

22. The percentage of Delaware PBCs that secured VC funding was far higher than is typical for traditional Delaware corporations. We cannot read too much into this fact, since it may be the result of a selection effect, but to the extent this data point is meaningful, it bodes well for Delaware PBCs' ability to raise VC funds.

23. *Id.*

24. Ina Steiner, "Etsy Gives Up B Corp Status to Maintain Corporate Structure," *eCommerce Bytes* (Nov. 30, 2017), https://www.ecommercebytes.com/2017/11/30/etsy -gives-b-corp-status-maintain-corporate-structure/ (last viewed Aug. 4, 2021).

25. Benjamin D. Stone & Sarah C. Palmer, "What Are My Exit Options as a Public Benefit Corporation?" *VC Experts*, Oct. 12, 2020), https://blog.vcexperts.com /2020/10/12/what-are-my-exit-options-as-a-public-benefit-corporation/ (last viewed Aug. 4, 2021).

26. Globe Newswire, "Kronos Advanced Technologies Plans Shareholder Meeting and to Become America's First OTC Public Benefit Corporation, Citing Purpose, Accountability, and Transparency," *StreetInsider.com* (July 15, 2020), https: //cooleypubco.com/2021/01/25/corporation-converts-to-pbc/ (last viewed Aug. 4, 2021).

27. Lauren Debter, "Allbirds Valued at over $4 Billion after Stock Surges in IPO," *Forbes*, Nov. 3, 2021, https://www.forbes.com/sites/laurendebter/2021/11/03/ allbirds-shares-soar-after-shoemaker-raises-over-300-million-in-ipo/?sh= 54b107369027 (last viewed Aug. 12, 2022).

28. Amalgamated Financial Corp., "Amalgamated Financial Becomes the First Publicly Traded Financial Services Company to Incorporate as a Public Benefit Corporation" (Mar. 1, 2021), https://www.bloomberg.com/news/articles/2021-03 -26/aerofarms-to-go-public-in-1-2-billion-spring-valley-spac-deal (last viewed Aug. 4, 2021).

29. Jon Swartz, "Greenhouse Company AppHarvest Soars 44% in SPAC Debut," *MarketWatch* (Feb. 1, 2021), https://www.marketwatch.com/story/greehouse -company-appharvests-spac-debuts-11612200621 (last viewed Aug. 4, 2021).

30. Christopher Marquis, "Public Benefit Corporations Flourish in the Public Markets," *Forbes* (June 14, 2021), https://www.forbes.com/sites/christophermarquis/2021/06/14/public-benefit-corporations-flourish-in-the-public-markets/?sh=6d28e524233d.

31. *Id.*

32. Michael Sheetz, "Satellite Imagery Company Planet Goes Public, With $300 Million 'War Chest' After SPAC Deal," *CNBC* (Dec. 8, 2021), https://www.cnbc.com/2021/12/08/satellite-imagery-company-planet-begins-trading-on-the-nyse.html#:~:text=Investing%20in%20Space-,Satellite%20imagery%20company%20Planet%20goes%20public%2C%20with%20%24300%20million,war%20chest'%20after%20SPAC%20deal&text=Satellite%20imagery%20and%20data%20specialist,the%20New%20York%20Stock%20Exchange. (last viewed Aug. 12, 2022).

33. United Therapeutics Corporation, "United Therapeutics Converts to a Public Benefit Corporation Following Shareholder Approval," *PR Newswire* (Sept. 30, 2021), https://www.prnewswire.com/news-releases/united-therapeutics-converts-to-a-public-benefit-corporation-following-shareholder-approval-301388821.html (last viewed Aug. 12, 2022).

34. Cydney Posner, "In a First, a Traditional Corporation Converts to a PBC—Will It Spark a Trend?" *Cooley PubCo* (Jan. 25, 2021), https://cooleypubco.com/2021/01/25/corporation-converts-to-pbc/ (last viewed Aug. 4, 2021).

35. Lauren Hirsch, "With Sales Soaring, Warby Parker Prepares for Its Market Debut," *New York Times*, Sept. 29, 2021), https://www.nytimes.com/2021/09/29/business/warby-parker-stock-price.html (last viewed Aug. 12, 2022).

36. Tomi Kilgore, "Zevia Stock Opens More Than 10% below IPO Price," *MarketWatch* (July 22, 2021), https://www.marketwatch.com/story/zevia-stock-opens-more-than-10-below-ipo-price-2021-07-22?siteid=yhoof2 (last viewed Aug. 4, 2021).

37. Marquis, *supra* note 30.

38. Rick Munarriz, "3 Hot IPO Stocks to Buy in Oct.," *Motley Fool* (Oct. 4, 2020), https://www.fool.com/investing/2020/10/04/3-hot-ipo-stocks-to-buy-in-Oct./ (last viewed Aug. 4, 2021).

39. Swartz, *supra* note 29.

## Chapter 8: How Should Benefit Corporations Balance Profit and Public Good?

1. Lucy Handley, "Dave Gilboa and Neil Blumenthal: A Vision for Business," *CNBC* (Apr. 8, 2020), https://www.cnbc.com/warby-parkers-dave-gilboa-and-neil-blumenthal-a-vision-for-business/ (last viewed Oct. 7, 2021).

2. Steve Denning, "What's Behind Warby Parker's Success?," *Forbes* (Mar. 23, 2016), https://www.forbes.com/sites/stevedenning/2016/03/23/whats-behind-warby-parkers-success/?sh=52a5e56a411a (last viewed Nov. 23, 2022); Handley, *supra* note 1.

3. Claire Ballentine & Francesca Maglione, "Warby Parker Debuts at $6 Billion Valuation. Should You Buy?," *Bloomberg Wealth*, Sept. 29, 2021, https://www.bloom

berg.com/news/articles/2021-09-29/warby-parker-direct-listing-should-you-buy
-now-that-the-company-is-public (last viewed Oct. 7, 2021).

4. Denning, *supra* note 2.

5. *Id.*

6. Warby Parker Prospectus (Sept. 29, 2021), https://www.sec.gov/edgar/browse
/?CIK=1504776&owner=exclude (last viewed Oct. 7, 2021).

7. Ballentine & Maglione, *supra* note 3.

8. Ryan Deffenbaugh, "Warby Parker Public Offering Brings Test for Companies Promising Societal Good," *Crain's New York Business* (Aug. 26, 2021), https://
www.crainsnewyork.com/technology/warby-parker-ipo-public-offering-brings
-test-companies-promising-societal-good (last viewed Oct. 7, 2021); Warby Parker
Prospectus, *supra* note 6, at 1, 7.

9. Del. Gen. Corp. L. § 362(a). *also* Del. Gen. Corp. L. § 365(a) (using almost
identical language to describe the directors' duties).

10. Warby Parker Prospectus, *supra* note 6, at 154.

11. *Id.* at 62.

12. See, *e.g.,* Allbirds, Inc. S-1 p. 52–53 (Aug. 31, 2021) https://www.sec.gov/Ar
chives/edgar/data/0001653909/000162828021017824/allbirdss-1.htm (last viewed
Oct. 12, 2021); Coursera, Inc. S-1 pp.169–170 (Mar. 5, 2021), https://www.sec.gov/
edgar/browse/?CIK=1651562&owner=exclude (last viewed Oct. 12, 2021); Laureate
Education, Inc. Schedule 14A at p. 13 (Apr. 16, 2021), https://www.sec.gov/Archives/
edgar/data/0000912766/000110465921051085/tm212461-1_def14a.htm (last
viewed Oct. 12, 2021); United Therapeutics Corporation Schedule 14A at pp. 5–6
(Sept. 30, 2021), https://www.sec.gov/Archives/edgar/data/1082554/000120677421
002244/uthr3924131-def14a.htm#OurViewonUnitedTherapeuticsPBCBalancing
Obligation5 (last viewed Oct. 12, 2021); Veeva Systems Inc. Schedule 14A at p.27
(May 10, 2021), https://www.sec.gov/Archives/edgar/data/0001393052/00011403
6121016621/nc10024207x1_def14a.htm (last viewed Oct. 12, 2021); Vital Farms
Inc. Schedule 14A (Apr. 26, 2021) (not mentioned at all), https://www.sec.gov/Ar
chives/edgar/data/0001579733/000119312521131467/d111648ddef14a.htm (last
viewed Oct. 12, 2021);

13. Allbirds S-1, *supra* note 12.

14. United Therapeutics Schedule 14A, *supra* note 12, at 6. *also* Coursera S-1,
*supra* note 12 ("[W]e believe that our commitment to achieving our public benefit
goals will not materially affect the financial interests of our stockholders.").

15. Mark J. Lowenstein, "Benefit Corporations: A Challenge in Corporate Governance," 68 *Business Lawyer* 1007 (2013).

16. Ian B. Lee, "Efficiency and Ethics in the Debate about Shareholder Primacy,"
31 *Delaware Journal of Corporate Law* 533, 537–38 (2006).

17. Robert Flannigan, "The Economics of Fiduciary Accountability," 32 *Delaware
Journal of Corporate Law* 393, 396 at n.12 (2007).

18. Brian Galle, "Social Enterprise: Who Needs It?" 54 *Boston College Law Review*

2025, 2031 (2013); David Groshoff, Contrepreneurship? "Examining Social Enterprise Legislation's Feel-Good Governance Giveaways," 16 *University of Pennsylvania Journal of Business Law* 233, 277 (2013); Lee, *supra* note 16; Brett H. McDonnell, "From Duty and Disclosure to Power and Participation in Social Enterprise," 70 *Alabama Law Review* 77, 91–92 (2018).

19. See, *e.g.,* Del. Gen. Corp. L. §§ 211(b), 216(3), 361; Cal. Corp. Code §§ 600(b), 14600(b).

20. See, *e.g.,* Del. Gen. Corp. L. § 367; Cal. Corp. Code § 14623.

21. McDonnell, *supra* note 18; Leo E. Strine Jr., "Our Continuing Struggle with the Idea That For-Profit Corporations Seek Profit," 47 *Wake Forest Law Review* 135, 151 (2012).

22. Chapter 2 for a discussion of the limits on boards' discretion.

23. Chevron Corporation, home page, www.chevron.com (last viewed Oct. 15, 2021).

24. Chevron Corporation, "Chevron Sets Net Zero Aspiration and New GHG Intensity Target," (Oct. 11, 2021), https://www.chevron.com/stories/chevron-sets-net-zero-aspiration-and-new-ghg-intensity-target (last viewed Oct. 15, 2021).

25. Warby Parker, "Buy a Pair, Give a Pair," https://www.warbyparker.com/buy-a-pair-give-a-pair#:~:text=The%20whole%20story%20begins%20with,distribution%20has%20been%20temporarily%20suspended. (last viewed Oct. 15, 2021).

26. "Lithium-ion Batteries Need to be Greener and More Ethical," *Nature* (June 29, 2021), https://www.nature.com/articles/d41586-021-01735-z (last viewed Oct. 19, 2021); Amit Katwala, "The Spiralling Environmental Cost of Our Lithium Addiction," *Wired* (May 8, 2018), https://www.wired.co.uk/article/lithium-batteries-environment-impact (last viewed Oct. 19, 2021).

27. Katwala, *supra* note 26.

28. Russell Gold, Jessica Kuronen, & Elbert Wang, "Are Electric Cars Really Better for the Environment?" *Wall Street Journal* (Mar. 22, 2021), https://www.wsj.com/graphics/are-electric-cars-really-better-for-the-environment/ (last viewed Oct. 19, 2021).

29. Katwala, *supra* note 26.

30. Jill E. Fisch & Steven Davidoff Solomon, "The 'Value' of a Public Benefit Corporation," in *Research Handbook on Corporate Purpose and Personhood* (Elizabeth Pollman & Robert B. Thompson, eds.) (Elgar 2021), https://ssrn.com/abstract=3712532 (last viewed Oct. 19, 2021).

31. *Id.* at 11 (citing Wallace Witowski, "Lemonade IPO: 5 Things to Know about the Online Insurer," *Marketwatch*, July 2, 2020, https://www.marketwatch.com/story/lemonade-ipo-5-things-to-know-about-the-online-insurer-2020-07-01 (last viewed Oct. 19, 2021).

32. Model Act § 401.

33. *Id.*. § 402.

34. Del. Gen. Corp. L. § 366.

35. Allbirds, "Our Materials—Wool," https://www.allbirds.com/pages/our-ma

terials-wool (last viewed Oct. 26, 2021); Allbirds, "Our Materials—Tree," https://
www.allbirds.com/pages/our-materials-tree (last viewed Oct. 26, 2021).

36. Tonya Garcia, "Allbirds IPO: 5 Things to Know about the Eco-Friendly
Shoe Company Before It Goes Public," *Marketwatch* (Oct. 26, 2021), https://www.
marketwatch.com/story/allbirds-ipo-5-things-to-know-about-the-eco-friendly
-shoe-company-before-it-goes-public-11630606746 (last viewed Oct. 26, 2021).

37. , *e.g.,* Khan Academy, "Lagrange Multipliers, Introduction," https://www.
khanacademy.org/math/multivariable-calculus/applications-of-multivariable-der
ivatives/constrained-optimization/a/lagrange-multipliers-single-constraint (last
viewed Oct. 28, 2021); Analytics Vidhya, "Introductory Guide on Linear Programming for (Aspiring) Data Scientists," (Feb. 28, 2017), https://www.analyticsvidhya
.com/blog/2017/02/lintroductory-guide-on-linear-programming-explained-in
-simple-english/ (last viewed Oct. 28, 2021).

## Chapter 9: The Publicly Traded Public Benefit Corporation

1. Laureate Education, Inc., "About Laureate," https://www.laureate.net/about
laureate/ (last viewed May 20, 2022).

2. Laureate Education, Inc., "Mission," https://www.laureate.net/mission/#:~:
text=Public%20Benefit%20Corporation,material%2C%20positive%20impact%
20on%20society (last viewed May 20, 2022).

3. Christopher Marquis, "Public Benefit Corporations Flourish in the Public
Markets," *Forbes*, June 14, 2021, https://www.forbes.com/sites/christophermarquis/
2021/06/14/public-benefit-corporations-flourish-in-the-public-markets/?sh=
3289c1e5233d (last viewed May 20, 2022).

4. Cydney Posner, "Renewed Interest in IPOs of Public Benefit Corporations,"
*Harvard Law School Forum on Corporate Governance* (July 31, 2020), https://corpgov.law.har
vard.edu/2020/07/31/renewed-interest-in-ipos-of-public-benefit-corporations/ (last
viewed May 23, 2022); Lauren Debter, "Allbirds Valued at over $4 Billion after Stock
Surges in IPO," *Forbes*, Nov. 3, 2021, https://www.forbes.com/sites/laurendebter/2021
/11/03/allbirds-shares-soar-after-shoemaker-raises-over-300-million-in-ipo/?sh=
54b107369027 (last viewed May 23, 2022); Amalgamated Financial Corp., "Amalgamated Financial Becomes the First Publicly Traded Financial Services Company to
Incorporate as a Public Benefit Corporation," May 1, 2021, https://www.globenews
wire.com/news-release/2021/03/01/2184277/0/en/Amalgamated-Financial-Be
comes-the-First-Publicly traded-Financial-Services-Company-to-Incorporate-as-a
-Public-Benefit-Corporation.html (last viewed May 23, 2022); United Therapeutics
Corporation, "United Therapeutics Converts to a Public Benefit Corporation following Shareholder Approval," https://www.prnewswire.com/news-releases/united
-therapeutics-converts-to-a-public-benefit-corporation-following-shareholder-ap
proval-301388821.html (last viewed May 23, 2022).

5. These include Allbirds, Amalgamated Bank, AppHarvest, Broadway Finan-

cial Corporation, Coursera, Kronos Advanced Technologies, Laureate Education, Lemonade, Planet, United Therapeutics, Veeva Systems, Vital Farms, Warby Parker, Zevia, and Zymergen.

6. Danone North America, "A Commitment to Growing Research: Danone North America Celebrates a Decade of Fellowship Grants for Gut Microbiome Yogurt and Probiotic Studies" (Dec. 21, 2021), https://finance.yahoo.com/news/commitment-growing-research-danone-north-153500773.html (last viewed May 23, 2022).

7. Michael B. Dorff, James Hicks, & Steven Davidoff Solomon, "The Future or Fancy? An Empirical Study of Public Benefit Corporations," 11 *Harvard Business Law Review* 113 (2021).

8. *Ernst & Ernst v. Hochfelder*, 425 U.S. 185, 195 (1976).

9. *New York Stock Exchange Listed Company Manual* §§ 303A.01 (requiring boards to have a majority of independent directors) 303A.04 (requiring nominating committees), 303A.05 (requiring audit committees), 303A.06 (requiring audit committees). *also* 17 C.F.R. § 240.10A-3 (establishing listing requirements for audit committees).

10. *Id.* § 303A.01.

11. For a list of these special events that trigger an obligation to file a Form 8-K, *see* U.S. Securities and Exchange Commission, "Fast Answers: Form 8-K," https://www.sec.gov/fast-answers/answersform8khtm.html (last viewed May 23, 2022).

12. For example, companies must disclose certain information when making a self-tender for their own stock. 17 C.F.R. §240.13e-4.

13. *Id.* § 229.

14. *Id.* § 240.12b-20.

15. See, *e.g., Basic, Inc. v. Levinson*, 485 U.S. 224, 231 (1988) (holding that a fact is material in the context of Rule 10b-5, the rule that bars fraud in connection with the purchase or sale of a security, when "there is a substantial likelihood that a reasonable shareholder would consider it important). *also TSC Industries, Inc. v. Northway, Inc.*, 426 U.S. 438 (1976) (adopting the same definition of materiality in the proxy voting context).

16. 17 C.F.R. § 229.

17. 15 U.S.C.A. § 78r.

18. 17 C.F.R. § 240.10b-5.

19. J. Haskell Murray, "An Early Report on Benefit Reports," 118 *West Virginia Law Review* 25 (2015); Maxime Verheyden, "Public Reporting by Benefit Corporations: Importance, Compliance, and Recommendations," 14 *Hastings Business Law Journal* 37 (2018).

20. 17 C.R.R. §240.10b-5.

21. *Id.* § 229.101.

22. *Id.*

23. *Id.*

24. 17 C.F.R. §229.105.

25. *Id.*

26. Allbirds, 2021 Form 10-K, at 7 (Mar. 16, 2022), https://www.sec.gov/ix?doc=/Archives/edgar/data/1653909/000165390922000016/bird-20211231.htm (last viewed May 27, 2022).

27. *Id.* at 10–18.

28. *Id.* at 15.

29. *Id.* at 45.

30. *Id.* at 9.

31. *Id.*

32. *Id.* at 19.

33. Allbirds, "2020 Sustainability Report," https://cdn.allbirds.com/image/upload/v1625161698/marketing-pages/Allbirds_Sustainability_Report_2020.pdf (last viewed May 27, 2022).

34. *Id.*

35. *Id.* at 69–70.

36. Warby Parker, 2021 Form 10-K (Mar. 18, 2022), https://www.sec.gov/ix?doc=/Archives/edgar/data/1504776/000150477622000007/wrby-20211231.htm#ia e8426288653402996b2073da6172088_118 (last viewed May 27, 2022).

37. Warby Parker, "2021 Impact Report," (2022), https://www.warbyparker.com/assets/img/impact-report/Impact-Report-2021-v2.pdf (last viewed May 27, 2022).

38. See, *e.g.,* Ronnie Cohen & Gabriele Lingenfelter, "Money Isn't Everything: Why Public Benefit Corporations Should Be Required to Disclose Non-Financial Information," 42 *Delaware Journal of Corporate Law* 115 (2017); Brent J. Horton, "Rising to Their Full Potential: How a Uniform Disclosure Regime Will Empower Benefit Corporations," 9 *Harvard Business Law Review* 101 (Winter 2019).

39. "The Enhancement and Standardization of Climate-Related Disclosures for Investors," Exchange Act Release Nos. 33–11042; 34–94478 (Mar. 22, 2022), https://www.sec.gov/rules/proposed/2022/33-11042.pdf (last viewed May 31, 2022).

40. *Id.* at 7.

41. Katanga Johnson, "U.S. SEC Extends Comment Period on Climate Risk Proposal," *Reuters* (May 10, 2022), https://www.reuters.com/legal/government/us-sec-gives-public-until-june-17-weigh-climate-risk-proposal-amid-significant-2022-05-09/ (last viewed May 31, 2022); Lawrence A. Cunningham, "Comment Letter on SEC Climate Disclosure Proposal by 22 Law and Finance Professors," (Apr. 25, 2022), https://ssrn.com/abstract=4109278 (last viewed May 31, 2022).

42. I am indebted to Professor Patrick Corrigan for the points in this section.

43. 15 U.S.C. §78m(b)(2)(A).

44. *Id.* § 78m(b)(2)(B).

45. *Id.* § 7241(a).

46. *Id.*

47. *Id.* §7262(b).

48. Jau-Yang Liu, "An Internal Control System that Includes Corporate Social Responsibility for Social Sustainability in the New Era," 10 *Sustainability* 3382 (2018).

49. *Matrixx Initiatives Inc. v. Siracusano* 563 U.S. 27, 37–38 (2011) (quoting *Stoneridge Investment Partners, LLC v. Scientific-Atlanta, Inc.*, 552 U.S. 148 [2008]).

50. Joan Heminway, "Corporate Purpose and Litigation Risk in Publicly Held U.S. Benefit Corporations," 40 *Seattle Law Review* 611, 641–45 (2017).

51. *Halliburton Co. v. Erica P. John Fund, Inc.*, 573 U.S. 258 (2014).

52. *Id.* at 286.

53. Annie Lowrey, "Could Index Funds Be 'Worse Than Marxism'?" *Atlantic*, Apr. 5, 2021 ($11 trillion is now invested in index funds, up from $2 trillion a decade ago), https://www.theatlantic.com/ideas/archive/2021/04/the-autopilot-economy/618497/ (last viewed June 1, 2022).

54. Rick Alexander, "One Small Step from Financial Materiality to Sesquimateriality: A Critical Conceptual Leap for the ISSB," *Harvard Law School Forum on Corporate Governance* (May 4, 2022), https://theshareholdercommons.com/wp-content/uploads/2022/05/2022-05-04-one-small-step-from-financial-materiality-to-sesquimateriality-a-critical-conceptual-leap-for-the-issb.pdf (last viewed June 1, 2022).

55. Del. Gen. Corp. L. § 367; Model Act §305.

56. Del. Gen. Corp. L. § 367.

57. Cal. Corp. Code § 14623.

58. Jill E. Fisch and Steven Davidoff Solomon, "The 'Value' of a Public Benefit Corporation," in *Research Handbook on Corporate Purpose and Personhood* (Elizabeth Pollman & Robert B. Thompson, eds.) (Elgar 2021).

59. Sean J. Griffith & Dorothy S. Lund, "A Mission Statement for Mutual Funds in Shareholder Litigation," 87 *University of Chicago Law Review Online* 1149 (2020), https://lawreview.uchicago.edu/volume-875-july-2020-1149-1477 (last viewed June 2, 2022).

60. Heminway, *supra* note 51, at 644–45.

61. *supra*, Chapter 6.

62. *Id.*

# INDEX